Writers on
Organizations

Fifth Edition

Writers on
Organizations

Derek S. Pugh
David J. Hickson
Authors

SAGE Publications
International Educational and Professional Publisher
Thousand Oaks   London   New Delhi

First published by Hutchinson, 1964
Subsequent U.K. publication by Penguin Books Ltd., 1971, 1973, 1975-1983, 1989, 1996

For information address:

SAGE Publications, Inc.
2455 Teller Road
Thousand Oaks, California 91320
E-mail: order@sagepub.com

Printed in the United States of America

Library of Congress Cataloging-in-Publication Data

Pugh, Derek Salman.
    Writers on organizations / authors, Derek S. Pugh and David J.
Hickson.—5th ed.
       p.   cm.
    Includes bibliographical references and index.
    ISBN 0-7619-0475-1 (cloth: acid-free paper).—ISBN
0-7619-0476-X (pbk.: acid-free paper)
    1. Organizational sociology.   2. Industrial management.
I. Hickson, David John. II. Title.
HM131.P74   1996
302.3'5—dc20   96-25180

This book is printed on acid-free paper.

97 98 99 00 01 02 10 9 8 7 6 5 4 3 2 1

Sage Production Editor: Astrid Virding
Sage Typesetter: Andrea D. Swanson
Cover Designer: Candice Harman

To our parents and to our professional forebears

Contents

Introduction to the Fifth Edition   ix

1. The Structure of Organizations   **1**

Max Weber   3
Derek Pugh and the Aston Group
    Including John Child and David Hickson   8
Alfred D. Chandler   18
Oliver E. Williamson   23
Henry Mintzberg   27
Charles Handy   34
Christopher Bartlett and Sumantra Ghoshal   39

2. The Organization in Its Environment   **44**

Tom Burns   46
Paul Lawrence and Jay Lorsch   50
James D. Thompson   56
Jeffrey Pfeffer and Gerald R. Salancik   62
Raymond E. Miles and Charles C. Snow   66
Michael T. Hannan and John Freeman   72
Geert Hofstede   77

3. The Management of Organizations   **84**

Henri Fayol   86
Frederick W. Taylor   91
Harry Braverman and the "Labor Process" Debate   95
Thomas J. Peters and Robert H. Waterman   99
Rosabeth Moss Kanter   105
Karl E. Weick   111

4. Decision Making in Organizations   **116**

Herbert A. Simon   117

James G. March   121
Victor H. Vroom   126
Michel Crozier   131

5. People in Organizations   **136**

Elton Mayo and the Hawthorne Investigations   138
Rensis Likert and Douglas McGregor   142
Edgar H. Schein   148
Frederick Herzberg   153
Eric Trist and the Work of the Tavistock Institute   158

6. Organizational Change and Learning   **165**

Paul J. DiMaggio and Walter W. Powell   167
Andrew Pettigrew   171
Chris Argyris   177
Peter Senge   180
Gareth Morgan   184

Name Index   189

Subject Index   191

About the Authors   205

Introduction to
the Fifth Edition

Since the first edition of this book appeared in 1964, it has been in gratifyingly continuous demand, having sold more than 250,000 copies. With changing organizational issues and with new work making an impact, it is appropriate now to offer a fifth edition, once again completely revised. We have added descriptions of new writers, brought others up to date, and made some rearrangement of the sections.

It is a commonplace of discussion among managers and administrators that all organizations are different. Even so, it is important to study these differences and to classify them. Something useful can thus be said about various kinds of organizations, the ways in which they function, and the behavior of members within them. This book describes the contributions that many prominent writers have made to the understanding of organizations and their management.

In presenting these contributions, our aim has remained the same over the years: to give a direct introductory exposition of the views of leading authors whose ideas are currently the subject of interest and debate. We conceive of this work as a resource book giving a general overview of the field, and so we have not essayed critical analysis, which would be a quite different task. It is our hope that readers will bring their own critical appraisal to each contribution. Even so, we are conscious of the very considerable selection and compression that is involved in presenting a writer's work in a few pages. Some distortions must inevitably result. We can only plead the best of intentions in that our hope is to entice the reader to go to the original listed sources, in their richness and complexity. A fully revised edition of the companion volume *Organization Theory: Selected Readings* (4th ed., Penguin Books, edited by D. S. Pugh) presents extracts from the work of many of the writers summarized here.

One attraction of this introductory book is that it should be a relatively slim volume. We have therefore had to balance the addition of new writers with the dropping of others. Their contributions, though, continue to form part of the flow of concepts and theories that nurture the field. We have therefore compiled an omnibus edition, which contains the descriptions of all the writers included in all the previous editions of this book. This hardback volume, entitled *Great Writers on Organizations: The Omnibus Edition* by D. S. Pugh and D. J. Hickson (1993, Dartmouth Publishing), will allow a fuller exploration of the subject.

In considering which changes to make in the current edition, we conducted a small informal survey of our professional colleagues in many countries. We should like to thank them very much for responding so promptly with their views, which helped us in our deliberations. The decisions on content were, of course, ours alone.

Our heartfelt thanks go to our wives, who for the fifth time around suffered most in the cause.

Derek S. Pugh
David J. Hickson

1 *The Structure of Organizations*

The decisive reason for the advance of bureaucratic organization has always been its purely technical superiority over any other form of organization.

Max Weber

It may not be impossible to run an effective organization of 5,000 employees nonbureaucratically, but it would be so difficult that no one tries.

The Aston Group

The visible hand of managerial direction has replaced the invisible hand of market mechanisms in coordinating flows and allocating resources in major modern industries.

Alfred D. Chandler

Transaction cost economizing is, we submit, the driving force that is responsible for the main institutional changes [in corporations].

Oliver E. Williamson

Adhocracy [the innovative configuration] is the structure of our age.

Henry Mintzberg

Increasingly your corporations will come to resemble universities or colleges.

Charles Handy

The task [of the transnational organization] is not to build a sophisticated matrix structure, but to create a "matrix in the minds of managers."

Christopher Bartlett and Sumantra Ghoshal

All organizations have to make provision for continuing activities directed toward the achievement of given aims. Regularities in such

1

activities as task allocation, supervision, and coordination are developed. Such regularities constitute the organization's structure, and the fact that these activities can be arranged in various ways means that organizations can have differing structures. Indeed, in some respects, every organization is unique. But many writers have examined a variety of structures to see whether any general principles can be extracted. This variety, moreover, may be related to variations in such factors as the objectives of the organization, its size, ownership, geographic location, and technology of manufacture, which produce the characteristic differences in structure of a bank, a hospital, a mass production factory, or a local governmental department.

The writers in this section are concerned with identifying different forms of organizational structures and exploring their implications. Max Weber presents three organizational types on the basis of how authority is exercised. He views one of these types—bureaucracy—as the dominant modern form. Derek Pugh and the Aston Group suggest that it is more realistic to talk in terms of dimensions of structures, rather than of types. Alfred Chandler shows how management structure flows from the company strategy. Oliver Williamson points to the way in which the pressures on the organization to process its information efficiently leads to the type of relationship, market or hierarchical, that is developed. Henry Mintzberg describes a range of types of modern organizations and their effectiveness. Charles Handy identifies some established structures of organization but suggests that a distinctively different new form is coming into being. Christopher Bartlett and Sumantra Ghoshal argue that, for multinational firms to be successful in the current global market environment, they must develop an innovative new structure and culture of working.

All the contributors to this section suggest that an appropriate structure is vital to the efficiency of an organization and must be the subject of careful study in its own right.

Max Weber

Max Weber (1864–1920) was born in Germany. He qualified in law and then became a member of the staff of Berlin University. He remained an academic for the rest of his life, having a primary interest in the broad sweep of the historical development of civilizations through studies of the sociology of religion and the sociology of economic life. In his approach to both of these topics, he showed a tremendous range in examining the major world religions, such as Judaism, Christianity, and Buddhism, and in tracing the pattern of economic development from prefeudal times. These two interests were combined in his classic studies of the impact of Protestant beliefs on the development of capitalism in Western Europe and the United States. Weber had the prodigious output and ponderous style typical of German philosophers, but those of his writings that have been translated into English have established him as a major figure in sociology.

Weber's principal contribution to the study of organizations was his theory of authority structures, which led him to characterize organizations in terms of the authority relations within them. This characterization stemmed from a basic concern with why individuals obey commands, why people do as they are told. To deal with this problem, Weber made a distinction between *power,* the ability to force people to obey regardless of their resistance, and *authority,* in which orders are voluntarily obeyed by those receiving them. Under an authority system, those in the subordinate role see the issuing of directives by those in the superordinate role as legitimate. Weber distinguished between organizational types according to the way in which authority is legitimated. He outlined three pure types, which he labeled "charismatic," "traditional," and "rational-legal," each of which is expressed in a particular administrative apparatus or organization. These pure types are distinctions useful for analyzing organizations, although any real organization may be a combination of them.

The first mode of exercising authority is based on the personal qualities of the leader. Weber used the Greek term *charisma* to mean any quality of individual personality by virtue of which the leader is set apart from ordinary people and treated as endowed with supernatural, superhuman, or at least specifically exceptional powers or qualities. This is the position of the prophet, messiah, or political leader, whose organization consists of a set of disciples: The disciples have the job of mediating between the leader and the masses. The typical case of this kind is a small-scale revolutionary movement either religious or political in form, but many organizations have had "charismatic" founders, such as Lord Nuffield (Morris Motors) and Henry Ford. Because the basis of authority is in the characteristics of one person and because commands are based on that person's inspiration, however, this type of organization has a built-in instability. The question of succession always arises when the leader dies and the authority has to be passed on. Typically, in political and religious organizations, the movement splits, with the various disciples claiming to be the "true" heirs to the charismatic leader. Thus, the process is usually one of fission. The tendencies toward this kind of breakdown can be seen in the jockeying for position of Hitler's lieutenants—Himmler and Göring—during the first few months of 1945. It exemplifies the problem of an heir to the leader, and even if the leader nominates a successor, that person will not necessarily be accepted. It is unlikely that another charismatic leader will be present, and so the organization must lose its charismatic form and become one of the two remaining types. If the succession becomes hereditary, the organization becomes traditional in form; if the succession is determined by rule, a bureaucratic organization develops.

The bases of order and authority in *traditional* organizations are precedent and usage. The rights and expectations of various groups are established in terms of taking what has always happened as sacred; the great arbiter in such a system is custom. Leaders in such a system have authority by virtue of the status they have inherited, and the extent of their authority is fixed by custom. When charisma is traditionalized by making its transmission hereditary, it becomes part of the role of the leader, rather than being part of the founder's personality. The actual organizational form under a traditional authority system can take one of two patterns. Under the *patrimonial* form, officials are personal servants, dependent on the leader for remuneration. Under the *feudal* form, the officials have much more autonomy, with their own sources of income and a traditional relationship of loyalty toward the leader. The feudal system has a material basis of tithes, fiefs, and beneficiaries all resting on past usage and a system of customary rights and duties. Although Weber's examples are historical, his insight is equally applicable to modern organizations. Managerial positions are often handed down from one generation to the next as firms establish their own dynasties based on hereditary transmission. Selection and appointment may be based on kinship, rather than on expertise. Similarly, ways of doing things in many organizations are justified in terms of always having been done that way *as a reason in itself,* rather than on the basis of a rational analysis.

The concept of rational analysis leads to Weber's third type of authority system—the rational-legal one—with its bureaucratic organizational form. This Weber sees as the dominant institution of modern society. The system is called "rational" because the means are expressly designed to achieve certain specific goals; that is, the organization is like a well-designed machine with a certain function to perform, and every part of the machine contributes to the attainment of maximum performance of that function. It is called "legal" because authority is exercised by means of a system of rules and procedures through the office an individual occupies at a particular time. For such organization, Weber uses the name "bureaucracy." In common usage, *bureaucracy* is synonymous with inefficiency, an emphasis on red tape, and excessive writing and recording. Specifically, it is identified with inefficient public administration. But in terms of his own definition, Weber states that a bureaucratic organization is technically the most efficient form of organization possible. "Precision, speed, unambiguity, knowledge of files, continuity, discretion, unity, strict subordination, reduction of friction and of material and personal costs—these are raised to the optimum point in the strictly bureaucratic administration." Weber himself uses the machine analogy when he says that the bureaucracy is like a modern machine, whereas other organizational forms are like non-mechanical methods of production.

The reason for the efficiency of the bureaucracy lies in its organizational form. Because the means used are those that will best achieve the stated ends, it is unencumbered by the personal whims of the leader or by traditional procedures that are no longer applicable. This is because bureaucracies represent the final stage in depersonalization. Such organizations have a series of officials whose roles are circumscribed by written definitions of their authority. These offices are arranged in a hierarchy, each successive step embracing all those beneath it. There is a set of rules and procedures within which every possible contingency is theoretically provided for. There is a "bureau" for the safe keeping of all written records and files, it being an important part of the rationality of the system that information is written down. A clear separation is made between personal and business affairs, bolstered by a contractual method of appointment in terms of technical qualifications for office. In such an organization, authority is based in the office, and commands are obeyed because the rules state that it is within the competence of a particular office to issue such commands. Also important is the stress on the appointment of experts. One sign of a developing bureaucracy is the growth of professional managers and an increase in the number of specialist experts with their own departments.

For Weber, this expansion adds up to a highly efficient system of coordination and control. The rationality of the organization shows in its ability to "calculate" the consequences of its action. Because of the hierarchy of authority and the system of rules, control of the actions of individuals in the organization is ensured; this is the depersonalization. Because of the employment of experts who have their specific areas of responsibility and the use of files, there is an amalgamation of the best available knowledge and a record of past behavior of the organization. These enable predictions to be made about future events. The organization has rationality: "the methodical attainment of a definitely given and practical end by means of an increasingly precise calculation of means."

This is where the link between Weber's interest in religion and organizations occurs. Capitalism as an economic system is based on the rational long-term calculation of economic gain. Initially for this to happen, as well as the expansion of world markets, a particular moral outlook is needed. Weber saw this as being supplied by the Protestant religion after the Reformation, with its emphasis on this world and the need for people to show their salvation through their industry on earth. Thus, economic activity gradually became labeled as a positive good, rather than as a negative evil. Capitalism was launched on its path, and this path was cleared most easily through the organizational form of bureaucracy, which supplied the apparatus for putting economic rationality into practice. Providing as it does efficiency and regularity, bureaucratic administration is a necessity for any long-term economic calculation. So, with increasing industrialization, bureaucracy becomes the dominant method of organizing, and so potent is it that it becomes characteristic of other areas of society, such as education, government, and politics. Finally, the bureaucratic organization becomes typical of all the institutions of modern society.

Most studies of the formal, structural characteristics of organizations over the past three decades started from the work of Max Weber. His importance lies in having made the first attempt to produce systematic categories for organizational analysis.

Bibliography

Gerth, H. H., and Mills, C. W. (eds.), *From Max Weber: Essays in Sociology,* Oxford University Press, 1946.

Weber, M., *The Protestant Ethic and the Spirit of Capitalism,* Allen & Unwin, 1930; rev. ed., Scribner, 1977; Peter Smith, 1984.

Weber, M., *The Theory of Social and Economic Organization,* Free Press, 1947, 1961.

Derek Pugh and the Aston Group Including John Child and David Hickson

In the late 1950s, Derek Pugh, now Visiting Research Professor of International Management at the Open University Business School, United Kingdom, brought to the Birmingham College of Advanced Technology (which became the University of Aston-in-Birmingham) a distinctive view of how to conduct research. His research experience as a social psychologist at the University of Edinburgh had placed him in close contact with researchers in other social sciences. He believed that the scope of empirical investigation and of understanding could be widened by multidisciplinary research founded on a common commitment to and ownership of results within the research team and on team management skills.

The Industrial Administration Research Unit at Aston, founded and led by Pugh between 1961 and 1970, included several "generations" of researchers whose academic origins were as diverse as psychology, sociology, economics, politics, and no specific discipline at all. The names that appear most frequently on publications are John Child, David Hickson, Bob Hinings, Roy Payne, Diana Pheysey, and Charles McMillan as the initiator with David Hickson of much subsequent international research, but there are many more. It is symptomatic of the nature of the group that it has not taken on the name of any one individual, even that of Derek Pugh, but is usually known as the Aston Group even though there is no longer any special link with that university. The program of research dispersed with the members of the group, and they and others in touch with them have pursued its work elsewhere in Britain and in several other countries.

The Aston Program contributed to organization theory by blending some of the research methods and assumptions of psychology with conceptions of organizations and their workings from sociology and economics. Its approach has three essential elements. First, because organizations and their members are changing and complex, numbers of their *attributes should be studied together and as matters of degree,* not as "either/or" phenomena—a multivariate approach to a changing world of grays, rather than blacks and whites. This approach also implies that there will be no single reason for the way in which an organization is set up and run, but many possible influences (multivariate causal explanation). What happens cannot be due to an organization's size alone, nor for that matter to its technology alone, but must in some degree be due to a number of these and other factors all acting together.

Second, because organizations outlast the comings and goings of individuals, it is *appropriate to study their nonpersonal or institutional aspects* by using information on their divisions of work, their control systems, and their formal hierarchies. For this, individuals can be interviewed as informants who describe these aspects, rather than be asked to indicate how they experience the organization personally, which they would be if asked to respond to questionnaires about themselves.

Third, because organizations are working wholes, they and their members *should be seen from more than one perspective* to give the fullest possible view. "The response to the recurring conundrum 'does man make organization or does organization make man?' must be to assume that both are happening all the time." Therefore, the Aston Program aimed to link

Organizational structure and functioning
Group composition and interaction
Individual personality and behavior

Early ambitions to include features of the surrounding society were not realized initially, but began to be included later, when research extended beyond Britain to organizations in other societies.

The program commenced with a project in the Birmingham area in England, from which has grown all further research. It focused on the organizational level by studying a highly diverse sample of 46 organizations: private sector and public sector, from manufacturers of cars and chocolate bars to municipal departments, public services, and chain stores. Their formal structures were analyzed in terms of their degrees of

Specialization of functions and roles
Standardization of procedures
Formalization of documentation
Centralization of authority
Configuration of role structure

These concepts reflect prevalent ideas about bureaucratization and how to manage, which can be found in the work of Weber (p. 3) and Fayol (p. 86).

Many ways of measuring these aspects of structure were devised that have been employed variously by many researchers since. The most distinctive kind of measure used, an innovation in research on organizations, was based on demonstrating that, for example, the number of functions (e.g., finance, public relations) an organization had specialized out of a set of possible specialisms could validly be added to give it a specialization score, and similarly with standardization, formalization, and centralization. This procedure enabled one organization to be compared with another in these terms for the first time.

Despite the range and ramifications of this research, its salient results took on a relatively simple outline. First, the measures of specialization, standardization, and formalization were simplified into a combined score for each organization. To distinguish this from its three constituents, it was called *structuring of activities*. An organization with highly structured activities has many specialized sections, such as buying, training, and work study, and many routine procedures and formal documents, the total effect being that what has to be done is marked out or structured. Second, centralization of decision making and the autonomy of an organization's decision making from any owning organization were together termed *concentration of authority*. An organization with concentrated authority not only has most of its decisions made at the top of its own hierarchy but also has many decisions made for it, over its head, by the management of another organization of which it is a wholly or partly owned subsidiary or subordinate section.

Thus, at its simplest, the Aston Group isolated two primary elements of any organization: (a) how far the activities of its personnel are structured and (b) how far its decision-making authority is concentrated at the top, which between them sum up much of what an organization is like. Know them and you know it, to a large extent, for they are its two fundamentals.

Although the Aston Program's approach assumes that organizations are what they are for many reasons, these first results were also relatively simple in the principal explanations they suggested. A series of features of the organization's context, including its purpose, ownership, technology, size, and dependence, were examined for any correlation with how far an organization had structured its activities or concentrated its authority. It was found that ownership (whether private or public, dispersed in thousands of shareholdings or in the hands of a family) made little difference to structuring and concentration, as did technology, which was reflected in only a few aspects of structure.

What did and does matter much more for the form taken by an organization is its *size* and its degree of *dependence on other organizations.* The larger it is, the more likely its employees are to work in very specialized functions, following standardized procedures and formalized documentation; that is, it will score highly on structuring of activities and have many of the appearances of bureaucracy. The more it is dependent on only a few owning, supplier, or customer units, or even just one—total dependence means an organization is wholly owned by another that supplies all its needs and takes all its outputs—the less autonomy it will have in its own decision making, and even those decisions that are left to it are likely to be centralized within itself, rather than decentralized.

Casting their results into an empirically derived taxonomy of forms of organizational structure, the Aston Group put forward from their first project a view of the forms prevalent in contemporary industrialized society, in Britain and probably elsewhere. Large firms, big businesses, are typically *workflow bureaucracies,* highly structured but not so highly concentrated in authority as some. Public service organizations of local and central governments are *personnel bureaucracies,* not very structured but with highly concentrated authority and procedures focused on hiring, promoting, and firing of personnel. Smaller units within large private or public groups are *full bureaucracies,* with the high structuring of the workflow type and the highly concentrated authority of the personnel type. Smaller firms in personal ownership have neither of these features to any great extent, being *nonbureaucracies* (or implicitly structured). There are other types, but these four main ones can be depicted thus:

		Personnel bureaucracies	Full bureaucracies
Concentration of Authority	High		
	Low	Non-bureaucracies	Workflow bureaucracies

Low   High
Structuring of Activities

The progression of the Aston Group into research on group and role characteristics and on the individual's experience of organizational "climate," in accordance with their program of linking organizational, group, and individual levels of analysis, is not so well known. Its results are not so clear-cut. If any construction can be placed on them overall, it is that they lift from bureaucracy the pall of gloom laid over it by widespread assumptions of its uniformly stifling and dreary nature. It may be like that, but if it is, then it is so for those in the lowest level jobs and not necessarily for those higher in the hierarchy. Life for them differs from one bureaucratic organization to another.

Through a mixture of surveys and of intensive case studies with batteries of methods, Aston researchers showed that although structuring of activities does tend to be associated with greater formality at the group interaction level and although concentration of authority does tend to be associated with less autonomy for individuals and with greater conventional attention to rules, a uniformly bureaucratic-type firm can be effective and its personnel can like working in it. At least, this was so in their case study of a small firm owned by a large international corporation, a "small effective bureaucracy" they code-named "Aston."

In organizations that showed both high structuring and high concentration of authority, which were loosely equated with bureaucracies, no evidence of less attractive climates (in terms of the way in which authority was exercised, of interest in work, of routine, and of personal relationships) was found. At the top, such organizations tended to have managers who were younger and better qualified, with more flexible and challenging attitudes. And firms with younger managers tended to show faster growth in sales and assets (although whether youth caused growth or growth attracted younger personnel is an unanswered question). So, those managing more bureaucratic-type firms were unlikely themselves to be cautious and conformist and were more likely to seek innovation and risk.

Greater confidence is shown in the Aston Program's achievements at the organization level of analysis, however. On such issues as the presence or absence of procedures, documents, defined authority, and control systems, the program demonstrated that significant comparisons can be made between organizations of virtually any kind. (But it must be remembered that the data do not tell how far these means are then used.) The Aston Program provides concepts and measures of organizational structure that have withstood use and reuse by researchers beyond the original team in a way that rarely happens.

John Child

John Child, now Guinness Professor of Management at the Judge Institute of Management Studies at the University of Cambridge, joined

Pugh at Aston in using the same methods to replicate the results in contrasting industries, stable compared with fast changing.

Most significantly, he made explicit what had remained implicit in the thinking behind the Aston Program. He highlighted *strategic choice* by emphasizing that all aspects of organizations were, in some sense, chosen by their managements. They did not just happen. Size, for example, does not "cause" specialization just like that. Growth in size enables, or pressures, managers who want to have effective organizations to add more specialist departments so that work can be divided clearly between more people, who thus acquire more specialized expertise. The managers choose what to do. More than that, they choose the growth in size to begin with. They decide to expand output, to add a new marketing department, or whatever, and so they increase the number of employees. Strategic choice by managers affects both context and structure.

But one choice constrains another; each choice (e.g., of size) constrains the options open for the next (e.g., of the degree of structuring to be adopted). A major instance is that the choice of how far to develop either of the two primary elements—structuring and concentration—is likely to limit to some extent what can be done with the other because there is a small negative relationship between them; that is, more of one probably means somewhat less of the other, and to that extent they are alternative means of controlling an organization, not mutually exclusive alternatives (because all organizations use both) but alternative emphases.

Later, Child spent some years in China during the transition from Maoist rule. In some of the first ever independent empirical research in that nation's industries, he and Chinese colleagues exposed the problems of devolving a centrally planned system. Decentralization was uneven and only partially effective. Central and local governments kept capital investment in their own hands, and formal delegation to managements of decisions on, for instance, purchasing and recruiting meant little if, in practice, managers had to go to state agencies to find sources of goods and personnel.

David Hickson

David Hickson, now Research Professor of International Management at Bradford Management Center, England, who was with the Aston Group from the beginning, shared with Pugh a particular responsibility for extending its work beyond Britain. Over the years, Aston-based projects took place in many nations, including the United States and Canada, Western Europe together with Poland and Sweden, the Middle East and Israel, India, Hong Kong, and Japan. Among the differences that have been found are notably high centralization of organizations under state central planning in Poland, high structuring (specialization and formalization) in Japanese companies that have adopted contemporary Western forms of organization and management, and comparatively less structuring in paternalistic Hong Kong firms.

Hickson, Hinings, and colleagues put forward a culture-free hypothesis that originated from a comparison of manufacturing firms in Britain, Canada, and the United States. As they saw it, this hypothesis stated the "boldest" possibility—namely, "Relationships between the structural characteristics of work organizations and variables of organization context will be stable across societies."

Greater size, for instance, would consistently go with greater specialization and greater formalization in any country, West or East. Lex Donaldson, of the Australian Graduate School of Management in Sydney, a former colleague of Pugh's at the London Business School and once a student of Hickson's at Aston itself, is a constant advocate of the kind of work accomplished by the Aston Group. He tested this hypothesis by using the published results of studies in 13 countries and found that it was supported. There were indeed stable relationships, especially with size of organization. Everywhere, bigger organizations are likely to be not only more structured but also less centralized (the latter relationship may be weaker in the East). In other words, once jobs and procedures are set up, top managers can delegate more because people know what they should do, and simultaneously they ask to be allowed to do it. This finding suggests, not that all organizations are the same, but that managers in all nations have similar constraints on their choices, which show up as a repeated pattern of relationships among size and dependence and structural features.

Again with Hinings, and with other colleagues in the Faculty of Business at the University of Alberta, Canada, Hickson went on to examine which managers most influence these choices and why. They proposed a *strategic contingencies theory of intraorganizational power* and verified it by studying departmental influence in firms in Canada and the United States. The theory gives three reasons why some departmental managers are powerful and others weak: how far they (a) *cope with uncertainty,* (b) are *centrally situated,* and (c) are *not substitutable.* If their department can cope with uncertainty, then the rest of the organization can function with fewer difficulties, as when a marketing department evens out erratic fluctuations in customer demands by astute advertising so that production can be more stable year round. If their department is central to the flows of work around the organization, then more others who feed work to it and wait for its work are dependent on it, as when a finance department receives their estimates and allocates their budgets. If their department cannot be substituted for because no one else in the organization or any external agency can do what it does, then it holds a monopoly-like position. Should there be an alternative, as when some of the work of a purchasing department could be contracted out to a buying agent, that position is fragile.

Departmental managers whose personnel are strong in all three respects have an overall control of strategic contingencies within their organization that gives them more influence over decisions outside their departmental concerns. Pfeffer and Salancik (p. 62) use this same idea in their theory about an organization's external relationships.

Hickson, together with colleagues at Bradford Management Center, England, then investigated how these managerial decisions, particularly the major ones, came to be made. Comparing 150 histories of decisions in 30 organizations in England, they found three prevalent ways of making such decisions. Decisions could be arrived at by a process that was (a) *sporadic,* "informally spasmodic and protracted"; or (b) *fluid,* "steadily paced, formally channelled, speedy"; or (c) *constricted,* "narrowly channelled."

Which type of process occurred depended more on what was being decided than on the kind of organization—manufacturer or hospital or utility or whatever it might be—in which it was being decided. The most complex and political matters (e.g., new products, major reorganizations) most often gave rise to a sporadic process; those that were still complex but less political (e.g., a big share issue) were likely to go through a smoother, fluid process; and those that were still political but less complex (e.g., the organization's corporate budget and business plan) were likely to go through a tighter, constricted process. As the Bradford researchers put it, "The matter for decision matters most."

Together with his colleagues, Hickson therefore draws attention to three of the more crucial features of what managers have to work with. First, wherever they may be, there will be consistent constraints, one decision after another, in the structural features—as defined by the Aston Program—that characterize organizations. Second, they must expect differing patterns of influence in different organizations; marketing may have great say in one firm, little in another, for instance.

Third, by contrast, they will be able to recognize what is going on when big decisions are made in organizations other than their own, easily fitting in if they change jobs; a similarly complex and political matter is likely to engender much the same process wherever it occurs.

Bibliography

Aston Program Books

Hickson, D. J., and McMillan, C. J. (eds.), *Organization and Nation: The Aston Program IV,* Gower, 1981.
Pugh, D. S., and Hickson, D. J., *Organizational Structure in Its Context: The Aston Program I,* Gower, 1976.
Pugh, D. S., and Hinings, C. R. (eds.), *Organizational Structure—Extensions and Replications: The Aston Program II,* Gower, 1976.
Pugh, D. S., and Payne, R. L. (eds.), *Organizational Behavior in Its Context: The Aston Program III,* Gower, 1977.

Aston Program Papers

Child, J., "Organizational Structures, Environment, and Performance: The Role of Strategic Choice," *Sociology, 6,* (1972), 2-22.
Donaldson, L., *Size and Bureaucracy in East and West: A Preliminary Meta Analysis,* in S. R. Clegg, D. C. Dunphy, and S. G. Redding, *The Enterprise and Management in East Asia,* University of Hong Kong, 1986.
Pugh, D. S., "The Measurement of Organization Structures: Does Context Determine Form?" *Organizational Dynamics,* (Spring, 1973), 19-34; reprinted in D. S. Pugh (ed.), *Organization Theory,* Penguin Books, 1997.

Further Work

Child, J., *Management in China During the Age of Reform,* Cambridge University Press, 1994.
Donaldson, L., *In Defense of Organization Theory,* Cambridge University Press, 1985.
Donaldson, L., *American Anti-Management Theories of Organization,* Cambridge University Press, 1995.
Hickson, D. J., Butler, R. J., Cray, D., Mallory, G. R., and Wilson, D. C., *Top Decisions: Strategic Decision-Making in Organizations,* Jossey-Bass, 1986.

Hickson, D. J., Hinings, C. R., Lee, C. A., Schneck, R. E., and Pennings, J. M., "A Strategic Contingencies Theory of Intraorganizational Power," *Administrative Science Quarterly, 16/2,* (1971), 216-229.

Hinings, C. R., Hickson, D. J., Pennings, J. M., and Schneck, R. C., "Structural Conditions of Intraorganizational Power," *Administrative Science Quarterly, 19/1,* (1974), 22-44.

Alfred D. Chandler

Alfred Chandler is Straus Professor of Business History in the Graduate School of Business Administration, Harvard University. He is an economic historian, and his research work has centered on the study of business history and, in particular, administration. He has long argued that this is a much neglected area in the study of recent history. His studies of big business have been carried out with grants from a number of sources, including the Alfred P. Sloan Foundation. His work has been internationally recognized, and his book, *The Visible Hand,* was awarded the Pulitzer Prize in history and the Bancroft Prize. Chandler has taught at a variety of universities in the United States and Europe.

All of Chandler's academic work has been concerned with the theme of the rise and role of the large-scale business enterprise during what he describes as the formative years of modern capitalism—the years 1850 to 1920. He suggests, from his many studies, that during this period a new economic institution was created—the multi-unit firm—controlled by a new class of managers operating within a new system of capitalism. These new managers had to develop strategies different from those of their entrepreneurial predecessors and be particularly innovative in creating structures to implement those strategies. The reasons for this shift are to be found in changes in demand bringing about mass markets and technological change that allowed high-volume production. The new organizational structures allowed the integration of mass production with mass distribution.

Although Chandler's analysis is historical, he makes general points about organizational change and the relationship between strategy and structure. In particular, from his studies, Chandler is clear that the structure of an organization follows from the strategy that is adopted. The distinction between these two is crucial. *Strategy* is the determination of basic long-term goals and objectives, together with the adoption of courses of action and the allocation of resources for carrying out those goals. *Structure* is the organization that is devised to administer the activities that arise from the strategies adopted. As such, it involves the existence of a hierarchy, the distribution of work, and lines of authority and communication. In addition, the concept of structure covers the information and data that flow along those lines.

Once an organization moves away from the small, owner-controlled enterprise toward the modern, multi-unit business enterprise, then the new class of managers appears. This is important for structural developments because the salaried manager is committed to the long-term stability of the enterprise. The managerial hierarchy gives positions of power and authority and as a result becomes a source of both permanence and continued growth. As part of this process, the careers of salaried managers become increasingly technical and professional.

The role of management in developing structure is central to Chandler's analysis. As he puts it, "The visible hand of management has replaced Adam Smith's invisible hand of market forces." Managers are both products of and developers of the multidivisional, decentralized structure that is the organizational outcome of technological change and rising demand. They become responsible for the administration of the enterprise—that is, coordinating, planning, and appraising work and allocating resources.

The structural arrangements of a large business enterprise have to allow for both the efficient day-to-day operations of its various units and dealing with the long-run health of the company. The developments that follow from this involve operating with a decentralized structure to deal with day-to-day manufacturing and services and building up a central office with functional departments to manage the long-run prospects of the company. These tasks are all part of the process of specialization of functions as a major structural device. The key distinctions are among the general office, divisions, departments, and field units. Each of these has a particular function, and one basic reason for the success of this type of structure is that it clearly removes from the immediate operations those executives responsible for long-term planning and appraisal. This separation is significant because it gives those executives the time, information, and psychological commitment for long-term activities.

The introduction of this distinctive organizational structure with its unique managerial hierarchy marked the transition from a family- or finance-based capitalism to managerial capitalism. But because, in Chandler's view, structure follows strategy, this transition could only occur in response to external pressures. Particularly important was the increasing volume of activity that arose in response to the new national and increasingly urban markets of the late 19th century. Together with this came technological change, which enabled enterprises to move into high-volume production.

In the face of such pressures, enterprises could adopt either positive or defensive strategies. A *positive strategy* occurs when an enterprise actively looks for new markets and new products to serve those markets. It is organized around product diversification. A *defensive strategy* occurs when an enterprise acts to protect its current position. The common way of achieving this protection is to form a vertically integrated company by means of mergers with similar enterprises, suppliers, and customers.

Both strategies lead to bigger organizations that have administrative problems. This effect begins a systematization of techniques for the administration of functional activities. An initial type of organization for achieving this is the centralized, functionally departmentalized structure. It enables the necessary new expert skills to be brought in but retains control by the owners. But the increase in scale of organizations involves building up capacity and enlarging the resources of people, money, and materials at the disposal of an enterprise. One result is further and continuing growth to ensure the full use of those resources, a result that emanates from the interests of the new managers, rather than of the owners. Growth becomes internally as well as externally generated and then produces the really innovative structure—that of the multi-unit decentralized form.

To illustrate his points in detail and to chart the process of structural innovation, Chandler looks at the cases of four companies: Du Pont, General Motors, Standard Oil of New Jersey, and Sears Roebuck. According to Chandler, the general pressures and needs facing these four companies were the same. Also in general terms, the structural outcome was very similar. But the process of diagnosing the issues and introducing the consequent administrative changes was quite different.

The particular structural innovation of Du Pont was to create autonomous divisions. The company reached the beginning of the 20th century as a loose federation with no central administrative control. The first strategy of the younger Du Ponts was to centralize control and concentrate manufacturing activity in a few, larger plants. This was the centralized, functionally departmentalized structure. Important to the operation of the company was the development of new forms of management information and forecasting. The introduction of the multi-unit, decentralized structure came with the need to maintain growth. It was done by basing the structure on a new principle: coordinating related effort, rather than like things. This innovative principle meant that different broad functional activities had to be placed in separate administrative units. To operate these units, the executives responsible were given enhanced authority. Eventually, these developed into product-based units backed by a central, general office to deal with strategic issues. This development left the autonomous units to get on with day-to-day operations.

The General Motors case underlines the need for structure to follow strategy. William Durant, the founder of General Motors, went for a volume strategy with many operating units in an extremely loose federation. A crisis occurred in 1920 because of lack of overall control. The response of Alfred P. Sloan, who became the chief executive officer in 1923, was to create a general office to be responsible for broad policies and objectives and to coordinate effort. A line-and-staff structure was developed that allowed the product divisions to ensure good use of resources and a proper product flow, with the headquarters staff appraising divisional performance and plans. The new structure took 5 years to put into place.

Sloan has described in *My Years With General Motors* the nature of the problems and the need for changes as he saw them from the chief executive's point of view. Top management has the basic tasks of providing motivation and opportunity for senior executives: motivation by incentive compensation through stock option plans, and opportunity through decentralized management. But coordination is also required, and good management rests on a reconciliation of centralization and decentralization. Through his attempts to obtain the correct structural balance between those extremes, Sloan enunciated his seemingly paradoxical principle of "coordinated decentralization." His aim was coordinated control of decentralized operations. Policy coordination is achieved through committees. It is evolved in a continuous debate to which all may contribute and is basically an educational process. Executive administration is the clear responsibility of people who carry out the evolving policy.

As with General Motors, Standard Oil of New Jersey was, for Chandler, a case of initial failure to adjust structure to strategy. The channels of authority and communication were insufficiently defined within a partly federated, partly consolidated company. As a result, a series of crises over inventories and overproduction during the 1920s led to ad hoc responses. The initial development was to build up a central office for resource allocation and coordination. A second stage was to set up a decentralized divisional structure. According to Chandler, the response in Standard Oil was slower and more tentative than in Du Pont or General Motors, partly because the problems were more difficult and partly because of a general lack of concern with organizational problems.

During the 1920s and 1930s, Sears Roebuck underwent the same process in its own particular way, partly planned and partly unplanned. The initial defensive strategy of vertical integration produced a centralized, functionally departmentalized structure. Continued growth produced the pressure for decentralized, regional organization and for sorting out the relationship between operating units and functional departments. Contributors to the book edited by Chandler and Daems trace similar processes in French, German, and British industry.

For Chandler, both his case studies and his broader work illustrate a number of general points about structural development and organizational innovation. One is that the market and technological pressures of an urban, industrial society push enterprises in the same structural direction, but the actual process of innovation can be quite different. In this process, it is important to distinguish between an adaptive response and a creative innovation. An *adaptive response* is a structural change that stays within the range of current custom and practice, as was the case with functional departments and a central office. A *creative innovation* goes beyond existing practice and procedures—developing decentralized field units, for example. The general adoption of a line-and-staff departmental structure meant that delegation of authority and responsibility to field units was possible.

From this process, says Chandler, arises a new economic function in society—that of administrative coordination and control. To carry out that function, a new species is created: the salaried manager. In carrying out the function, the modern business enterprise is produced, with its two specific characteristics: (a) the existence of many distinct operating units and (b) their management by a hierarchy of salaried executives.

Bibliography

Chandler, A. D., *Strategy and Structure,* MIT Press, 1962.

Chandler, A. D., *The Visible Hand: The Managerial Revolution in American Business,* Harvard University Press, 1977.

Chandler, A. D., and Daems, H., (eds.), *Managerial Hierarchies: Comparative Perspectives on the Rise of the Modern Industrial Enterprise,* Harvard University Press, 1980.

Chandler, A. D., and Tedlow, R. S., *The Coming of Managerial Capitalism,* Irwin, 1985.

Sloan, A. P., *My Years with General Motors,* Doubleday, 1972.

Oliver E. Williamson

Oliver Williamson, an American economist, began his working life as a project engineer in U.S. government service but soon moved into academic life, taking degrees at Stanford and Carnegie-Mellon Universities. His career has taken him through leading U.S. universities, and he is now TransAmerica Professor of Business, Economics, and Law at the University of California, Berkeley.

Williamson probes beneath the usual questions about what organizations are like and how their members behave to ask why they are there at all. Why organizations? His answer is that they lower the cost of transactions. He sees society as a network of transactions—contracts in the widest sense of that term—and suggests that a "transactional paradigm" will yield the reasons for organizations. These reasons are not size—that is, the economies of scale that have been supposed to explain large organizations—nor large-scale technologies, but the information cost of transactions. Size and technology are important, not in themselves, but because of the demands they make for information.

Each of the multitude of recurrent transactions that take place in a society can be conducted either in a market or within an organization. Which mode of transacting is used depends on the information available and the costs to the transacting parties of adding to that information should they require more. So, as the requirements for information change, transactions may be conducted more in markets or more and more within organizations. The trend has been for more transactions to be gathered within the boundaries of organizations, and Williamson's discussion is primarily about change in that direction. He has been concerned mainly with societies moving that way, but if the starting point were a society in which central planning and non-market transactions predominated, the analysis could, as appropriately, deal with the shifting of transactions from within organizations out to markets. Analysis of transaction costs can answer "Why not organizations?" as well as "Why organizations?"

Williamson's point of view joins market economics to organization theory in a form of institutional economics. He looks forward to the

23

possibility that measures of market structure will eventually combine with measures of the internal structure of organizations (see Derek Pugh and the Aston Group, p. 8).

Markets and *hierarchies* are alternatives for conducting transactions. So, transactions are brought within the hierarchical structures of organizations when the market mode is no longer efficient. For example, mergers or takeovers bring into a single organization contracting parties whose transactions will then be regulated by the internal rules of a hierarchy, and not by the rules of a market. Or, organizations are set up to transact within themselves business that might alternatively have been done by separate parties contracting between themselves in market terms.

Which mode is adopted depends on the degree of *information impactedness*. This exists when the "true underlying circumstances" of a transaction are known to one or more parties but not to others. Where there is less than complete trust between the parties, those who lack information could only obtain parity by incurring costs, which may be high, even prohibitive. Thus, a buyer who is offered supplies may be unsure whether the quality will be what is required, whether delivery is likely to be on time, or how far the proposed price is more than need be paid. This uncertainty may arise because no one, not even the seller, has adequate information on these matters; or, it may be that even if information is available, the buyer cannot trust it because the seller will have interpreted it to favor the selling vantage point.

A market is the most efficacious mode of conducting transactions when all necessary information is conveyed between parties by a price, and this single item of information is sufficient. Transactions are better brought within a hierarchy when much more must be known, much less is certain, and there may be "quasi-moral" elements, because the hierarchy brings the inadequately informed parties to a transaction together under some degree of control.

Transactions will be shifted out of a market and into the hierarchy of a firm or other form of organization when information impactedness is high—that is, when the uncertainties and distrust inherent in transactions become too great for prices to be acceptably determined. At this point, the advantages of a hierarchy become the greater. First, it extends the bounds on rationality. Although the rationalities of each party within an organization are still restricted, specialization enables each to deal with a part of the overall problem that is small enough to be comprehended, the results of all their work being brought together by specialized decision makers at the apex. More information is exchanged or can be required to be handed over. Common numbering and coding systems and occupational jargon cut down communication costs. Second, subsections of an organization can each attend to a given aspect of the uncertainty-complexity of a situation, thus making manageable a problem that would, in total, be too uncertain-complex. Aspects can be attended to as the situation unfolds, rather than all at once, and decisions that might otherwise be too complex can be split into smaller sequential steps. Third, a hierarchy curbs opportunism. Pay, promotion, and control techniques ensure that the parties work in some degree toward common goals. Confidence may not be complete, but it is greater. Parties cannot use their gains entirely for their own ends, and what they do can be more effectively checked and audited. Should disputes arise, superior hierarchical levels can decide them. Fourth, where there are small numbers, a situation that opportunistic parties are inclined to take advantage of, the hierarchy can overrule bargaining.

In general, then, hierarchy more nearly approaches parity of information and, in particular, provides for quasi-moral and reciprocal obligations over and above strictly economic ones.

What, then, stops hierarchies from taking over more and more transactions indefinitely? The limits begin to appear as firms grow larger and as vertical integration between firms extends. Costs then rise to a level at which the marginal costs of administering the incremental transaction begin to exceed those of completing transactions through a market. The goals of groups or subsections within an organization start to outweigh the common aims; the proliferation of specialists in control systems to combat this tendency becomes more and more expensive; sunk costs encourage the persistence of existing ways of doing things even if they would not now be done that way, were they to be started afresh; and communication is increasingly distorted. Leaders become more distant from those they lead—"bureaucratic insularity"—and cooperation between those at lower levels becomes perfunctory, rather than wholehearted. Coordination and common purpose lapse.

These costs rise in the unitary structure of hierarchy (called U-form) when the top management of the single large organization tries to control transactions within it. The U-form is therefore a vanishing breed among large U.S. corporations, although the Reynolds Metal Company and the Quaker Oats Company retained this form through the 1960s. Organizational transaction costs can be relatively reduced by the adoption of a multidivisional structure (called M-form), as in the examples described by Chandler (see p. 20) of Du Pont, General Motors, Standard Oil of New Jersey, and Sears Roebuck, which changed to the M-form in the 1920s and 1930s. To be effective, this form of organization requires a general overall management that concentrates on monitoring the performance of the constituent divisions and on strategic planning. Management can use the multidivisional structure as a miniature capital market in which funds are moved into the most profitable uses more effectively than by the external capital market because, internally, there is more complete information about the firm than parties in the external capital market have about comparative investment opportunities.

But if general management gets involved in the day-to-day operation of the divisions, then information costs will again be forced up, in what is called the "corrupted M-form." One large corporation is quoted as attempting to move from the corrupted M-form by releasing 5,000 nonproduction personnel. It also reduced corporate staff—that is, people not reporting to profit centers—by more than 1,300, down to a new total of 132. The aim was to decentralize into true profit centers, in which each divisional manager's performance could be accurately evaluated without the allocation of heavy corporate overheads.

If the change from the corrupted M-form cannot be achieved and the information costs remain high, then market transactions will become more attractive. Ultimately, the relative cost of overcoming information impactedness determines whether the transactions in a society are conducted through markets or within organizations.

Bibliography

Williamson, O. E., *Markets and Hierarchies: Analysis and Antitrust Implications,* Free Press, 1975.
Williamson, O. E., *Economic Organization,* New York University Press, 1986.

Henry Mintzberg

Henry Mintzberg is Bronfman Professor of Management at McGill University, Montreal. He graduated from the Sloan School of Management at the Massachusetts Institute of Technology. Among a variety of consulting assignments and visiting appointments, he has been Visiting Professor at the University of Aix-en-Provence in France. He has studied what managers actually do as they manage and what kinds of organizations they are managing.

Mintzberg shows a substantial difference between what managers do and what they are said to do. On the basis of work-activity studies, he demonstrates that a manager's job is characterized by pace, interruptions, brevity, variety and fragmentation of activities, and a preference for verbal contacts. Managers spend a considerable amount of time in scheduled meetings and in networks of contacts outside meetings.

The fragmentary nature of what managers do leads to the suggestion that they have to perform a wide variety of roles. Mintzberg suggests 10 managerial roles that can be grouped into three categories: interpersonal, informational, and decisional.

The *interpersonal category* covers the relationships that a manager has to have with others. The three roles within this category are figurehead, leader, and liaison. Managers have to act as *figureheads,* representing their organizations, because of their formal authority and symbolic position. As *leaders,* managers have to bring together the needs of an organization and those of the individuals under their command. The third interpersonal role, that of *liaison,* deals with the horizontal relationships that work-activity studies have shown to be important for a manager. A manager has to maintain a network of relationships outside the organization.

Managers have to collect, disseminate, and transmit information and have three corresponding roles in the *informational category*—namely, monitor, disseminator, and spokesperson. A manager is important as a *monitor* of what goes on in the organization, receiving information about both internal and external events and transmitting it to others. This process of transmission is the role of *disseminator,* passing on information of both a factual and value kind. A manager often has to give information concerning the organization to outsiders, taking the role of *spokesperson* to both the general public and those in positions of influence.

As with so many writers about management, Mintzberg regards the most crucial part of managerial activity as that concerned with making decisions—the *decisional category.* The four roles that he places in this category are based on different classes of decisions—namely, entrepreneur, disturbance handler, resource allocator, and negotiator. As *entrepreneurs,* managers make decisions about changing what is happening in an organization. They may have to both initiate change and take an active part in deciding exactly what is to be done. In principle, they are acting voluntarily. This is very different from their role as *disturbance handlers,* in which managers have to make decisions that arise from events beyond their control and unpredicted. The ability to react to events, as well as to plan activities, is an important managerial skill in Mintzberg's eyes.

The managerial role of *resource allocator* is central to much organizational analysis. Clearly, a manager has to make decisions about the allocation of money, people, equipment, time, and so on. Mintzberg points out that, in doing so, a manager is actually scheduling time, programming work, and authorizing actions. Mintzberg puts the *negotiator* role in the decisional category because it is "resource trading in real time." A manager has to negotiate with others and, in the process, must be able to make decisions about the commitment of organizational resources.

For Mintzberg, these 10 roles provide a more adequate description of what managers do than any of the various schools of management thought. In these roles, the information is crucial; the manager is determining the priority of information. Through the interpersonal roles a manager acquires information, and through the decisional roles it is put into use.

The scope for each manager to choose a different blend of roles means that management is not reducible to a set of scientific statements and programs. Management is essentially an art, and it is necessary for managers to try to learn continuously about their own situations. Self-study is vital. At the moment, there is no solid basis for teaching a theory of managing. According to Mintzberg, "The management school has been more effective at training technocrats to deal with structured problems than managers to deal with unstructured ones."

Table 1.1 Seven Organizational Types

Organizational Configuration	Prime Coordinating Mechanism	Key Part	Type of Decentralization
Entrepreneurial	Direct supervision	Strategic apex	Vertical and horizontal centralization
Machine	Standardization of work processes	Technostructure	Limited horizontal decentralization
Professional	Standardization of skills	Operating core	Horizontal decentralization
Diversified	Standardization of outputs	Middle line	Limited vertical decentralization
Innovative	Mutual adjustment	Support staff	Selected decentralization
Missionary	Standardization of norms	Ideology	Decentralization
Political	None	None	Varies

SOURCE: Mintzberg (1989).

Mintzberg presents a way of understanding the design of organizations and suggests seven types. As shown in Table 1.1, the first of these types are differentiated according to which basic part of the organization forms the key to its operations. In the *entrepreneurial organization,* the "strategic apex" is key. In a manufacturer, for example, this would be the president or chief executive, the board of directors, and their personal staff. In a *machine organization,* the "technostructure" is key; this includes those in planning, finance, training, operations research and work study, and production scheduling. The key part in a *professional organization* is the "operating core," those at the working base of the organization. Whereas in a manufacturer this would be the buyers, machine operators, salespeople, and dispatchers, in a professional bureaucracy it might be doctors and nurses (in a hospital) or teaching staff (in a college). The "middle line" is the key part in the *diversified organization,* being the personnel who "manage managers" in the hierarchy between the strategic apex and the operating core. In manufacturing, these would include the heads of the production and sales functions and the managers and supervisors beneath them. In an *innovative organization,* what Mintzberg calls an adhocracy, the "support staff" are the key part. In a typical manufacturer, they might be in public relations, industrial relations, pricing, payroll, even the cafeteria, as well as in research and development, but in an adhocracy the focus is on the latter, the "R&D." In the final two configurations, no part of the organization itself is key. *Missionary organizations* are pulled by "ideology," and *political organizations* have no key feature.

In each of the first five types, its key part exerts a "pull" on the organization. "To the extent that conditions favor one over the others, the organization is drawn to structure itself as one of the configurations," or designs. It is pulled toward one more than toward the others.

The first type, the entrepreneurial organization, in which the strongest pull is by the *strategic apex* toward centralization, is as simple as its name indicates. It has little or no technostructure, few support staff, minimal differentiation between departments, and a small hierarchy. Coordination is by direct supervision, downward from the strong apex where power is in the hands of the chief executive; therefore, it does not need formal planning or training or similar procedures and can be flexible and "organic" (see also Burns, p. 46). The conditions favoring this form are those of the classic entrepreneurial owner-managed firm— a small organization in a simple yet dynamic environment that can be understood by one leading individual. Most organizations pass through this structure in their formative years, and some stay small enough to continue it. They could be as diverse as an automobile dealership, a retail store, a new governmental department, or a vigorous manufacturer on a small scale.

Some people enjoy working in such an organization because of the sense of mission it gives and its flexibility. Others resent the domination from the top; they see it as paternalistic or autocratic, unfashionable in democratic times. The organization is also precarious: "One heart attack can literally wipe out the organization's prime coordinating mechanism."

The machine organization is far more secure (see Weber, p. 5). It does not depend on a single person. The strongest pull on it is from its *technostructure,* the planners, financial controllers, production schedulers, and their kind. They pull toward standardization. Once work has been divided into standard routine tasks, it can be controlled by them through formalized rules and regulations. Control is almost an obsession. It is second only to the entrepreneurial organization in centralization, but in it power is divided between the strategic apex and the technostructure. A post office, a steel manufacturer, a prison, a major airline, and a vehicle assembler are all like this. They have the conditions favoring this design, mainly that they are older, larger organizations carrying out repetitive work in stable environments, probably themselves subject to control from a remote corporate head office or government.

Although efficient at repetitive work, this form of organization is riddled with conflict between top and bottom and between departments. To many of its personnel, the work they do is meaningless. Its managers spend much of their energy just holding it together. It was fashionable at the height of the Industrial Revolution, but like the entrepreneurial organization, it is no longer so.

The third kind of configuration or design, the professional organization, is pulled by its *operating core* toward professionalized autonomy; that is, it is dominated by highly trained professional specialists. These have to be employed because the work is too complex to be controlled and coordinated in any other way. So, it is broken into specialisms, and people who already have standardized skills are hired to do it—that means professionals already trained and indoctrinated who can be relied on to do what has to be done. This is the situation in universities, hospitals, schools, accountancy firms, social work agencies, and some firms that employ highly skilled craftspeople—for example, in fashion textiles designing. Because others without the training cannot interfere, the professionals are relatively independent. Their working autonomy is usually reinforced by a high demand for the service they give. Hence, whereas the machine organization is run by hierarchical authority, the professional organization emphasizes the power of expertise. Whereas the machine organization sets its own standards, the bureaucratic administrative framework of a professional organization accepts standards set externally by professional bodies such as the medical and accounting institutions.

This design of organization is uniquely democratic, but it suffers from difficulties of coordination and jurisdiction. Who should teach the statistics course in the management degree—the staff of the Mathematics Department or the Business Department? And who can declare a professor incompetent, and what then can be done about it?

The diversified organization is most widely used by large, private, industrial corporations, but it can also be seen in those U.S. universities that have several campuses, or in health administrations that control several hospitals, and generally in socialist economies in which government ministries control numbers of enterprises. It piggybacks on the machine organization because a headquarters is controlling several of them. These make a powerful *middle line,* in Mintzberg's terminology, the key part around which the organization functions. It is pulled toward Balkanization because each division is relatively self-sufficient, with its own marketing, purchasing, and manufacturing (or equivalent) and so on, and each operates in its own market. Indeed, the diversified form is usually the result of a machine organization diversifying across more than one market, either into different products or into different geographic areas.

Although each division has a great deal of autonomy, headquarters decides how much capital each shall have and watches numerical performance indicators, such as profits, sales, and return on investment. This is where the problems arise. Headquarters may meddle too much in divisional decisions, and its concentration on numerical indicators may neglect other considerations, such as product quality or environmental preservation. Mintzberg suspects that although the diversified organization is a fashionable sign of the times, it may be the most vulnerable of the five designs to legal and social changes.

In contrast, a space agency, an avant-garde film company, a factory making complex prototypes, or a petrochemicals company is likely to be designed as an innovative organization, or adhocracy. These are young, research-based organizations that need to innovate in rapidly changing conditions. The primary key part of an adhocracy is the *support staff* in research and development, but there may also be key *operating core personnel,* experts on whom innovation depends. Unlike the professional organization, the adhocracy is not seeking the repetitive use of professionally standardized skills. Instead, it groups its highly trained specialists into mixed project teams, hoping to generate new ideas. It is pulled toward coordination within and between teams by "mutual adjustment" (see Thompson, p. 58)—that is, by direct cooperation. Unified bureaucratic controls might get in the way. Of the five designs of organization, "Adhocracy shows the least reverence for the classical principles of management" (e.g., as promulgated by Fayol, p. 86). It is uniquely both organic and decentralized.

Adhocracy has two variants. An *operating adhocracy* works directly for clients, as in an advertising agency, whereas an *administrative adhocracy* serves itself, as did the National Aeronautics and Space Administration (NASA) in building up U.S. space exploration.

Inevitably, adhocracy creates difficulties as well as innovations. People talk a lot, and this costs time. There is confusion over who is doing what. It is the most politicized design, breeding internal competition and conflict. But its strength in enabling flexibility of response means that new industries rely on this configuration. Mintzberg maintains that adhocracy is the structure of the present age, and he also confesses that this is the type of organization he likes best.

The missionary organization does not have a key part, as such. Its key glue, which holds everything together, is the possession of an *ideology*—that is, a rich system of distinctive values and beliefs shared by all the members. It is rooted in a deep sense of mission, associated with charismatic leadership and developed through strongly held traditions that reinforce the identification of the individual with the organization. Coordination is through standardization of norms, reinforced by selection and indoctrination of members. The West had thought this approach to be appropriate to religious institutions, but Japanese corporations have shown that it can be successfully applied in business settings—and not only in the Japanese culture. Many U.S. firms have an overlay of the missionary approach (e.g., McDonald's, Hewlett-Packard) and build their effectiveness on an organizational ideology.

The final configuration is the political organization, which does not have overall coordinating mechanisms, but is characterized by conflict. All organizations have a degree of conflict in which some "political" activity takes place. This does not prejudice the organization's functioning; indeed, it has a positive role to play in stimulating change. But when the conflict is pervasive, the organization has become politicized. This form characterizes some large, public-sector institutions riven by conflicting approaches about both methods and objectives and by private corporations in post-takeover and merger situations. If the conflict cannot be reduced, then the organization will not survive—unless it is artificially protected by, for example, the government.

It is important for managers to understand the configuration of their particular organization to ensure that the various parts "fit together" and are consistent in what they do. But, Mintzberg warns, do not forget there will always be contradictions among the forces in organizations. Managers should use these contradictions creatively, not ignore or try to suppress them.

Bibliography

Mintzberg, H., *The Nature of Managerial Work,* Harper & Row, 1973; Prentice Hall, 1980.

Mintzberg, H., "The Manager's Job: Folklore and Fact." *Harvard Business Review,* (1975), 49-61; reprinted in D. S. Pugh (ed.), *Organization Theory,* Penguin Books, 1997.

Mintzberg, H., *The Structuring of Organizations,* Prentice Hall, 1979.

Mintzberg, H., *Mintzberg on Management,* Free Press, 1989.

Charles Handy

Charles Handy is a British writer and broadcaster. Born in Ireland, he has been an oil company executive, a business economist, and a professor at the London Business School. He was Warden of St. George's House in Windsor Castle, which is a center for discussion of issues of business ethics, on which topic he takes a Christian approach. He has served as Chair of the Royal Society for the Encouragement of Arts, Manufacture, and Commerce and was the 1994 British Business Columnist of the year. His concern is with the changing nature of work and organizations in modern economy and society.

Handy distinguishes four types of organizations, each symbolized by its characteristic ancient Greek god. Each generates a distinctive organizational culture that pervades all its activities. The first type is the *club culture,* thought of as presided over by Zeus, who epitomizes the strong leader who has power and uses it. The visual image of this culture is a spider's web. Although there may be formal organizational departments and lines of authority, the only lines that matter are those, formal or informal, leading to the boss at the center of the web. Most organizations begin in this culture, where the strength is in speed of decision. A limitation is that the quality of the decisions depends entirely on the caliber of the boss and the inner circle because others can make little impact. You advance in this organization by learning to think and act as the boss would have done in your situation.

The second type of organization is the *role culture,* with its patron god Apollo, the god of order and rules. It is pictured as a Greek temple. The pillars represent the functions and divisions of the organization. Within them, it is assumed, people are rational and roles are defined, allocated, and carried out according to systems of rules and procedures. It is the culture that Weber (p. 5) called bureaucratic and that Burns (p. 46) called mechanistic, and many large organizations that value stability and predictability are of this type—for example, government administration, insurance corporations, and organizations with a long history of success with one product or service. Its strength is shown when tomorrow can be expected to be like yesterday; conversely, its weakness is its slowness to recognize the need for strategic change and inability to adapt.

The third type is the *task culture* of Athena, goddess of knowledge. In this culture, management is regarded as a series of problems to be solved. First define the problem and then allocate resources for its solution, including people, machines, and money. The visual image of the organization is a net because it draws resources from all parts of the system. It is a network of loosely linked matrix structures in which task forces, working parties, ad hoc groups, and so on are brought together to achieve a particular goal. It is the culture that Burns (p. 46) called organic (or organismic). It works well when flexibility is required because the organization's output is a series of solutions to particular problems (e.g., in consultancy companies, advertising agencies, R&D departments). But these cultures do not function well when repetition and predictability are required or when low costs are a major factor in success.

The final type of organization is the *existential culture,* presided over by Dionysus, god of wine and song. The key difference here is that, unlike the other types, in which the individual is subordinate to the aims of the organization, in this type the organization exists to help in the achievement of the individual's aims. For example, groups of professionals such as doctors, lawyers, or architects can come together to create an organization so as to share an office, a telephone, a secretary. In these organizations, the individual professionals are supreme; they recognize no "boss," although they may accept coordination from a committee of their peers. These organizations are so democratic that few sanctions are available to administrators. Management, which is regarded as a chore, requires general consent, which leads to endless negotiation to obtain any coordinated effort.

No business or industrial organizations operate completely within this last culture. But an important change is occurring in the nature of organizations, which find it efficient to contract out more and more of their work to independent professionals. Organizations will therefore have to deal more and more with those who take a Dionysian view of the world.

This is only one of a number of changes currently being experienced in employment. They are not part of a predictable pattern, but rather are *discontinuous* changes in society. Such discontinuities happen from time to time in history. The change in the basis of economic activity from agriculture to industry is an example. The change now is from profitability based on machine power and brawn to profitability based on intelligence and professional skills. McKinsey and Company, the management consultants, has estimated that, by the year 2000, 80% of all jobs will require cerebral rather than manual skills, a complete reversal from 50 years earlier.

In this new situation, both the nature of work and the nature of organizations are changing. In general, people can no longer expect to work their lives in one occupation, perhaps for one employer. Organizations can no longer afford the overhead of carrying large numbers of people who may only be wanted for part of the time. Instead, work must be reconceptualized in a much more flexible way as a "portfolio of activities" based on professional knowledge and skill, which a person is able to offer to a number of organizations.

Handy uses the Irish national emblem—the shamrock—to characterize the ways in which people are linked to modern organizations. The *shamrock organization* has three parts, comparable to the three leaves the cloverlike shamrock has on each stem. Each part represents a different category of contribution to the organization by separate groups of people who have differing expectations and who are managed and paid differently.

The first part of the shamrock is the *professional core* of qualified professionals, technicians, and managers. They are essential to the organization, owning the organizational knowledge that distinguishes it from its competitors. They are therefore hard to replace, and the organization pays them high salaries and fringe benefits. In return, the organization wants commitment, hard work, and long hours. They are managed in the task culture and thus are expected to be flexibly available to go anywhere at any time and to do what is required. For this, they are paid more and more. Thus, they are expensive, and organizations look for ways to reduce their numbers. Downsizing has been characteristic of organizations in recent years, but output has gone up: Half the number, paid twice as much, producing three times the output, appears to be the aim.

With a smaller core, more and more work is contracted out to specialists who can do it more efficiently and inexpensively. So, a *contractual fringe* has come into being and is taking a larger and larger proportion of the work. This is the second part of the shamrock. Manufacturing firms typically make fewer and fewer of the components of their products. They have become assemblers of parts manufactured by suppliers, hence the importance of Japanese just-in-time delivery systems. Organizations regularly contract out activities that were once regarded as a normal part of their work—for example, advertising and market research, computing, and catering. The contractual fringe is made up of people and organizations who are paid for the results achieved (fees, not wages), and this has great importance for the way in which they are managed. They are paid for output achieved, not for hours spent at work. But organizations are much more used to paying employees for time and have to learn to manage the contractual relationship effectively across a very wide range of activities.

The third part of the shamrock is the *flexible labor force*. These are the part-time and temporary workers who are the fastest growing part of the employment market. Because organizations want to both increase their ability to respond to variations in demand and improve profitability, they turn to this force to give them additional flexibility. Because people in this force are part-time or seasonal employees, the problem is that employers may regard this part of the organization as merely casual labor. But if these workers are treated casually, they will be casual in their attitudes to the organization and its outputs, which means that the standards aimed for will not be reached. They are managed in the role culture, and although they will never have the commitment of the core, they have to be treated fairly if they are to be adequate in their roles.

Along with the development of the shamrock organization has come another discontinuous change in the nature of authority in organizations: the emergence of the *federal organization*. This is more than just a decentralized organization; the logic of that form implies that knowledge and power are at the top of the hierarchy and that certain amounts of them are handed down to the component parts. In the federal organization, the logic goes the other way, with the subsidiaries federating together to get benefits of scale, but the drive and energy coming mostly from the parts. The center is small. It does not direct or control the activities of the parts; rather, it advises and influences, only reserving to itself a few key decisions (e.g., capital allocations, appointment of top executives). Its vital task is to give a vision that shapes and gives point to the work of all the parts. Handy compares this form of organization to a university or college, where the top management group can have only limited understanding about the large range of teaching and research activities being carried out.

For federalism to work well, two key principles must be understood and practiced. The first is *subsidiarity,* the principle that the larger and higher body should not exercise functions that can be carried out efficiently by smaller and lesser bodies. For those at the center, this a much more difficult concept to put into practice than it appears because a considerable amount of trust and confidence is required. The center cannot be sure whether the subsidiary organization can carry out the function efficiently before it has actually done so. But, in a catch-22 situation, if it uses this lack of experience as an argument against allowing them to try, then subsidiarity will never occur.

The second principle refers to those in the subsidiaries: They must want to increase the range of activities in their roles. Handy uses the analogy of the *inverted doughnut* to focus on the changing nature of organizational roles. A doughnut (or bagel) has a hole in the middle; the inverted doughnut is filled in the middle, but the surround is empty up to the round contours of the edge. The core represents which part of the job is fully prescribed, often in a job description, which if not done well will be seen as a clear failure on the part of the job occupant. But a job will also have discretionary opportunities that no one has specified but that, if carried out effectively, will be regarded as showing appropriate initiative. These can fill the space up to the outside rim of the doughnut, which represents the boundaries of the discretion allowed in the job.

Traditionally, jobs in organizations have had large cores and small areas of discretion, as in an Apollo role culture. This structure allows control of the processes and of the behavior of the people. In federal organizations, the cores are much smaller because the exercise of discretion by subsidiary staff is key for subsidiarity to occur. These are more likely to be the task cultures of Athena. Controls can only be exercised after the event through "management by results," and mistakes will inevitably occur. Managements have to learn to forgive mistakes and not always punish them, because this is how learning takes place.

Bibliography

Handy, C., *The Gods of Management,* Souvenir Press, 1978; Pan Books, 1979.

Handy, C., *Understanding Organizations,* 3rd ed., Penguin Books, 1985.

Handy, C., *The Age of Unreason,* Business Books, 1989.

Handy, C., *The Empty Raincoat,* Hutchinson, 1994. (published in the United States as *The Age of Paradox,* Harvard Business School Press)

Handy, C., *Beyond Certainty,* Hutchinson, 1995.

Handy, C., "Trust and the Virtual Organization," *Harvard Business Review* (May-June 1995), 40-50; reprinted in D. S. Pugh (ed.), *Organization Theory,* Penguin Books, 1997.

Christopher Bartlett and Sumantra Ghoshal

Christopher Bartlett and Sumantra Ghoshal are business school academics who have studied the functioning of corporations that operate internationally. Bartlett is a Professor at the Harvard Business School; Ghoshal is at the London Business School. Their research leads them to propose that a new type of organizational structure, with its concomitant distinctive managerial thinking, is required for success in the current global business environment.

Bartlett and Ghoshal maintain that the world's largest companies are in flux because global pressures have forced them to rethink their traditional worldwide strategies. Although some firms have prospered, most are struggling for survival. Even within particular industries, big differences have been manifested in performance. For example, within the consumer electronics industry, the Japanese Matsushita corporation has prospered, whereas the American General Electric was eventually forced to sell off its business in this sector. It is not just a matter of the Japanese being better at it than the Americans. In the soap and detergent market, the American Procter & Gamble was able to mount a major thrust into international markets, whereas the international efforts of Kao, the dominant Japanese competitor in this industry, have stalled.

The key is the organization's capability for effective international operations. This is a combination of its strategic posture, its organization structure, and its attitude toward learning and innovation. For each firm, the particular characteristics of its organizational capability have been built up over previous decades in response to the problems faced then. This administrative heritage is an organizational asset, but it has to be examined very carefully and questioned because it is also a constraint in adapting to new global environmental demands.

In the 1980s, three distinct types of cross-national firms, each with different capabilities, could be identified: multinational companies, global companies, and international companies.

Multinational companies have developed a strategic posture and structure that allow them to be very sensitive to differences in national environments. Their key capability is *responsiveness*. They build a strong local presence by responding to local market opportunities and are prepared to vary their products and even their businesses as necessary in the different countries. Firms such as the Anglo-Dutch Unilever and the American International Telephone and Telegraph (ITT) were pioneers in developing links to each host country's infrastructure and thus creating conglomerates. These are relatively decentralized confederations with distributed resources and responsibilities. The control exercised may be limited to little more than the supervision of financial results.

Global companies are driven by the need for common global operations and are thus much more centralized in their strategic and operational decisions. Their key capability is *efficiency*. They obtain cost advantages through building world-scale facilities to distribute standard products to markets everywhere. It is a form pioneered in the auto industry by Ford and is the approach taken by many Japanese companies, such as Matsushita and Toyota. The center retains strong control in decision making, and foreign operations are seen as delivery mechanisms to global markets. Products and strategies are developed to exploit what is regarded as a worldwide unitary market.

International companies base their strategy primarily on transferring and adapting the parent company's knowledge and expertise to foreign markets. Their key capability is *transfer of learning*. The parent company retains considerable influence, but local units can adapt products and ideas coming from the center. Firms such as the American IBM and the Swedish Ericsson run a "coordinated federation" in which the subsidiaries have more autonomy than in the global company but less than in the multinational firm. Particular functions, such as R&D, product development, and market development, as well as finance, are kept close to the center. So, both responsiveness to local markets and integrated global development have a degree of benefit.

Within the last decade, because of the turbulence of the global environment, not one of these three types of structures and its accompanying capability has been adequate for success. For example, customers are demanding differentiated products as provided by the multinational company, but with the same high quality and low costs as standard products provided by the global company. Also, frequent changes in economic, technological, political, and social environments require the firm to be readily responsive. But in addition, the organization has to build in the capability to continue to be responsive to the inevitable changes that occur in tastes, technologies, and exchange rates.

A new form of organization has been emerging to cope with this complex and changing global situation. It does not demand responsiveness *or* efficiency *or* learning as the key capability, but rather requires all three to be achieved simultaneously. This is the *transnational organization,* in which managers accept that each of the three previous types is partially true and has its own merits but that none represents the whole truth. Bartlett and Ghoshal put forward the transnational organization concept as a managerially sophisticated ideal type toward which cross-national organizations will have to develop in order to obtain and retain global competitiveness.

In the transnational company, an *integrated network* structure is developed in which neither centralization nor decentralization is embraced as a principle but selective decisions about location and authority have to be made. Certain activities may be best centralized within the home country (e.g., basic research, treasury function), but others are best concentrated in certain subsidiaries (e.g., component production in low-wage economies, technical development in countries with a technically sophisticated infrastructure), whereas yet others are decentralized to many national operations (e.g., differentiated product assembly, sales). So, for example, a U.S. transnational may obtain the benefits of world-scale production for labor-intensive products by building in a low-wage economy like Mexico while obtaining the benefits of producing technically sophisticated products in Germany and assembling both in Britain for the European market. Thus, there is a considerable degree of functional and national specialization, which requires the interdependencies to be well managed. Frequently, these interdependencies are designed to build self-enforcing cooperation among different units, such as when the French subsidiary depends on Spain for one range of products while the Spanish one depends on France for another.

The transnational organization requires a distinctively different approach from previous forms of international operations. Its management has the key task of developing a set of strategic capabilities and relevant organizational characteristics as shown in Table 1.2.

To obtain global competitiveness with the transnational's dispersed and interdependent assets and resources requires balancing diverse capabilities and perspectives. As Crozier (p. 131) and Hickson (p. 14) have shown, the group that copes with the most critical strategic tasks of the organization gains power. So, for example, in Unilever (a "multinational" company), the geographic managers became dominant because their contribution was crucial to achieving the dispersed responsiveness

Table 1.2 Building and Managing the Transnational Organization

Strategic Capability	Organizational Characteristics	Management Tasks
Global competitiveness	Dispersed and interdependent assets and resources	Legitimating diverse perspectives and capabilities
Multinational flexibility	Differentiated and specialized subsidiary roles	Developing multiple and flexible coordination processes
Worldwide learning	Joint development and worldwide sharing of knowledge	Building shared vision and individual commitment

SOURCE: Bartlett and Ghoshal (1989).

required. But in Matsushita (a "global" company), the product division managers dominated because they were the key to the company's world-scale efficiency. In IBM (an "international" company), the strong technical and marketing functional groups retained their power through all reorganizations because they were the basis of the company's strategy of building and transferring its core competencies for worldwide learning. The transnational company, however, must develop a multidimensional organization structure that legitimates diversity and eliminates any bias that favors the management of any particular function, product, or geographic area.

Similarly, the transnational needs to develop flexible coordination processes among the highly specialized and differentiated roles of its subsidiaries. It cannot rely on one preferred way of obtaining control. The preferred American way of a formalized control system (e.g., as in ITT), the preferred Japanese way of a centralized decision-making structure (e.g., as in Kao), and the preferred European way of a socialization process for instilling a common culture (e.g., as in Unilever) are all inadequate by themselves for the transnational. A portfolio of highly flexible coordination processes calling on all these approaches is required. These are used in appropriate ways for different types of national subsidiaries.

One type of national subsidiary may act as a *strategic leader* in a particular product market. For example, the Phillips subsidiary in the United Kingdom is the lead company for the whole corporation in the teletext market. The dominant approach to coordination in this case is the process of socialization. A second type of subsidiary may act in a *contributor* role. This type has a good local resource capability but is operating in a market of limited strategic importance. An example is Ericsson's Australian subsidiary, which made important contributions to the development of its telephone switching business but whose home market is limited. It therefore has to be developed to contribute more widely to international operations. In this case, direct headquarters coordination is appropriate. A third type of national subsidiary is the *implementer,* which carries out the corporation's operations in a market of limited potential. For example, Procter & Gamble created teams to develop Euro Brands, which could be marketed on a coordinated European basis. This plan required its subsidiaries in various European countries to refrain from modifying the formula, changing the packaging, or adjusting the advertising approach in order for the company to obtain efficiencies of scale. This implementer type of subsidiary is coordinated by formalized systems, which require the least corporate management time.

The internal differentiation both of subsidiary company roles and of types of coordination processes—which may change from issue to issue—can lead to severe conflict in a transnational. The need for worldwide sharing of knowledge can cause difficulties too. Therefore, a final key task of the central management is the need to unify the organization through a shared corporate vision. This task requires clarity, continuity, and consistency of purpose. Transnational organizations have to work to establish and communicate these attributes if they are to form the basis for the generation of individual commitment. It requires, among other things, a sophisticated human resource management system that pays particular attention to training and development and to career management in an international setting.

Bartlett and Ghoshal are very clear that the complex transnational structure is not just a more sophisticated matrix structure. It is much more than that because a new management mind-set is needed to understand the multidimensional nature of the tasks and to be prepared to interact openly and flexibly on them with others. As they put it, "The task is not to build a sophisticated matrix structure, but to create a 'matrix in the minds of managers.'"

Bibliography

Bartlett, C. A., and Ghoshal, S., *Managing Across Borders: The Transnational Solution,* Century Business, 1989.

2 The Organization in Its Environment

The beginning of administrative wisdom is the awareness that there is no one optimum type of management system.

Tom Burns

The effective organization has integrating devices consistent with the diversity of its environment. The more diverse the environment and the more differentiated the organization, the more elaborate the integrating devices.

Paul Lawrence and Jay Lorsch

Uncertainties pose major challenges to rationality.

James D. Thompson

The key to organizational survival is the ability to acquire and maintain resources.

Jeffrey Pfeffer and Gerald R. Salancik

Efficient organizations establish mechanisms that complement their market strategy.

Raymond E. Miles and Charles C. Snow

An ecology of organizations seeks to understand how social conditions affect the rates at which new organizations and new organizational forms arise, the rates at which organizations change forms, and the rates at which organizations and forms die out.

Michael T. Hannan and John Freeman

Whether they like it or not, the headquarters of multinationals are in the business of multicultural management.

Geert Hofstede

All organizations are situated in an environment, be that, for example, business, governmental, educational, or voluntary service. In this environment are other organizations and people with whom transactions have to take place. These will include suppliers, clients or customers, and competitors. In addition, more general aspects of the environment will have important effects, such as legal, technological, and ethical developments.

The writers in this section have analyzed how the need to function successfully in different environments has led organizations to adopt different structures and strategies. Tom Burns examines the effects of rapidly changing technological developments on the attempts of old established firms to adjust to new environments. Paul Lawrence and Jay Lorsch emphasize that the appropriateness of an organization's structure in relation to its environmental requirements is the basis of effectiveness.

James Thompson portrays organizations as open systems having to achieve their goals in the face of uncertainty in their environments. Jeffrey Pfeffer and Gerald Salancik argue for a "resource dependence perspective," which sees all organizational functioning as resulting from the organization's interdependence with its environment. Raymond Miles and Charles Snow emphasize the strategic choices that managements have to make to adapt to the environmental pressures they face, whereas Michael Hannan and John Freeman take an ecological and evolutionary view of the chances of organizations surviving in their particular environments.

Geert Hofstede highlights national culture as it affects management values and processes. This environmental feature is particularly important in the ever more frequent international activities of organizations.

Tom Burns

Tom Burns spent more than 30 years at the University of Edinburgh, retiring in 1981 as Professor of Sociology. His early interests were in urban sociology, and he worked with the West Midland Group on Postwar Reconstruction and Planning. While he was at Edinburgh, his particular concern was with studies of different types of organizations and their effects on communication patterns and on the activities of managers. He has also explored the relevance of different forms of organizations to changing conditions—especially to the impact of technical innovation.

In collaboration with a psychologist (G. M. Stalker), Burns has studied the attempt to introduce electronics development work into traditional Scottish firms, with a view to their entering this modern and rapidly expanding industry as the markets for their own well-established products diminished. The difficulties these firms faced in adjusting to the new situation of continuously changing technology and markets led him to describe two "ideal types" of management organizations, which are the extreme points of a continuum along which most organizations can be placed.

The *mechanistic* type of organization is adapted to relatively stable conditions. In it, the problems and tasks of management are broken down into specialisms within which each person carries out his or her assigned, precisely defined task. The hierarchy of control is clear, and the responsibility for overall knowledge and coordination rests exclusively at the top of the hierarchy. Vertical communication and interaction (between superiors and subordinates) is emphasized, and there is an insistence on loyalty to the concern and obedience to superiors. This system corresponds quite closely to Weber's rational-legal bureaucracy (see p. 5).

The *organismic* (also called *organic*) type of organization is adapted to unstable conditions when new and unfamiliar problems continually arise that cannot be broken down and distributed among the existing specialist roles. There is, therefore, a continual adjustment and redefinition of individual tasks, and the contributive rather than restrictive nature of specialist knowledge is emphasized. Interactions and communication (information and advice, rather than orders) may occur at any level as required by the process, and a much higher degree of commitment to the aims of the organization as a whole is generated. In this system, organizational charts laying down the exact functions and responsibilities of each individual are not found, and indeed their use may be explicitly rejected as hampering the efficient functioning of the organization.

The almost complete failure of the traditional Scottish firms to absorb electronics research and development engineers into their organizations leads Burns to doubt whether a mechanistic firm can consciously change into an organismic one. This is because individuals in a mechanistic organization not only are committed to the organization as a whole but also are members of a group or department with a stable career structure and sectional interests in conflict with those of other groups. Thus, power struggles develop between established sections to obtain control of the new functions and resources. These struggles divert the organization from purposive adaptation and allow out-of-date mechanistic structures to be perpetuated and "pathological" systems to develop.

Pathological systems are attempts by mechanistic organizations to cope with new problems of change, innovation, and uncertainty while sticking to the formal bureaucratic structure. Burns describes three of these typical reactions. In a mechanistic organization, the normal procedure for dealing with a matter outside an individual's sphere of responsibility is to refer it to the appropriate specialist or, failing that, to a superior. In a rapidly changing situation, the need for such consultations occurs frequently, and in many instances the superior has to put the matter higher still. A heavy load of such decisions finds its way to the chief executive, and it soon becomes apparent that many decisions can only be made by going to the top. Thus, what develops is Burns's first typical reaction—the *ambiguous figure system* of an official hierarchy and a nonofficially recognized system of pair relationships between the chief executive and some dozens of people at different positions in the management structure. The head of the concern is overloaded with work, and many senior managers whose status depends on the functioning of the formal system feel frustrated at being bypassed.

Some firms attempt to cope with the problems of communication by creating more branches of the bureaucratic hierarchy (e.g., contract managers, liaison officers). This is Burns's second typical reaction—a system described as the *mechanistic jungle,* in which a new job or even a whole new department may be created whose existence depends on the perpetuation of these difficulties.

Burns's third type of typical reaction is the *superpersonal* or *committee system.* The committee is the traditional way of dealing with temporary problems that cannot be solved within a single individual's role without upsetting the balance of power. But as a permanent device, it is inefficient, in that it has to compete with the loyalty demanded and career structure offered by the traditional departments. This system has been tried only sporadically by firms because it has been disliked as being typical of inefficient governmental administration; attempts to develop the committee as a superperson to fulfil a continuing function that no individual could carry out have met with little success.

For a proper understanding of organizational functioning, Burns maintains, it is therefore always necessary to conceive of an organization as the simultaneous working of at least three social systems. The first of these is the *formal system,* derived from the aims of the organization, its technology, and its attempts to cope with its environment. This is the overt system in terms of which all discussion about decision making takes place. But organizations are also cooperative systems of people who have career aspirations and a career structure and who compete for advancement. Thus, decisions taken in the overt structure inevitably affect the differential career prospects of the members, who will therefore evaluate them in terms of the second social system—the *career system*—as well as the formal system, and will react accordingly. This action leads to the third social system that is part of an organization—its *political system.* Every organization is the scene of "political" activity in which individuals and departments compete and cooperate for power. Again, all decisions in the overt system are evaluated for their relative impact on the power structure, as well as for their contribution to the achievement of the organization's goals.

It is naive to consider the organization as a unitary system equated with the formal system, and any change to be successful must be acceptable in terms of the career structure and the political structure as well. This is particularly so with modern technologically based organizations that contain qualified experts who have a career structure and a technical authority that goes far beyond the organization itself and its top management. Thus, the attempt to change from a mechanistic to an organismic management structure has enormous implications for the career structure (which is much less dependent on the particular organization) and the power system (which is much more diffuse, deriving from technical knowledge as much as formal position).

Concern with the interaction of these three social systems within the organization continues in Burns's study of the British Broadcasting Corporation (BBC). The BBC is a very segmented organization both horizontally, where many departments (e.g., Drama, Outside Broadcasts, Finance) appear to be competing as much as cooperating, and vertically, where in order to rise in the grading structure, executives soon lose contact with the professional skills (e.g., journalism, engineering) they are supposed to administer. In this situation, the career and the political systems can become more important than the formal authority system.

Burns charts the rise in power of the central management of the BBC at the expense of the creative and professional staff, which stems from the corporation's financial pressures. He maintains that the corporation can only develop as a creative service dedicated to the public good if it is freed from its financial client relationship to the government.

"A sense of the past and the very recent past is essential to anyone who is trying to perceive the here-and-now of industrial organization." If the organizational structure is viewed as a result of a process of continuous development of the three social systems of formal organization, career structure, and political system, a study of this process will help organizations avoid traps into which they would otherwise fall. Adaptation to new and changing situations is not automatic. Indeed, many factors militate against it. An important one is the existence of an organizational structure appropriate to an earlier phase of development. Another is the multifaceted nature of the commitments of organizational members—to their careers, to their departments, and to their specialist subunits. These are often stronger than their commitment to the organization as a whole.

Bibliography

Burns, T., "Industry in a New Age," *New Society,* 31 January 1963, no. 18; reprinted in D. S. Pugh (ed.), *Organization Theory,* Penguin Books, 1997.

Burns, T., "On the Plurality of Social Systems," in J. R. Lawrence (ed.), *Operational Research and the Social Sciences,* Tavistock, 1966.

Burns, T., *The BBC: Public Institution and Private World,* Macmillan, 1977.

Burns, T., and Stalker, G. M., *The Management of Innovation,* Routledge Chapman & Hall, 1961; 3rd ed., Oxford University Press, 1994.

Paul Lawrence and Jay Lorsch

Paul Lawrence and Jay Lorsch were professorial colleagues in Organizational Behavior at the Harvard Business School. Together with many collaborators (who include S. A. Allan, S. M. Davis, J. Kotter, H. Lane, and J. J. Morse), they conducted a series of studies into the appropriate structure and functioning of organizations using what has become known as the "organization and environment" approach, described in their seminal book of that title.

Lawrence and Lorsch began their analysis with the question of why people seek to build organizations. Their answer is that organizations enable people to find better solutions to the environmental problems facing them. This explanation immediately highlights three key elements in their approach to understanding organizational behavior: (a) People, not organizations, have purposes; (b) people have to come together to coordinate their different activities into an organization; and (c) the effectiveness of an organization is judged by the adequacy with which the members' needs are satisfied through planned transactions with the environment.

To cope effectively with their external environments, organizations must develop segmented units, each of which has as its major task the problem of dealing with some aspect of the conditions outside the firm. For example, in a manufacturing firm with production, sales, and design units, the production unit deals with production equipment sources, raw materials sources, and labor markets; the sales unit faces problems with the market, the customers, and the competitors; and the design unit has to cope with technological developments, governmental regulations, and so on. This *differentiation* of function and task is accompanied by differences in cognitive and emotional orientation among the managers in different units, and differences, too, in the formal structure of different departments. For instance, the development department may have a long-term time horizon and a very informal structure, whereas the production department may be dealing with day-to-day problems in a rigidly formal system, with the sales department facing the medium-term effects of competitors' advertising with moderate formality.

Even so, the organization is a system that has to be coordinated so that a state of collaboration exists to obtain for members the benefits of effective transactions with the environment. This is the required *integration,* and it, too, is affected by the nature of the external conditions.

The basic necessity for both appropriate differentiation and adequate integration to perform effectively in the external environment is at the core of Lawrence and Lorsch's model of organizational functioning. The approach was developed in an important study they carried out on 10 firms in three industries—plastics (6 firms), food (2 firms), and containers (2 firms)—that constituted very different environments for the enterprises concerned.

The study recognized that all the firms involved segment their environment. Each of the 10 was dealing with a market subenvironment (the task of the sales department), a technoeconomic subenvironment (the task of the manufacturing unit), and a scientific subenvironment (the task of the R&D or design department). The greater the degree of uncertainty within each subenvironment and the greater the diversity between them, the greater the need of the firms to *differentiate* between their subunits of sales, production, and research in order to be effective in each subenvironment. For example, on the one hand, in the plastics industry, which was found to have great diversity, with the science subenvironment highly uncertain but the technoeconomic one relatively stable, a considerable degree of differentiation within effective firms was found. In the container industry, on the other hand, all parts of the environment were relatively certain, and so a much lower degree of differentiation was apparent.

But greater differentiation brings with it potential for greater interdepartmental conflicts as the specialist groups develop their own ways of dealing with the particular uncertainties of their own subenvironments. These differences are not just minor variations in outlook; they may involve fundamental ways of thinking and behaving. In the plastics industry, a sales manager may be discussing a potential new product in terms of whether it will perform in the customers' machinery, whether they will pay the cost, and whether it can be got onto the market in 3 months' time. The research scientist at the same meeting may be thinking about whether the molecular structure of the material could be changed without affecting its stability and whether doing this would open a line of research for the next 2 years that would be more interesting than other projects. These two specialists not only think differently but also dress differently, have different habits of punctuality, and so

Table 2.1 Comparison of Integrative Devices in Three High-Performing Organizations

	Plastics	*Food*	*Container*
Degree of differentiation	10.7	8.0	5.7
Major integrative devices	(1) Integrative department	(1) Individual integrators	(1) Direct managerial contact
	(2) Permanent cross-functional teams at three levels of management	(2) Temporary cross-functional teams	(2) Managerial hierarchy
	(3) Direct managerial contact	(3) Direct managerial contact	(3) Paper system
	(4) Managerial hierarchy	(4) Managerial hierarchy	
	(5) Paper system	(5) Paper system	

SOURCE: Lawrence and Lorsch (1967).

on. It becomes crucial, therefore, that a highly differentiated firm should have appropriate methods of *integration* and conflict resolution if it is to perform well in the environment.

Table 2.1 lists the integrative devices that were found to be operating in three high-performing organizations, one from each of the industries studied. The top row gives the rating for the degree of differentiation. The need to operate effectively in the plastics environment led the firm to develop a high degree of differentiation, the container firm had the lowest differentiation, and the food firm was in between.

Each of these firms used a different combination of devices for achieving integration. All of them, to some extent, used the traditional methods of paper systems, the formal managerial hierarchy, and direct managerial contact between members of the different departments. For the container firm, with the least differentiation, these methods were sufficient; but in the food firm, which had a greater need for integration, temporary teams made up of specialists from the units involved were set up to deal with any particularly urgent issue. Managers within functional departments were also assigned integrating roles, such as that of liaison officer. Clearly, the effective food firm was devoting more time and effort to integrating activity.

The plastics organization had, in addition, established a special department, one of whose primary activities was integration. It also had an elaborate set of permanent integrating teams, each made up of members from the various functional units and the integrating department. The purpose of these teams was to provide a formal setting in which interdepartmental conflicts, such as the one described above between the sales manager and the research scientist, could be resolved with the help of an integrator. The effective plastics firms drew on the whole range of integrative devices and needed to do so because its necessary differentiation was so high.

The appropriateness of the three-way relationships among the uncertainty and diversity of the environment, the degree of organizational differentiation, and the state of integration and conflict resolution achieved will lead to effective functioning. Inadequacy in any of these relationships was associated with lower performance. Thus, for example, the high performers in the plastics and food industry had *both* greater differentiation *and* greater integration than the low performers because both were required. By contrast, in the low-performing container organization, no evidence was found that the integrating unit it possessed was serving a useful purpose, given its low level of differentiation.

Effective conflict resolution, which is the behavioral basis of integration, was found to have a pattern in which inter-unit conflict is dealt with by managers working in a problem-solving mode to face the issues and work through to the best overall solution—rather than smoothing over the issues to avoid conflict or letting the party with the greater power force its solution on others. It was also found that, in dealing with conflict effectively, the people primarily involved in achieving integration (whether they be superiors in the line hierarchy or persons appointed specifically to coordinating roles) need to have their authority based not just on their formal position, but largely on their knowledge of and competence on the issues as perceived by all the groups involved, together with a balanced orientation between the parties. The power and influence to make decisions leading to the resolution of conflict must, therefore, be located at the points where the knowledge to reach such decisions also exists.

The Lawrence and Lorsch framework, by emphasizing that the appropriate organizational structure will depend on the environmental demands, takes a "contingency" approach, rejecting the formulation that one particular structural form (e.g., bureaucracy; see Weber, p. 5) or one particular motivational approach (e.g., Theory Y; see Likert and McGregor, p. 146) is always best. Appropriateness is the key.

Lorsch and Morse, in a further study, compared two manufacturing plants (one high-performing, one low-performing) with two research laboratories (similarly high and low performers). The organizational structures and processes of the high-performing manufacturer in a relatively certain environment were high formality, short time-horizon, and highly directive management. The people working in this organization were found to have low cognitive complexity, low tolerance for ambiguity, and dependence in authority relationships. The high-performing research laboratory in a relatively uncertain environment had low formality, long time-horizons, and high participation. Its members had high cognitive complexity, high tolerance for ambiguity, and independence in authority relationships. Yet, both organizations were effective because they were appropriately organized with appropriate members for their environmental tasks. Indeed, the less effective organization in each pair did not show most of the distinctive characteristics of structure and process to the same degree; however, the characteristics of the members were as clearly differentiated as in the successful organizations. The less effective organizations, it seems, could obtain the appropriate people but could not organize them in the appropriate way. But equally, in other cases, failure could be a result of having inappropriate people even though they were appropriately organized.

In a later study of seven major U.S. industries, including those of steel, agriculture, hospitals, and telecommunication, Lawrence and Dyer developed the "competitive principle." This principle maintains that an industry needs to experience an appropriate degree of vigorous competition in its environment if it is to be economically strong. Either too little or too much competition will lead to inefficient and non-innovative performance. They argue for the setting up of a governmental agency to monitor the competitive pressures in each industry and thus determine whether the pressures need to be increased or reduced.

The analysis of matrix organizations has been a particular concern of Davis and Lawrence. Matrix organization structures are those with a multiple command system—many managers having two bosses. For example, finance managers would have a finance director to whom they would be responsible for professional standards and who would be concerned with their career development and promotion. In addition, each of the finance managers would also report to a project director to whom they would be responsible for giving the appropriate cost accounting services needed for their current project and who would therefore be in charge of the day-to-day work allocation. Clearly, this form of structure violates Fayol's principle of "unity of command" (see p. 89), and its greater complexity would be the preferred structure only in certain situations: (a) when several highly salient sectors (e.g., products, markets, functions) are simultaneously necessary for goal achievement; (b) when the tasks are uncertain, complex, and interdependent; and (c) when there is a need to realize economies by using scarce resources effectively. In these circumstances, the need is for complex differentiation and integration via the matrix mode.

Bibliography

Davis, S. M., and Lawrence, P. R., *Matrix,* Addison-Wesley, 1977.

Donaldson, G., and Lorsch, J. W., *Decision Making at the Top,* Basic Books, 1983.

Lawrence, P. R., and Dyer, D. *Renewing American Industry,* Free Press, 1983.

Lawrence, P. R., and Lorsch, J. W., *Organization and Environment,* Harvard Business School Press, 1967.

Lawrence, P. R., and Lorsch, J. W., *Developing Organizations: Diagnosis and Action,* Addison-Wesley, 1969.

James D. Thompson

After leaving the U.S. armed forces subsequent to World War II, James Thompson (1920–1973) became a sociologist. Yet, he made his contribution to the understanding of organizations through research in business schools. He was the founding editor of the world's leading research journal in organization theory—the *Administrative Science Quarterly*. He died prematurely, only 6 years after the publication in 1967 of his classic book *Organizations in Action*. This book draws together a range of ideas that were forming at the time it was written and that have continued to be at the center of organization theory. It is a portrayal of complex organizations "as open systems, hence indeterminate and faced with uncertainty, but at the same time as subject to criteria of rationality and hence needing determinateness and certainty." It pictures organizations continually striving to act rationally in the face of technological and environmental uncertainties. Their basic problem is how to cope with these uncertainties.

In other words, organizations—or rather, their members—aspire to be reasoned and orderly despite circumstances and events that may prevent their being so. These standards, or *norms of rationality* to which they aspire, demand of organizations both coordination within and adjustment without. The twin tasks of administration are to provide the needful coordination within the organization and the adjustment to circumstances outside it.

The first task, therefore, is to achieve the stable coordination of those basic work activities, which Thompson calls the *technical core* of an organization. For example, in factory production work, supplies of components must be continuously in the right places at the right times if assembly is to proceed smoothly, just as in a college the teachers and students must be in the right rooms at the right times.

The second task of administration is to regulate transactions across the boundary of the organization—that is, its contacts with the world outside itself. This might be done by negotiating with outside interests for, say, assured financial credit or raw materials or by changing with the environment, as when a chain of toy stores changes what it sells in response to rising public standards of safety for children. Or, it might be done by *buffering*. Buffering protects the technical core from the uncertainties of acquiring resources and of disposing of outputs, for example, by having a purchasing department to handle suppliers and a sales department to deal with customers. A public relations department can cope with challenges to the rightfulness of what the organization is doing, as in the cases of nuclear power and cigarette manufacture. Such *boundary spanning units* are placed between the technical core and the outside world to buffer it from external shocks. Another possibility is to move the boundaries of the organization to encircle sources of uncertainty and bring them under control—for instance, to ensure supplies by buying up a supplier firm.

Hence, organizations come to be made up of a variety of parts. These can be linked together in fundamentally different ways, and so internal interdependence may differ from one organization to the next and within any one organization. Interdependence can be pooled, sequential, or reciprocal. In *pooled interdependence,* the work of each part of an organization is not directly connected to that of the others but is a "discrete contribution to the whole." Yet, because each is supported by that whole organization, which in turn would be threatened by the failure of any of its parts, they have a pooled interdependence within it. Such is the situation in a university, where the departments of biology, French language, and management, for example, are not linked in any way other than by their common reliance on the university as a whole.

In *sequential interdependence,* one part cannot do its job until others have done theirs. Tasks have to be done in sequence—first this, then that. Such is the situation in a factory where one workshop must machine components to the correct sizes before the next can put them through a hardening treatment, and so on through successive stages up to the final product.

In *reciprocal interdependence,* each does something for the other. Unlike the one-way flow in sequential interdependence, the outputs of both become inputs for the other. That is the situation in an airline where the flight operations section constantly makes aircraft available to the maintenance engineers for servicing, and the engineers constantly turn out aircraft ready for the operations people to fly.

Reciprocal interdependence requires the closest coordination, sequential interdependence less, and pooled interdependence least. Although all organizations have a certain amount of pooled interdependence, and in some it may be the prevalent form, not all have sequential interdependence in addition to pooled, and fewer still have within them all these three kinds of interdependence.

The various units are grouped in the hierarchy of an organization in such a way as to minimize the costs of coordinating what they do. The means of coordination differ. Reciprocally interdependent units have to coordinate what each does for the other by *mutual adjustment,* so they are likely to be placed together in the hierarchy under common superiors who can ensure that they cooperate. If units are sequentially interdependent, then their work can be coordinated by *planning or scheduling,* the work of each being planned to dovetail in sequence with that of the next in line. In a factory, a prior department in the sequence has to turn out enough components so that the next department in the sequence is not left standing idle. If there is merely pooled interdependence, then some coordination within the whole can be achieved by *standardization* of the rules that link each part to the whole. In a university, for example, although departments differ in their contributions to the whole, in principle they are all to be dealt with in the same manner when it comes to examination procedures or budget allocations (which is not to say that they all get the same budget).

Organizations also differ in the activities undertaken by their technical core. They have one or more of three technologies. First, a *long-linked technology,* as in manufacturing, performs a series of tasks in a set order, giving rise to the sequential interdependence of units referred to earlier. Second, a *mediating technology* links other parties, as where banks mediate between lenders and borrowers or an employment agency mediates between prospective employers and employees. Third, an *intensive technology* functions in response to feedback from the object worked on, as where what is done and when it is done depend, for example, in a hospital, on the patient's condition, or at a construction site, on the condition of the ground.

The ways in which organizations attempt to encircle external sources of uncertainty by extending their boundaries are determined by these kinds of technology. Those with long-linked technologies tend to go for a corresponding vertical integration, as when oil refiners own roadside service stations and automobile manufacturers own suppliers of components. Those with mediating technologies try to increase the populations they serve, so airlines increase their route networks and banks put branches into new areas. Finally, organizations with intensive technology attempt to incorporate the object worked on so as to control it better—for instance, universities making their students also their members and therefore subject to their rules, and mental hospitals bringing patients inside for observation.

This extension of boundaries is not the only way of coping with environmentally derived uncertainty. As also mentioned before, organizations can buffer their technical core by setting up boundary-spanning units that allow the core to operate as if there were stability. By stockpiling supplies and outputs, for example, work can continue as if there were a steady stream of supplies and a steady demand by the market. Alternatively, fluctuations may be prevented, as when utilities offer inexpensive off-peak gas or electricity to smooth out demand, or may be anticipated, as when ice-cream production is adjusted to seasonal changes. If buffering, smoothing, and anticipating fail, organizations can resort to rationing. So the U.S. Postal Service gives priority to first-class mail, a hospital may deal only with urgent cases, and a manufacturer may limit the proportion of popular items taken by any one wholesaler.

The relation between technical core and boundary-spanning activities gives rise to appropriate types of structure. Where technical core and boundary-spanning activities can be isolated from one another, there is likely to be in the hierarchy a layer of functionally specialized departments, such as purchasing and sales and finance, comparatively remote from the core and under central control. Where core and boundary activities are more closely interdependent, there is more likely to be a divisionalized structure, decentralized into "self-sufficient clusters" of units. Each cluster has only so much to deal with, for instance, as in a divisionalized multinational firm that has one multidepartment division covering Europe, another covering Southeast Asia, and so on.

Norms of rationality, which Thompson repeatedly stresses are assumed in all that he has to say about organizations, require that organizations "keep score" so that their performances can be assessed. The problem is how to do this. Where it is possible to trace clearly the consequences of what is done—for instance, where there is a clear presumption that new equipment has reduced costs—then efficiency measures can be used. These assume understanding of cause and effect and known standards of performance, as is the case with many financial indicators in industry. If *intrinsic criteria,* which indicate relatively directly the standard of work done, are lacking, however, then *extrinsic criteria* have to be used. From these, the quantity and quality of the work can be inferred, but they do not show it directly. Hence, university research is measured by counting the money gained for it in competitive applications to funding institutions and by the number of publications about it, rather than by its results as such, and mental hospitals emphasize discharge rates, rather than the extent to which patients are cured.

Organizations are torn between the differing assessments made by a variety of assessors. The potential users of a public health service will look at it in one way; the government providing the money will look at it in another. The users are concerned with the treatment given; the government is concerned more with the cost of the treatment. Shareholders stress dividend and profits; customers stress prices. So, each organization tries to do best on the criteria used by those on whom it is most dependent. Furthermore, it will try to score well on the most *visible criteria.* These are the most obvious to the most important assessors. Business firms are sensitive to the price of their stock on the stock exchange, schools announce the examination performances of top students, and so on. Less visible criteria may be neglected even if they are intrinsically more desirable.

According to Thompson, the more sources of uncertainty there are, the more possibilities there are for gaining power (also see Crozier, p. 131) and the more likely it is that "political" positions will be taken up. In general, people higher in management have discretion in decisions, and so what should be done is subject to their personal judgment, including their assessment of what will be acceptable to others. This political assessment would be crucial in deciding whether two departments could be successfully merged, for example.

The making of decisions involves beliefs or assumptions as to what will happen if this, rather than that, is done and preferences as to what is most desirable. There is less certainty about some beliefs and preferences than there is about others, as illustrated by Thompson's matrix:

| | | Preference regarding possible outcomes | |
		Certainty	Uncertainty
Beliefs about cause/effect relations	Certain	Computational Strategy	Compromise Strategy
	Uncertain	Judgmental Strategy	Inspirational Strategy

The matrix shows four likely kinds of *decision-making strategies.* The two left-hand boxes represent situations in which there is relative certainty on what is wanted. Those concerned are clear on what outcome they prefer. In the top left-hand box, they are also certain of what the consequences of their decision may be. Such all-around certainty might occur if they were considering increasing existing production capacity in response to a steady rise in sales. Agreed on the need to expand, and knowing the technology from past experience, the managers could confidently calculate likely costs and returns in a *computational* manner. The bottom left-hand box, however, represents a situation in which cause and effect are less well known. Here, the same managers still want to expand capacity, but if they do, they will have to buy new machinery of an untried design. This decision is less susceptible to computation, more a *judgmental* matter assessing the risk involved.

In the two right-hand boxes, managers are not sure what they want, and they may be divided in their opinions. Alternative outcomes may each be attractive—for instance, increasing capacity either for mass production of low-quality products or for a smaller volume of high-quality products. If the technology for both is well known and if market forecasts are confident that either can be profitable, a *compromise* strategy results in some of each. If there is all-around uncertainty, as in the bottom right-hand box, then an *inspirational* strategy is more likely. There are neither clear preferences for high-volume against low-volume production, nor confidence in what the consequences of new production machinery or of launching more goods onto the market will be. The strategy has to be an inspired leap in the dark.

In Thompson's view, the aim of management and administration when designing organizations and making decisions must be the effective alignment of organizational structure, technology, and environment. This central conception has been and continues to be at the heart of organization theory, and it is a constant stimulus to research. Again and again, his analysis is returned to as a source of ideas, few of which have been as yet supplanted.

Bibliography

Thompson, J. D., *Organization in Action,* McGraw-Hill, 1967.

Jeffrey Pfeffer and
Gerald R. Salancik

Jeffrey Pfeffer and Gerald Salancik are, respectively, professors at the Stanford University Graduate School of Business, California; and at Carnegie-Mellon University, Pittsburgh. Pfeffer and Salancik contend that organizations should be understood in terms of their interdependence with their environments. They advocate a *resource dependence perspective.* For example, explaining discontent among the employees of a fast-food chain in terms of poor human relations and poor pay is irrelevant if the organization can draw on a pool of easily recruited youthful labor; and because its competitors can do so, too, the organization is not going to incur the costs of better human relations and pay.

Organizations are not self-directed and autonomous. They need resources, including money, materials, personnel, and information, and to get these they must interact with others who control the resources. This interaction involves them in a constant struggle for autonomy as they confront external constraints. They become "quasi markets" in which influence is bartered not only between internal sections but also between those sections or subunits and external interests.

Interdependence with others lies in the availability of resources and the demand for them. It is of many kinds—for instance, the direct dependence of a seller organization on its customers; and the indirect dependence on each other of two seller organizations, not in mutual contact, via a set of potential customers for whom they compete.

Three conditions define how dependent an organization is. First is the importance of a resource to it. This is a combination of the magnitude of that resource—in other words, the proportion of inputs and outputs accounted for by the resource—and of its criticality, best revealed by how severe the consequences would be if it were not available. Second is how much discretion those who control a resource have over its allocation and use. If they have completely free access to it and can make the rules about it, then an organization that needs it can be put in a highly dependent position. Third is how far those who control a resource have a monopoly of it. Can an organization that needs it find an alternative source or a substitute? Thus, "the potential for one organization's influencing another derives from its discretionary control over resources needed by that other and the other's dependence on the resource and lack of countervailing resources or access to alternative sources." Because the others on whom an organization depends may not be dependable, its effectiveness is indicated more by how well it balances these dependencies than by internal measures of efficiency of a financial or similar nature.

To Pfeffer and Salancik, the possible strategies that an organization may use to balance its dependencies are of four kinds:

1. It may adapt to or alter external constraints.
2. It may alter the interdependencies by merger, diversification, or growth.
3. It may negotiate its environment by interlocking directorships or joint ventures with other organizations or by other associations.
4. It may change the legality or legitimacy of its environment by political action.

The first kind of strategy—adapting to or altering external constraints—may be carried out in numerous ways. An organization can pay sequential attention (see March, p. 121) to the demands made on it, attending first to one and then to another as, in turn, they become more pressing. For example, for a time, customers may take priority, and then attention may switch to financial economies required by owners or lenders. An organization can play one interest against another (e.g., blaming different unions for current difficulties). It can influence the formulation of demands (e.g., by advertising); it can claim that it cannot comply because of, say, legal restrictions; and it can minimize its dependence by stocks of materials or money.

Merging, diversifying, and growing are each ways of pursuing the second kind of strategy—altering the interdependent relationships. Mergers do this by bringing control of critical resources within one organization, stabilizing the exchange of which they are part. They may be backward, sideways, or forward, incorporating suppliers, competitors, or purchasers. Diversification shifts and widens the interdependencies in which an organization is enmeshed, extricating it from overdependence in any one field. Growth in size increases the power of an organization relative to others and makes more others interested in its survival. Size has been found to improve stability more than profitability.

Negotiating the environment, the third kind of strategy, is a more common strategy than total absorption by merger. Interlocking directorships whereby boards include members of the boards of other organizations, cartels to control supplies, trade agreements, memberships in trade associations and coordinating industry councils and advisory bodies, joint ventures in which two or more organizations work together, and the like are commonplace. Such links help keep the participating organizations informed about what is happening outside themselves and ensure mutual commitment. Normative expectations about what each other will do build up, making each more sure of the other's reliability.

Finally, if none of the other strategies are open to them, organizations resort to the fourth strategy—political action. They endeavor to obtain and sustain favorable taxation, or tariffs, or subsidies, or licensing of themselves or their members (e.g., as where the practice of medicine or law is restricted to defined categories of qualified people), or they charge others with violating regulations (as when competitors are accused of prohibited monopolistic arrangements). Political activity by organizations that give to political party funds, that lobby members of legislatures, and that are represented on governmental and related agencies and councils is constant. Indeed, if the level of state regulation is high, the decisions of lawmakers and governmental agencies become more important to an organization than those of its customers or clients.

How are the effects of the environment, with whose elements an organization is interdependent, transmitted to that organization? It is generally accepted that environments affect organizations, but how that happens is not made explicit. Pfeffer and Salancik suggest that one means is *executive succession*—that is, the removal of executives and their replacement by others. Through this method, the environment influences the political processes within organizations from which action emerges.

Pfeffer and Salancik's argument has three causal steps. In the first step, changes in which sectors of the environment are uncertain and in which sectors are less so mold the pattern of power in an organization. This molding occurs as posited by the "strategic contingencies theory of intraorganizational power," formulated by Hickson, Hinings, and their colleagues (see Pugh and the Aston Group, p. 13). According to this theory, those sections or subunits of organizations most able to cope with what is uncertain in an organization (e.g., a marketing department smoothing out erratic fluctuations in orders by shrewdly timed advertising, a maintenance department keeping production flowing by skilled attention to breakdowns) gain power, subject to two conditions: (a)

They must be non-substitutable (no one else can do what they do), and (b) they must be central (many others in the organization are affected by what they do, and the organization's main outputs would be affected immediately if they ceased to do it).

In the second step, the resulting distribution of power then affects the choice of top personnel. As Pfeffer and Salancik put it, "We view administrative succession as a political process of contested capability, where the contest is resolved by subunit power." The tendency is to blame top management for difficulties, the counterpart to top management's own tendency to take credit for successes in a world over which they have limited control. So, they tend to be removed if things go badly, and who is removed and who replaces them follows the perceptions of the powerful as to who can best cope with the perceived uncertain dependencies.

The third step is that once executives and administrators are appointed, they can and do influence the main directive decisions. Although their control over their world is limited, it is sufficient to shape decisions. They take part in what Child has called "strategic choice" (see Pugh and the Aston Group, p. 13), which delineates the intended future course of their organization. They "enact" an environment, acting according to how they see it and trying to change it to their organization's advantage. Further, changes in top personnel permit movement between organizations, and this can be a tacit means of coordination. The managers of one organization know the managers in another.

Top managements are especially concerned with (a) scanning the environment to find out what is happening and what may happen, (b) loosening dependencies so that the organization does not become too dependent on any one or few others, and (c) managing conflicting external demands. It has been fashionable to forecast that the environment they face will become more and more dispersed and turbulent, but Pfeffer and Salancik do not agree. They foresee "an increasingly interconnected environment in which power is increasingly concentrated." Although they write in terms of the U.S. variant of the capitalist system, their resource dependence perspective generalizes beyond that.

Bibliography

Pfeffer, J., and Salancik, G. R., *The External Control of Organizations: A Resource Dependence Perspective,* Harper & Row, 1978.

Raymond E. Miles and Charles C. Snow

Raymond Miles and Charles Snow are both professors in U.S. business schools. Miles is Professor of Business Administration at the University of California, Berkeley. He has studied and advised a wide variety of organizations in the public and private sectors. Snow is Professor of Organizational Behavior at Pennsylvania State University.

Miles and Snow ask how and why organizations differ in strategy, in structure, in technology, and in administration. Why do some offer a broad range of products or services and others offer a narrower range? Why are some structured around functional specialisms and others around product lines or services? Why are some more centralized, others more decentralized? For Miles and Snow, the answers can be found with Thompson (see p. 56) in what he termed the "alignment of organization with environment."

To align organization and environment successfully, management has to solve three problems, and solve them continuously: the entrepreneurial, engineering, and administrative problems. The *entrepreneurial problem* is to choose a general market domain, or field of operation, in which the organization can be viable, to specify the precise target market, and to decide on the right products or services for it. Solving this problem, however, requires also solving the *engineering problem,* taking the word *engineering* in a wide sense. Ways of making the products or of offering the services have to be found. Technologies must be appropriate. Then, the *administrative problem* is to organize and manage the work.

The aim should be an effective *adaptive cycle.* This means the entrepreneurial, engineering, and administrative problems are tackled in coherent, mutually complementary ways that enable the organization as a whole to survive.

In studies of a variety of kinds of organizations, Miles and Snow named four types of *adaptation strategies* pursued by organizations: Defenders, Prospectors, Analyzers, and Reactors. Defenders and Prospectors are at opposite ends of the continuum of possible strategies. Analyzers are somewhere in between, with some features of both. Each of these three types has its own typical solutions to the entrepreneurial, engineering, and administrative problems. Reactors are different again. They seem unable to pursue consistently any of the other three types of strategy, reacting to events in an inconsistent way.

The first type, the *Defenders,* choose to solve the entrepreneurial problem by aiming at a narrow and stable domain. They set themselves to sustain a prominent position in a narrow market segment, competing on quality and/or price to keep a particular clientele satisfied. They grow cautiously, step by step, by deeper penetration of this limited market. They reap the benefits of familiarity with it and with what they are doing, but they tend to miss new developments because their managerial personnel have a restricted range of external contacts. They risk being caught by a major market shift to which they cannot adapt quickly enough.

Defenders are inclined to concentrate mostly on their engineering problem. Solving it is the key to their success. They succeed by being cost-efficient in doing what they know how to do well. They concentrate on improving quality control, production scheduling, materials handling and inventory control, distribution, and the like. They buffer their core technology from external disturbance, as Thompson would put it, by carrying stocks of supplies and of products so that, although there may be ups and downs in stocks, the production work itself can proceed steadily. Buffering may be helped through vertical integration with other organizations—that is, by mutual ownership or contracts that ensure supplies and orders. Although a Defender may work efficiently, however, here again is a risk. It may be a long time before the investment in technology pays off.

The Defender-type approach leads to a typical solution to the administrative problem. Efficient supplying of a limited clientele requires relatively centralized support. Instructions flow down from the top, and reports and explanations flow upward, via a "long-looped vertical information system." A central array of specialist departments, such as accounting and sales and personnel, administer a range of formalized documented procedures, such as budget returns, work schedules, and stock listings. Together with the chief executive, the crucial finance and production functions dominate the centralized system. As always, there are risks. Although the system is orderly, novel opportunities may pass it by.

A Defender strategy has been pursued successfully by a food company in Northern California described by Miles and Snow. It has stayed within a specialty market for dried fruits and fruit juices. Beginning just by growing these fruits, it met competition by extending into processing the fruit for consumption. This work has been mechanized, costs of growing fruit have been held down, and a small team specializes in improving quality. Control is centralized on the president and the heads of field operations, sales, and finance, and higher-than-average wages ensure a stable labor force. The firm has a long-term coherence of entrepreneurial, engineering, and administrative solutions.

The second type, *Prospectors,* the opposites to the Defenders, aim to find and exploit new opportunities. They stress "doing the right things," rather than "doing things right," as Defenders do. They may value a reputation for innovation more than they value profitability. Solving the entrepreneurial problem in this way requires keeping in touch with trends and events across a wide field of view. A variety of individuals and sections in the organization brings in news of current happenings, not necessarily only the more obvious ones, such as the market research or research and development departments. Growth comes from new products or services and from new markets, rather than from deeper penetration of the same market, as with a Defender. It is likely to occur in spurts as opportunities are successfully taken up, rather than gradually. The gain to Prospectors from being open to fresh possibilities has to be balanced against the risks. In their case, these are, respectively, that they may not be fully efficient in any one activity and that they may overextend themselves by taking on too much without sufficient recompense.

Their enterprising approach to the entrepreneurial problem requires a flexible solution to the engineering problem, so they use a variety of technologies. They do many things at once and can switch between them. Each line of work can be built up or discontinued fairly readily. There has to be trial-and-error work on prototypes. The gain is a flexible workforce; the cost is the difficulties of coordinating such a diversity of differing activity.

These solutions to the entrepreneurial and engineering problems are accompanied by a typical solution to the administrative problem. In the case of a Prospector, the administrative problem is how to facilitate all this activity, rather than how to control it. How can resources be deployed effectively without impeding the work by imposing inappropriately rigid central control?

The answer is to plan broadly, but not in detail. Skilled personnel can be relied on to know their jobs without detailed overseeing from the top. Small groups are gathered in project teams or task forces to work on new initiatives, and these, together with easy lateral contact between departments, create "short horizontal feedback loops." In other words, lines of communication are comparatively short. People can communicate quickly with anyone else they need to contact without having to go to the top first. The structure is comparatively decentralized, and the marketing and R&D functions are more influential than in a Defender. The advantage of this administrative solution overall is that it can respond rapidly to change, but inevitably there are risks. Some attempts to launch new products or services will be wasteful failures, costly in capital and in the time of highly paid personnel.

Miles and Snow exemplify the Prospector strategy by the success of an electronics corporation. This huge enterprise, with 30,000 employees, makes and sells an extensive range of equipment, including small computers and calculators, electric meters, and electrical testing equipment. Its entrepreneurial strategy is to keep one step ahead. It frequently launches new products with novelty value that fetch high prices. By the time prices fall, either the firm can manufacture cheaply just as its competitors have learned to, or another new launch is ready. Teams of scientists and engineers work on new possibilities, backed by the powerful marketing function whenever a new product is ready. The tendency is to create relatively autonomous divisions in each new product area. The company has a widely active and decentralized entrepreneurial, engineering, and administrative pattern, quite different from the focused, centralized Defender pattern.

Analyzers attempt to achieve some of the strengths of both Defenders and Prospectors. They try to balance the minimizing of risk and the maximizing of profits. Their solution to the entrepreneurial problem is a mixture of stable and changing products and markets. Their stable activities generate earnings sufficient to enable them to move into innovative areas already opened up by Prospectors, who have taken the early risks. The Analyzer is a follower of change, not an initiator.

Because Analyzers have something of both the Defender and the Prospector entrepreneurial solutions, they are likely to have something of both engineering solutions. They are likely to have a dual technical core; that is, the work will be partly stable and routinized, partly shifting, as new products are accepted and put into production quickly without the prolonged experimentation that a Prospector has to do. This combined solution to the engineering problem demands a corresponding dual administrative solution. There is both detailed control of stable lines and broad planning of innovations. Production and marketing both are influential because they are critical to getting new products into production. There are both central functional specialisms and also autonomous self-contained product groups.

Among examples of Analyzers, Miles and Snow cite a medium-sized U.S. general hospital. After many years of stability as a Defender, it underwent a series of changes. These were intended to enable it to offer new services already offered by more innovative hospitals while still sustaining its traditional, relatively conventional patient care. This change in solution to its entrepreneurial problem required it to move toward Prospector-type engineering and administrative solutions. While retaining existing medical technology, it acquired modern diagnostic equipment and the technical and medical staff to go with it. Administratively, its previous unitary structure was broken down into three semiautonomous divisions, one of which contained all the new diagnostic services and clinics. It succeeded in following others into this kind of work and in attracting a fresh range of low-income patients while keeping its established high-income clientele.

Defenders, Prospectors, and Analyzers have viable strategies, but *Reactors* do not. They are an unstable form. They fail to achieve or hold to an appropriate defending, prospecting, or analyzing strategy. As a result, they are liable merely to react to change and to do so in ways that are both inconsistent and inappropriate, so they perform poorly. This makes them hesitant over what to do next. There are many possible reasons for this condition; Miles and Snow give examples of three. First, perhaps the strategy is not "articulated," so that managers are not fully aware of it, as when a strategy pursued successfully by a firm's founder died with him and left the managers in disarray, not knowing what to do without him. Second, perhaps even though there is a recognized strategy, the technology and the structure do not fit it, as when a publishing firm aspired to an Analyzer strategy but could not separate its stable lines of work, which needed careful central control, from its changing lines, which needed scope for trial and error. Third, perhaps both strategy and structure persist inappositely, as when a foods firm clung to its long-established Defender strategy and structure even though declining profitability in a changing market pointed to the need for change.

Miles and Snow look beyond this typology of strategies to conjecture about signs of the future emergence of yet another type. They call this the *market-matrix* form of organization. It would "pursue mixed strategies with mixed structures." Some recent kinds of organizations, such as conglomerates, multinational corporations, aerospace firms, and certain educational institutions, have moved toward it. They have matrix sections, where lines of authority deliberately intersect or double up—for instance, where a department head also has responsibility for a major innovative project. A further step is then to expect such a project manager to bargain internally, market-fashion, for resources and for skilled personnel, the personnel having to be "purchased" from existing departments. So, a new form may be arising that is fitted to complex tasks.

Miles and Snow intend their typology to help managers determine what kind of strategy to pursue. They present a diagnostic checklist of questions on an organization's present and potential strategies to use for this purpose.

Bibliography

Miles, R. E., and Snow, C. C., *Organizational Strategy, Structure, and Process,* McGraw-Hill, 1978.

Miles, R. E., and Snow, C. C., "Fit, Failure, and the Hall of Fame," *California Management Review, 26,* (1984), 10-28; reprinted in D. S. Pugh (ed.), *Organization Theory,* Penguin Books, 1997.

Miles, R. E., and Snow, C. C., *Fit, Failure, and the Hall of Fame,* Free Press, 1994.

Michael T. Hannan and John Freeman

Michael T. Hannan and John Freeman are both social scientists at Cornell University. After a period at Stanford University, Hannan moved to Cornell, where his coauthor Freeman had been for many years. Hannan is Scarborough Professor of Social Science. Freeman is Professor of Behavioral and Organizational Sciences and a former editor of the journal *Administrative Science Quarterly*.

It has been the shared aim of Hannan and Freeman to lift the view taken of organizations to a wider perspective. They have done this by looking at organizations much as a bioecologist or naturalist looks at animal life. They see populations of organizations surviving or thriving or declining in particular environments, just as populations of, say, rabbits survive or thrive in a particular ecological situation but die out in another. Just as the understanding of wildlife has been enhanced by the study of ecology, so can the understanding of organizations be enhanced. The wider ecological perspective goes beyond the problems each organization alone has in coping with the environment, to see an organization as one of a population of organizations that coexists with or competes with other populations of organizations. The environment of each organization consists mainly of other organizations, so the existence of each is bound up with that of its own kind and of other kinds—hence, the *population ecology of organizations.*

Societies engage in many kinds of activities, and many kinds of service and manufacturing organizations are available to do these activities. Why this many, and why does the number of kinds rise and fall? This question is the same as "Why are there so many species of animals?" For both organizations and animals, population ecology explains the replacement of outmoded forms by new forms.

Indeed, the ability of a whole society to keep up with change depends on the development of new forms of organization. If a society contains many differing forms of organization, then there is a good chance that one or more of these may fit some new circumstances that arise. These new circumstances can then be taken advantage of quickly. If a society has comparatively few forms of organization, the society has to adapt to change by modifying one or more of these or by creating a new form; the latter takes longer. So, a society that already has among its hospitals some that specialize in advanced surgery can readily add on heart transplant techniques; but if it has only a uniform range of general hospitals that deal with the most common and inexpensively treated ailments, it has more difficulty in doing so.

This view assumes that populations of organizations evolve much as populations of biological species evolve. Those that fit their situation survive and thrive, and those that do not die out. This is a "Darwinian evolutionary position." It argues that change takes place more by the growth of new forms of organizations than by the intended reform of existing ones. Many theorists have pointed out that change in an organization is largely uncontrolled. Although its management may believe they are making changes according to plan, what happens is more haphazard than that. Differing views, unreliable information, and unforeseen eventualities make it uncertain whether they will get what they want, even if they know what they want (March, p. 121; Thompson, p. 56). Therefore, a Darwinian explanation that some forms fit the situation and prosper whereas others fail to fit and so decline is more tenable than supposing that managements succeed in deliberately redesigning existing organizations to bring them up to date. Burns (p. 46) describes an example of this. Several well-established firms in Britain were unable to change sufficiently to move into the new field of electronics even though they were offered every encouragement to do so. Their form of organization was too fixed.

The evolution of populations of organizations is not necessarily a steady process. It is more likely that there are periods of rapid change as new forms are tried out, interspersed with comparative stability during which existing forms persist. This explanation would match contemporary views of biological evolution that regard it as "punctuated equilibria"—long periods of comparatively balanced stability broken by shorter spasms of change. U.S. labor unions did not grow steadily in number. Spurts of activity occurred at the end of the 19th century, again after World War I, and again in the 1930s, when many new unions were founded. Between these peaks, relatively few new ones appeared.

Hannan and Freeman concentrate on the density within each population—that is, the number of organizations of a particular form. The density of a population is determined by how many organizations come and go. In other words, it is determined by how many are newly founded or come in from elsewhere and by how many cease to exist or leave to do something different.

Density has limits. Each *niche* in an environment can support a population density up to the limit of the *carrying capacity* of that niche. When the resources of a niche are exhausted, density can rise no further; that is, when competition for money and supplies and customers (or whatever else is needed) reaches an unsustainable level, some organizations will be squeezed out. This is analogous to what happens to wildlife when numbers become too great. Those who study wildlife regard a niche for animals as "the set of environmental conditions within which a population can grow or at least sustain its numbers." In the niches inhabited by organizations, too, there is only room for so many.

Given these assumptions about organizations, Hannan and Freeman consider first how fast new organizations in a population are founded (the rate of *founding*) and then how fast they die out (the rate of *disbanding*). Consider founding. The fact that there is a growing number of a particular form of organization relative to the capacity of an environmental niche does not necessarily stop new entrants. Indeed, Hannan and Freeman contend that, at first, the rate of founding increases as density increases. The more there are, the more new ones attempt to get in. This push occurs because a higher density means more of that form of organization are around, so people become accustomed to them. Their existence is less likely to be questioned. They acquire greater legitimacy, as labor unions did after precarious early years when their right to exist was challenged. Further, the rate of new foundings may increase as total numbers grow, because there are more and more people who have experience in how to set up such an organization. The know-how is available.

But there comes that level at which the niche can take no more, the level at which some are being squeezed out, and then launching new ones is no longer attractive. Then, the rate of founding falls. So, Hannan and Freeman argue, as the total number of organizations of a given form grows, first there are more new entrants and then there are fewer, because "density increases legitimacy at a decreasing rate" but "increases competition at an increasing rate." If foundings are plotted against density, an inverted U-shaped curve should result.

This is shown in the United States in populations of organizations as different as labor unions, newspapers, and semiconductor electronics firms. The history of unions and newspapers shows the pattern of first a rise and then a fall in foundings, while total numbers (density) increase; this pattern originated far back in the 19th century. Electronics is a much more recent and volatile population of the mid-20th century. Here, density increased rapidly as firms rushed to join this new industry, and so competition forced the rate of entry to the industry down much more quickly than was the case with the unions and newspapers.

Disbanding, or "mortality," is held to be the other way around. As the total number of organizations in a population grows, first fewer disbandings occur and then more. Of course, the number of disbandings—the "fatalities" in a population through closures or withdrawals from the field—may actually start quite high for the same reason that foundings start low: because legitimacy and know-how are hard to get when few of a kind exist. But the rate of disbandings soon drops as survival becomes easier, and so there are fewer and fewer disbandings, and more and more survivors. Once again, however, when density reaches a level where the niche can support no more, the trend changes. It swings around from a falling rate of disbandings to an increasing rate. Competition forces organizations out, and the number of disbandings begins to rise and may go on rising as long as density goes on rising.

Plotting disbandings against density should produce a U-shape. So indeed it did for the unions, newspapers, and electronics populations. The rate of disbanding dropped sharply for all three as their total number increased, and then rose again under the pressure of competition. But the force of competitive pressure appeared to differ. It seemed weakest for newspapers, stronger for electronics firms, and strongest for unions. Unions squeezed each other out more and more, once the critical density of union population was reached. The existence of a large number of craft unions, with members from the same occupations in many industries, seemed especially detrimental to industrial unions with members from many occupations in a single industry, for as the density of craft unions rose, so too did the disbanding of industrial unions.

Disbandings are also influenced by age and size of organization. Hannan and Freeman do not agree with assertions that modern organizations are (or should be) in a state of constant flux and innovation. As they see it, organizations persist because of their reliability in outputs of goods and services and their accountability for the use of resources, each of which increases with institutionalization and stability. So, the stability of age improves the chances of survival, despite the inertia that aging can bring. Fewer disbandings occur in populations of older organizations. Older unions and older firms are less likely to close down or merge than are younger ones.

Growth, too, improves the chances. Although bigger organizations similarly may have greater structural inertia, they have the resources to withstand shocks from their environments. "Small organizations are more likely than large ones to attempt change, but are more likely to disappear in the process."

Within populations, subpopulations are found to respond differently to different environmental niche conditions. Thus, among both restaurants and semiconductor firms, generalists (with a relatively wide range of services or products) are found to do better under variable conditions. Specialists (with a narrower range) do better in stable cyclical conditions, called "coarse-grained environments" (where there are known long-term business cycles). In further work, Hannan and his colleague Glenn Carroll show that these characteristics also apply to other niches. These include the U.S. brewing and banking industries and the population of newspapers in both Argentina and Ireland.

As applied to organizations by Hannan and Freeman, population ecology theory questions the usefulness of the efforts commonly made to reform existing organizations as managements attempt to keep up with change. It implies that populations or organizations change more effectively by selection and replacement than by adaptation. To effect change, start a new organization.

Here, population ecology theory becomes practical because, potentially, it can show whether "the dice are loaded for or against a particular way of doing business." There is no best form of organization, but many forms for many niches.

Bibliography

Hannan, M. T., and Carroll, G. R., *Dynamics of Organizational Populations,* Oxford University Press, 1992.
Hannan, M. T., and Freeman, J., *Organizational Ecology,* Harvard University Press, 1989.

Geert Hofstede

Geert Hofstede is a social psychologist who, until his retirement, was Professor of Organizational Anthropology and International Management at the University of Limburg, the Netherlands, and Director of the Institute for Research on Intercultural Cooperation there. In the early 1970s, he and his colleagues carried out a major systematic study of work-related attitudes. The study was based on two questionnaire surveys that produced more than 116,000 questionnaires from more than 70 countries; it was by far the largest organizationally based study ever to have been carried out.

Those respondents whose replies Hofstede used for research purposes were all sales and service employees of subsidiaries of IBM, a U.S.-based multinational corporation that operates in most countries. Within the sales and service function, all types of employees were surveyed—for example, sales clerks, professional engineers, top managers—by using the language of each country. Twenty different language versions of the questionnaire had to be made. The IBM employees represented well-matched subsets from each country: same company, job, and education but different nationalities. National cultural differences found within the company, therefore, are likely to be a conservative estimate of those existing within the countries at large. The survey was repeated after 4 years, with stable results, underlining the cultural nature of the differences found.

Hofstede identifies four basic dimensions of the differences between national cultures—power-distance, uncertainty-avoidance, individualism, and masculinity—based on the 40 larger subsidiaries on which the first analyses were made. Each of the national cultures can be positioned from high to low on each of the four scales and thus has a distinctive cultural profile.

The *power-distance dimension* is concerned with how close or how distant subordinates feel from their superiors. This is not physical distance, but how big the personal gap is felt to be. In a high power-distance culture (e.g., France, India), being a boss means exerting power and keeping that gap open. Inequality is accepted: "a place for everyone and everyone in his place." So, employees are frequently reluctant to express disagreement with their boss and prefer to work for a manager who makes the decisions—and takes the responsibility—and then simply tells them what to do.

In a low power-distance culture (e.g., Austria, Israel), superiors and subordinates consider each other to be colleagues, and both believe that inequalities in society should be minimized. So, those in power should try to look less powerful than they are. Employees are seldom afraid to disagree, and they expect to be consulted before decisions are made.

The *uncertainty-avoidance dimension* is the ease with which the culture copes with novelty. In strong uncertainty-avoidance cultures (e.g., Japan, Greece), people feel the need for clarity and order. They feel threatened by uncertain situations, and high anxiety and stress are experienced. This experience is combated by hard work, career stability, and intolerance of deviancy. Thus, employees believe that company rules should not be broken—even when it is shown to be in the company's best interest—and look forward to continue working with the firm until they retire.

In a weak uncertainty-avoidance culture (e.g., Denmark, Hong Kong), the uncertainty inherent in life is more easily accepted, and each day is taken as it comes. A very pragmatic view is taken about keeping or changing the existing rules, and employees expect to be working for the firm for much shorter periods.

The *individualism* dimension focuses on the degree to which the culture encourages individual, as opposed to collectivist, group-centered concerns. In an individualist culture (e.g., United States, Britain), the emphasis is on personal initiative and achievement, and everyone has the right to a private life and opinion. By contrast, a collectivist culture (e.g., Iran, Peru) is characterized by a tighter social framework, in which people are members of extended families or clans that protect them in exchange for loyalty. Careers are pursued to increase standing in the family by being able to help its other members. The emphasis is on belonging, and the aim is to be a good member; whereas in the individualist culture, the ideal is to be a good leader.

The *masculinity dimension* highlights "masculine" cultures (e.g., Australia, Italy), in which performance is what counts. Money and material standards are important; ambition is the driving force. Big and fast are beautiful; "machismo" is sexy. In contrast, in "feminine" cultures (e.g., the Netherlands, Sweden), the quality of life is what matters. People and the environment are important, service provides the motivation, small is beautiful, and unisex is attractive. The expected relationship of men to women differs considerably along this dimension. In "masculine" cultures, the sex roles are clearly differentiated. Men should be assertive, dominating; women should be caring, nurturing. In "feminine" cultures, the sex roles are more flexible, and there is a belief in equality between the sexes. It is not "unmasculine" for a man to take a caring role, for example.

Equipped with measurements that locate the 40 cultures along the four dimensions, Hofstede then offers a set of cultural maps of the world. Two points should be remembered in interpreting the results. The first point is that countries spread along the whole of each of the four dimensions, not only at the extremes. So, cultures are not only masculine like Italy, or feminine like Sweden. Many countries are in between; for example, Belgium is exactly in the center, Britain on the masculine side, and France on the feminine one.

The second point is that the position of a culture along a dimension is based on the averages for all the respondents in that particular country. Characterizing a national work culture does not mean that every person in the nation has all the characteristics ascribed to that culture; there are bound to be many individual variations. For example, many Japanese are risk takers, and many from Hong Kong avoid uncertainty; many Indians have low power-distance values, and many Israelis have high power-distance attitudes. What these scales are doing is describing the common values of the central core of the culture that come about through the "collective mental programming" of a number of people (a tribe, a nation, or a national minority) who are conditioned by the same life experience and the same education. Although this commonality will not make everybody the same, a country's nationals do share a cultural character—which is indeed more clearly visible to foreigners than to themselves.

Table 2.2 gives a classification of the nations grouped by cultural similarity according to the statistical technique of cluster analysis. They fall into eight areas. Because a culture's work-related values are so distinctive and different, it is to be expected that its organizational processes and behavior would be so too. So, Hofstede argues very strongly that we should not expect the same conceptions and prescriptions about management to be appropriate for all culture areas.

Some years later, Hofstede joined Michael Bond, a Canadian social psychologist working in Hong Kong, in research that added a fifth dimension to the previous four. Bond, realizing that most questionnaires

Table 2.2 Country Clusters and Their Characteristics

I: More developed Latin

high power-distance
high uncertainty-avoidance
medium to high individualism
medium masculinity

BELGIUM
FRANCE
ARGENTINA
BRAZIL
SPAIN
(ITALY)

II: Less developed Latin

high power-distance
high uncertainty-avoidance
low individualism
whole range on masculinity

COLOMBIA
MEXICO
VENEZUELA
CHILE
PERU
PORTUGAL

III: More developed Asian

medium power-distance
high uncertainty-avoidance
medium individualism
high masculinity

JAPAN

IV: Less developed Asian

high power-distance
low to medium uncertainty-avoidance
low individualism
medium masculinity

PAKISTAN
TAIWAN
THAILAND
HONG KONG
INDIA
PHILIPPINES
SINGAPORE

V: Near Eastern

high power-distance
high uncertainty-avoidance
low individualism
medium masculinity

GREECE
IRAN
TURKEY
(YUGOSLAVIA)

VI: Germanic

low power-distance
medium to high uncertainty-avoidance
medium individualism
medium to high masculinity

AUSTRIA
ISRAEL
GERMANY
SWITZERLAND

VII: Anglo

low to medium power-distance
low to medium uncertainty-avoidance
high individualism
high masculinity

AUSTRALIA
CANADA
BRITAIN
IRELAND
NEW ZEALAND
UNITED STATES
(SOUTH AFRICA)

VIII: Nordic

low power-distance
low to medium uncertainty-avoidance
medium to high individualism
low masculinity

DENMARK
FINLAND
NETHERLANDS
NORWAY
SWEDEN

SOURCE: Hofstede (1980).

have questions devised by Westerners, as did Hofstede's IBM surveys, investigated what would happen if the questions were developed by Asians. He asked Chinese social scientists in Hong Kong and Taiwan to define some Chinese cultural values. From these, a questionnaire was made up in Chinese and then translated into English and other languages—the other way around from the usual practice. The questionnaire was given to matched sets of students in different countries, East and West.

The most compelling finding was that three of the dimensions obtained were compatible with those found previously. Power-distance, individualism, and masculinity again differentiated among the national groups. The most distinctive finding was that a new dimension replaced Hofstede's, possibly Western-biased, uncertainty-avoidance. It distinguishes cultures in which persistence, thrift, and a firm status order in society, plus a keen sense of shame, are much more important than are respect for tradition, saving face socially, personal steadiness, and mutual honoring of favors and gifts. Insofar as what is most important is more forward looking, Bond called this Eastern-oriented characteristic *Confucian dynamism*. Hofstede subsequently preferred to call it "long-term versus short-term orientation."

Remarkably, all the most vigorous Asian economies—Japan, Taiwan, South Korea, Hong Kong, Singapore, and China itself—were high in Confucian dynamism (had a long-term orientation). Could this element in the cultures of their peoples partly explain their economic success, much as the so-called Protestant work ethic of earlier centuries in the West has been held to partly explain the industrial revolution (see Weber, p. 3)?

Hofstede illustrates the difficulties of applying management practices insensitively in very different cultures by what befell a U.S. idea when attempts were made to introduce it elsewhere. Management by objectives (MbO) started in the United States and has had most success there, particularly in situations in which the manager's results can be objectively measured.

Why is this so? MbO requires that

Subordinates are sufficiently independent to negotiate meaningfully with the boss (low power-distance)

Both are willing to take some risks—the boss in delegating power, the subordinate in accepting responsibility (low uncertainty-avoidance)

The subordinate is personally willing to "have a go" and make a mark (high individualism)

Both regard performance and results achieved as important (high masculinity)

This is the Anglo work culture pattern as Table 2.2 shows.

But how would MbO work out in other culture areas? For example, the Germanic culture area has low power-distance, which fits, as does the results orientation of high masculinity. The Germanic group, however, is high on uncertainty-avoidance, which would work against the risk taking and ambiguity involved in the Anglo process. But the idea of replacing the arbitrary authority of the boss with the impersonal authority of mutually agreed objectives fits well in this culture. This is, indeed, the way MbO has developed in Germany, emphasizing the need to develop procedures of a more participative kind. The German name for MbO is "management by joint goal setting," and elaborate formal systems have been developed. Also, great stress is put on team objectives (as opposed to the individual emphasis in the Anglo culture), and this fits in with the lower individualism of this culture area.

The More Developed Latin group, as represented by France, has high power-distance and high uncertainty-avoidance—completely the opposite to the Anglo group—so MbO is bound to encounter difficulties there. It did gain some popularity in France for a time, but it was not sustained. The problem was that, in a high power-distance culture, attempting to substitute the personal authority of the boss for self-monitored objectives is bound to generate anxiety. The boss does not delegate easily and will not stop short-circuiting intermediate hierarchical levels if necessary—and subordinates will expect this to happen and to be told what to do. And in a high uncertainty-avoidance culture, anxiety will be alleviated by sticking to the old ways.

Cultural differences, then, have an important impact on how organizations function, and manufacturing cars or treating the sick will call for different structures and processes in France or Japan or Britain. So, it is important even for international organizations to have a dominant national culture to fall back on (e.g., as the American or Japanese multinationals). Organizations without a home culture, in which the key decision makers can come from any country (e.g., UNESCO, the European Commission), find it very difficult to function effectively because of this lack. It is less of a problem for the political part of such organizations because negotiation between representatives is their task. But for the administrative apparatus, where the members represent not their countries but the organization as a whole, it is crippling—and most such "cultureless" organizations are inefficient and wasteful.

Bibliography

Hofstede, G., *Culture's Consequences: International Differences in Work-Related Values,* Sage, 1980.

Hofstede, G., "Motivation, Leadership, and Organization: Do American Theories Apply Abroad?" *Organizational Dynamics,* (Summer 1980), 42-63; reprinted in D. S. Pugh (ed.), *Organization Theory,* Penguin Books, 1997.

Hofstede, G., *Cultures and Organizations: Software of the Mind,* McGraw-Hill, 1991.

3 The Management of Organizations

To manage is to forecast and plan, to organize, to command, to coordinate and to control.

Henri Fayol

Scientific Management will mean, for the employers and the workmen who adopt it, the elimination of almost all causes for dispute and disagreement between them.

Frederick W. Taylor

It [modern management] was to ensure that as a craft declined the worker would sink to the level of general and undifferentiated labor power, adaptable to a large range of simple tasks, while as science grew, it would be concentrated in the hands of management.

Harry Braverman

Excellent companies were above all, brilliant on the basics.

Thomas J. Peters and Robert H. Waterman

The degree to which the opportunity to use power effectively is granted or withheld from individuals is one operative difference between those companies which stagnate and those which innovate.

Rosabeth Moss Kanter

An organization . . . . quite literally does impose the environment that imposes on it.

Karl E. Weick

Organizations with different structures, functioning in different environments, have to be managed. As long as there is management, there will be the problem of how to manage better. In one sense, attempts at answers to the problem will be as numerous as managers, for each will bring an individual approach to the task. Nonetheless, at any one time, there is enough in common for broad similarities to exist in what is thought and what is taught on this issue. The writers of this section have each sought to improve the understanding of administration and its practice. They have looked for the ingredients of a better management.

Henri Fayol puts forward a classic analysis of the management task, based on his long practical experience of doing the job and the personal insights he gained. F. W. Taylor's name is synonymous with the term *scientific management.* His extremely influential ideas made him a controversial figure in his own day and have remained a subject for much argument. Harry Braverman, from a Marxist perspective, mounts a critique on the degradation that Taylor's ideas bring to modern work.

Thomas Peters and Robert Waterman, in an influential analysis, report a set of eight attributes that characterize excellent firms, and they propose that these attributes should be widely adopted. Rosabeth Moss Kanter proposes ways in which organizations should be managed to draw more fully on the total human resources within them. Karl Weick points to the way in which each individual's subjective attempts to make sense of the organization must be understood and taken into account in the management process.

Henri Fayol

Henri Fayol (1841–1925) was a mining engineer by training. A French-man, he spent his working life with the French mining and metallurgical combine Commentry-Fourchamboult-Decazeville, first as an engineer, but from his early 30s onward in general management. From 1888 to 1918, he was Managing Director.

Fayol is among those who have achieved fame for ideas made known very late in life. He was in his 70s before he published them in a form that came to be widely read. He had written technical articles on mining engineering and a few preliminary papers on administration, but in 1916, the *Bulletin de la Société de l'Industrie Minerale* printed Fayol's *Administration Industrielle et Générale—Prévoyance, Organisation, Commandement, Coordination, Contrôle.* He is also among those whose reputation rests on a single short publication still frequently reprinted as a book; his other writings are little known.

The English version appears as *General and Industrial Management,* translated by Constance Storrs and first issued in 1949. There has been some debate over this rendering of the title of the work, and in particular of expressing the French word *administration* by the term *management.* It is argued that this title could simply imply that Fayol is concerned only with industrial management, whereas his own preface claims, "Management plays a very important part in the government of under-takings; of all undertakings, large or small, industrial, commercial, political, religious or any other." Indeed, in his last years, he studied the problems of state public services and lectured at the *École Supérieure de la Guerre.* So, it can be accepted that his intention was to initiate a theoretical analysis appropriate to a wide range of organizations.

Fayol suggests,

All activities to which industrial undertakings give rise can be divided into the following six groups:

1. Technical activities (production, manufacture, adaptation)
2. Commercial activities (buying, selling, exchange)

3. Financial activities (search for and optimum use of capital)
4. Security activities (protection of property and persons)
5. Accounting activities (stocktaking, balance sheet, costs, statistics)
6. Managerial activities (planning, organization, command, coordination, control)

Be the undertaking simple or complex, big or small, these six groups of activities or essential functions are always present.

Most of these six groups of activities will be present in most jobs but in varying measure, with the managerial element in particular being greatest in senior jobs and least or absent in direct production or lower clerical tasks. Managerial activities are specially emphasized as being universal to organizations. But it is commonplace to ask What is management? Is it anything that can be identified and stand on its own, or is it a word, a label, that has no substance?

Fayol's answer was unique at the time. The core of his contribution is his definition of management as comprising five elements:

1. To forecast and plan (in the French, *prévoyance*): "Examining the future and drawing up the plan of action"
2. To organize: "Building up the structure, material and human, of the undertaking"
3. To command: "Maintaining activity among the personnel"
4. To coordinate: "Binding together, unifying and harmonizing all activity and effort"
5. To control: "Seeing that everything occurs in conformity with established rule and expressed command"

For Fayol, managing means looking ahead, which makes the first element—the process of *forecasting and planning*—a central business activity. Management must "assess the future and make provision for it." To function adequately, a business organization needs a plan that has the characteristics of "unity, continuity, flexibility, and precision." The problems of planning that management must overcome are (a) making sure the objectives of each part of the organization are securely welded together (unity), (b) using both short- and long-term forecasting (continuity), (c) being able to adapt the plan in the light of changing circumstances (flexibility), and (d) attempting to accurately predict courses of action (precision). The essence of planning is to allow the optimum use of resources. Interestingly, Fayol in 1916 argued the necessity of a national plan for France, to be produced by the government.

To *organize,* the second element, is "building up the structure, material and human, of the undertaking." The task of management is to build up an organization that will allow the basic activities to be carried out in an optimal manner. Central to this is a structure in which plans are efficiently prepared and carried out. There must be a unity of command and direction, clear definition of responsibilities, and precise decision making backed up by an efficient system for selecting and training managers.

Fayol's third element—*to command*—comes logically after the first two. An organization must start with a plan, a definition of its goals. It then must produce an organizational structure appropriate to the achievement of those goals. Next, the organization must be put in motion, which is *command,* maintaining activity among the personnel. Through an ability to command, the manager obtains the best possible performance from subordinates. This must be done through example, through continuous contact with the staff, and by maintaining a broad view of the directing function. In this way, the manager maintains a high level of activity by instilling a sense of mission.

Command refers to the relationship between a manager and the subordinates in the area of the immediate task. But organizations have a variety of tasks to perform, so the fourth element—*coordination*—is necessary, "binding together, unifying and harmonizing all activity and effort." Essentially, this is making sure that one department's efforts are coincident with the efforts of other departments and keeping all activities in perspective with regard to the overall aims of the organization. This can only be attained by a constant circulation of information and regular meetings of management.

The fifth element—*control*—is logically the final element that checks that the other four elements are, in fact, performing properly: "seeing that everything occurs in conformity with established rule and expressed command." To be effective, control must operate quickly and there must be a system of sanctions. The best way to ensure this is to separate all functions concerned with inspection from the operation departments whose work they inspect. Fayol believed in independent, impartial staff departments.

Fayol uses this classification to divide up his chapters on how to administer or manage. It is probable that when he wrote of *"une doctrine administrative,"* he had in mind not only the above theory but also the addition of experience to theoretical analysis to form a doctrine of good management. He summarizes the lessons of his own experience in a number of general principles of management. These are his own rules, and he does not assume that they are necessarily of universal application or that they have any great permanence. Nonetheless, most have become part of managerial know-how, and many are regarded as fundamental tenets. Fayol outlines the following fourteen principles:

1. *Division of work:* Specialization allows the individual to build up expertise and thereby be more productive.

2. *Authority:* This is the right to issue commands, along with which must go the equivalent responsibility for its exercise.

3. *Discipline:* This is two-sided, because employees only obey orders if managers play their part by providing good leadership.

4. *Unity of command:* In contrast to F. W. Taylor's functional authority (see p. 94), Fayol was quite clear that each worker should have only one boss, with no other conflicting lines of command. On this issue, history has favored Fayol because his principle has found most adherents among managers.

5. *Unity of direction:* People engaged in the same kind of activities must have the same objectives in a single plan.

6. *Subordination of individual interest to general interest:* Management must see that the goals of the firm are always paramount.

7. *Remuneration:* Payment is an important motivator although, by analyzing a number of possibilities, Fayol points out that there is no such thing as a perfect system.

8. *Centralization or decentralization:* Again, this is a matter of degree, depending on the condition of the business and the quality of its personnel.

9. *Scalar chain:* A hierarchy is necessary for unity of direction, but lateral communication is also fundamental as long as superiors know that such communication is taking place.

10. *Order:* Both material order and social order are necessary. The former minimizes lost time and useless handling of materials; the latter is achieved through organization and selection.

11. *Equity:* In running a business, a "combination of kindliness and justice" is needed in treating employees if equity is to be achieved.

12. *Stability of tenure:* This is essential because of the time and expense involved in training good management. Fayol believes that successful businesses tend to have more stable managerial personnel.

13. *Initiative:* Allowing all personnel to show their initiative in some way is a source of strength for the organization even though it may well involve a sacrifice of "personal vanity" on the part of many managers.

14. *Esprit de corps:* Management must foster the morale of its employees and, to quote Fayol, "Real talent is needed to coordinate effort, encourage keenness, use each person's abilities, and reward each one's merit without arousing possible jealousies and disturbing harmonious relations."

But Fayol's pride of place in this field is due not so much to his principles of how to manage, enduring though these are, as to his definition of what management is. He is the earliest known proponent of a theoretical analysis of managerial activities—an analysis that has withstood a half-century of critical discussion. There can have been few writers since who have not been influenced by it; and his five elements have provided a system of concepts with which managers may clarify their thinking about what it is they have to do.

Bibliography

Fayol, H., *General and Industrial Management,* Pitman, 1949; translated by Constance Storrs from the original *Administration Industrielle et Générale,* 1916; paper edition by David S. Liake, 1987.

Frederick W. Taylor

Frederick Taylor (1856–1917) was an engineer by training. He joined the Midvale Steel Works as a laborer and rose rapidly to be a foreman and later Chief Engineer. He was afterward employed at the Bethlehem Steel Works and then became a consultant and devoted his time to the propagation of his ideas.

He first published his views on management in a paper entitled "A Piece Rate System," read to the American Society of Mechanical Engineers in 1895. These views were expanded into the book *Shop Management* (1903) and further developed in *Principles of Scientific Management* (1911). As a result of labor troubles caused by the attempt to apply his principles in a government arsenal, a House of Representatives' Special Committee was set up in 1911 to investigate Taylor's system of shop management. (A full description of events at the arsenal is given in Aitken's [1960] case study.) In 1947, *Shop Management,* the *Principles,* and Taylor's testimony to the special committee were collected together and published under the title *Scientific Management.*

Taylor was the founder of the movement known as *scientific management.* "The principal object of management," he states, "should be to secure the maximum prosperity for the employer, coupled with the maximum prosperity of each employee." For the employer, "maximum prosperity" means not just large profits in the short term but also the development of all aspects of the enterprise to a state of permanent prosperity. For the employees, maximum prosperity means not just immediate higher wages but also their development so that they may perform efficiently in the highest grade of work for which their natural abilities fit them. The mutual interdependence of management and workers and the necessity of their working together toward the common aim of increasing prosperity for all seemed completely self-evident to Taylor. He was thus driven to ask, Why is there so much antagonism and inefficiency?

He suggests three causes: (a) the fallacious belief of the workers that any increase in output would inevitably result in unemployment, (b) the defective systems of management that make it necessary for workers to restrict their output in order to protect their interests ("systematic soldiering"), and (c) inefficient rule-of-thumb effort-wasting methods of work. Taylor conceived it to be the aim of scientific management to overcome these obstacles. This could be achieved by a systematic study of work to discover the most efficient methods of performing the job and then a systematic study of management leading to the most efficient methods of controlling the workers. These methods would bring a great increase in efficiency and, with it, prosperity to the benefit of all because a highly efficient, prosperous business would be in a much better position to ensure the continuing well-paid employment of its workers. As Taylor put it: "What the workmen want from their employers beyond anything else is high wages and what employers want from their workmen most of all is low labor cost of manufacture . . . the existence or absence of these two elements forms the best index to either good or bad management."

To achieve this, Taylor lays down four "great underlying principles of management."

1. The Development of a True Science of Work

Taylor points out that no one really knows what constitutes a fair day's work; a boss, therefore, has unlimited opportunities for complaining about workers' inadequacies, and workers never really know what is expected of them. This dilemma can be remedied by the establishment, after scientific investigation, of a "large daily task" as the amount to be done by a suitable worker under optimum conditions. For this, the workers would receive a high rate of pay—much higher than the average worker would receive in "unscientific" factories. They would also suffer a loss of income if they failed to achieve this performance.

2. The Scientific Selection and Progressive Development of the Worker

To earn this high rate of pay, workers would have to be scientifically selected to ensure that they possess the physical and intellectual qualities to enable them to achieve the output. Then, they must be systematically trained to be "first class." Taylor believes that every worker could be first class at some job. It was the responsibility of management to develop workers, offering them opportunities for advancement that would finally enable them to do "the highest, most interesting, and most profitable class of work" for which they could become first class.

3. The Bringing Together of the Science of Work and the Scientifically Selected and Trained Workers

This is the process that causes the "mental revolution" in management, and Taylor maintains that, almost invariably, the major resistance to scientific management comes from the side of management. The workers, he finds, are very willing to cooperate in learning to do a good job for a high rate of pay.

4. The Constant and Intimate Cooperation of Management and Workers

The division of work and responsibility between management and workers is almost equal. The management takes over all the work for which it is better fitted than the workers—that is, the specification and verification of the methods, time, price, and quality standards of the job and the continuous supervision and control of the workers doing it. As Taylor saw it, hardly a single act should be done by any worker that is not preceded by and followed by some act on the part of management. With this close personal cooperation, the opportunities for conflict are almost eliminated because the operation of this authority is not arbitrary. The managers are continually demonstrating that their decisions are subject to the same discipline as the workers—namely, the scientific study of the work.

By *science,* Taylor means systematic observation and measurement, and an example of his method that he often quotes is the development of "the science of shoveling." He is insistent that, although shoveling is a very simple job, the study of the factors affecting efficient shoveling is quite complex—so much so that a worker who is phlegmatic enough to be able to do the job and stupid enough to choose it is extremely unlikely to be able to develop the most efficient method alone. But this is, in fact, what is hoped will happen. The *scientific* study of shoveling involves the determination of the optimum load that a first-class worker can handle with each shovelful. Then, the correct size of shovel to obtain this load, with different materials, must be established. Workers must be provided a range of shovels and told which one to use. They must then be placed on an incentive payment scheme that allows them to earn high wages (double what they would earn in "unscientific" firms) in return for high output.

The insistence on maximum specialization and the removal of all extraneous elements in order to concentrate on the essential task is fundamental to Taylor's thinking. He applies this concept to management too. He considers that the work of a typical factory supervisor is composed of a number of different functions (e.g., cost clerk, time clerk, inspector, repair boss, shop disciplinarian), and he believes that these could be separated out and performed by different specialists who would each be responsible for controlling different aspects of the work and the workers. He calls this system "functional management" and likens the increased efficiency that it would bring to that obtained in a school where students go to specialist teachers for different subjects, compared with a school in which one teacher teaches all subjects. He also formulates "the exception principle," which states that management reports should be condensed into comparative summaries giving in detail only the exceptions to past standards or averages—both the especially good and especially bad exceptions. Thus, the manager would obtain an immediate and comprehensive view of the progress of the work.

Taylor's methods have been followed by many others, among them Gantt, Frank and Lillian Gilbreth, Bedaux, Rowan, and Halsey. They have developed his thinking into what is now called *work study,* or *industrial engineering.* But even in his lifetime, Taylor's ideas led to bitter controversy over the alleged inhumanity of his system, which was said to reduce workers to the level of efficiently functioning machines. In fairness to Taylor, it must be said that his principles were often inadequately understood. For example, few managements have been willing to put into practice one of his basic tenets—that the earnings of a high-producing worker should have no limit; many incentive schemes involve such limits. This unwillingness may inhibit the "mental revolution" Taylor sought, which requires that "both sides take their eyes off the division of the surplus as the all important matter and together turn their attention towards increasing the size of the surplus."

Bibliography

Aitken, H. G. J., *Taylorism at Watertown Arsenal,* Harvard University Press, 1960.
Taylor, F. W., *Scientific Management,* Harper & Row, 1947.

Harry Braverman and the "Labor Process" Debate

Harry Braverman (1920–1976) was an American Marxist theorist concerned with analyzing the effects of the modern capitalist economy on the organization of work. His interest in this subject was stimulated by what he regarded as the unrealistic nature of much of what was written about productive labor. Braverman himself had very practical experience to bring to his analysis: He was trained as a craftsman coppersmith and worked at that trade and at pipe fitting and sheet metal work. He was employed in a naval shipyard, a railroad repair shop, and two sheet steel plants, in all of which he experienced the impact of technological change on craft employment. In later years as a journalist, book editor, and then publishing executive, he again had experience of the impact of modern technology, this time on administrative work such as marketing, accounting, and book production routines. His basic thesis is that, in a capitalist economy, all these changes act to de-skill work and to remove more and more power away from workers and into the hands of owners and managers. His book expounding this theme, *Labor and Monopoly Capitalism: The Degradation of Work in the Twentieth Century,* was awarded the 1974 C. Wright Mills Prize of the Society for the Study of Social Problems.

Braverman uses the framework for analyzing the nature of the capitalist system presented by Karl Marx in *Capital,* Volume 1 (published in 1867), and applies it to modern work and its organization. Marx used the term *the labor process* to refer to the ways by which raw materials are transformed into goods by human labor using tools and machines. In a capitalist system, by definition, the tools and machines are not owned by the workers but by the capitalists, and so the resulting goods become commodities to be sold on the market for the owners' profit. Workers themselves also have only a commodity to offer: their labor in exchange for wages. In this system, it is inevitable that owners will "exploit" workers—that is, obtain as much as possible as a contribution to profit while paying as little as possible in return as wages.

In modern times, according to Braverman, this "exploitation" requires managers (as representatives of owners) to design and redesign work in order to achieve competitive levels of profit. They need to have maximum control of workers and to look continually for ways of increasing that control. Typically, this has been achieved by increasing the division of labor into smaller and smaller, less and less demanding fragments of tasks. In this way, increased output may be obtained from a workforce that is less expensive because it is less skilled and less trained. Ford-type mass production epitomizes the results. Car workers on an assembly line, for example, who drive to their place of work will have already exercised their highest level of skill for that day.

This de-skilling and the abolition of craft ownership of work leads to alienation. This is another reason for the owning class (and its representatives—the managers) to need to control the working class. The workers are seen as untrustworthy members of an opposing class who are likely to obstruct, undermine, or otherwise resist the legitimate capitalist objective of maximizing profit. From this point of view, ways of organizing the labor and production process are not rationally determined in order to increase objective efficiency: rather, organizations take the form they do in order to enhance the domination of capital over labor.

The prime advocate of this approach to efficiency in the organization of production was F. W. Taylor (see p. 91). Braverman sees "scientific management," so called, as the classic and inevitable method used to control labor in growing capitalist enterprises. It is, of course, not scientific because it does not attempt to discover the actual case, but accepts management's view that it has a refractory workforce that has to be kept under control. It is not a "science of work," but a "science of the management of others' work under capitalist conditions." Its three basic tenets are (a) that knowledge of the labor process must be gathered in one place, (b) that it must be the exclusive preserve of management and not available to the workers, and (c) that this monopoly of knowledge must be used by management to control each step of the labor process. In total contrast to craft working, Taylor advocated a complete separation of conception from execution.

Braverman insists that scientific management is in full flow as the dominant approach to capitalist organization of the labor process. He is very dismissive of those social science writers of the human relations approach (see Herzberg, p. 153; Likert and McGregor, p. 142; and Mayo and the Hawthorne Investigations, p. 138) who maintain the need to humanize work and improve the quality of working life. In industry, these ideas are relegated to the sidelines of the personnel and training departments, with little real impact on the management of worker or work. In the production departments, where the labor process is actually carried out and controlled, Taylorism reigns supreme. It is, indeed, being extended to an even wider range of occupations, such as clerical and administrative routines, that are continually being de-skilled with the use of new computer technology. Braverman rejects the idea that automation is qualitatively different in the skill demands it makes of workers, as compared with mechanization. He argues that it, too, will decrease skill, as will any other technological development. This result is not a matter of a particular technology, but of how it is inevitably used to increase the control of the labor process by capital in the interests of profit.

The de-skilling and cheapening of such white-collar jobs as those of clerks and computer operators leads to an increase in the alienated working class. In the situation of "monopoly capitalism" (where giant corporations control the markets), new commodities are brought into being to shape the consumer to the needs of capital. All of society becomes a gigantic marketplace in the pursuit of profit. Printing and television, for example, become largely vehicles for marketing, rather than for information and education. Thus comes not only the degradation of work but also the degradation of family and community.

In the aftermath of Braverman's book, Marxist sociologists have been discussing its adequacy. Two particular issues have been taken up. The first issue concerns the inevitability of de-skilling on Taylorist lines in capitalist production. Braverman argued it was the one classic form that gave cheapness and control to the labor process and therefore was the inevitable result. Later writers have suggested that de-skilling may not be universal and that work under capitalism can take a variety of forms. Managements may use different ways to achieve their objectives of control. Richard Edwards (1979), in a historical survey of workplace relations, argues that although a hierarchy has remained constant, various additional forms of control have been used (e.g., coercive, technical, bureaucratic), depending on the struggle of owners, workers, and others to protect and advance their interests.

The second issue has focused on Braverman's argument that the de-skilling of white-collar workers will lead to an increase in the working class. As Graeme Salaman (1986) argues, this argument neglects the important element of subjective identification of workers.

This means that even de-skilled administrators and computer operators, for example, consider themselves—and therefore act and vote—as middle class.

Bibliography

Braverman, H., *Labor and Monopoly Capitalism: The Degradation of Work in the Twentieth Century,* Monthly Review Press, 1974.
Edwards, R., *Contested Terrain: The Transformation of the Workplace in the Twentieth Century,* Heinemann, 1979.
Salaman, G., *Working,* Tavistock, 1986.

Thomas J. Peters and Robert H. Waterman

Thomas J. Peters and Robert H. Waterman had been partners in McKinsey and Company, a leading management consultancy firm, for many years when they undertook a study of excellence in U.S. business. Their report, *In Search of Excellence,* became the most popular management book of recent years, with up to 5 million copies sold worldwide. Peters now runs his own organization founded to develop and propagate the ideas.

Peters and Waterman were concerned with examining and drawing lessons from big companies (those with annual turnovers of more than $1 billion) and that were well established (more than 20 years old). From the *Fortune* 500 list of the largest U.S. companies, 43 companies were chosen that satisfied a number of performance criteria. They had to be of above-average growth and financial return over a 20-year period, plus have a reputation in their business sector for continuous innovation in response to changing markets. For all these firms, a full study of the published information on them over 25 years was carried out. In addition, about half the cases were the subject of extensive interview studies of the top managers involved; more limited interviews were conducted in the remaining half of the sample.

The companies designated as excellent by this process include such leading names as Boeing, Hewlett-Packard, IBM, Johnson & Johnson, McDonald's, Procter & Gamble, and 3M. It is not claimed for these firms and for the others classified as excellent that they are without fault; they have made plenty of well-publicized mistakes. But overall, they have performed well over long periods, and they are in a good position to continue as innovative in the future.

The interviews were concerned with top management organizing for success and how it is tackled in these excellent companies. Peters and Waterman soon decided they could not stick to the formal aspects of managing: the organization chart, the budget plan, the balance sheet, and the control graph. These highly analytical tools and concepts are inherently conservative. They lead to detailed forecasting and planning and tight control: Cost reduction becomes the priority, and not revenue enhancement, for example. Above all, the philosophy behind the use of these narrowly rational techniques is to abhor mistakes, and therefore it does not value experimentation.

Such an approach cannot capture the distinctive nature of the excellent firms that innovate. A much wider range of processes must be considered, including those classified as informal, intuitive, irrational, and intractable, but that cannot be ignored. Indeed, the range must be managed because it has as much or more to do with the way in which companies excel (or fail) as do the formal structures and strategies.

Together with their colleagues Richard Pascale and Anthony Athos, Peters and Waterman developed a set of concepts to focus on what happens in the process of organizing; it became known as the McKinsey 7-S Framework. This is a series of seven interdependent aspects of organizing—all conveniently beginning with the letter *s:* structure, strategy, systems (and procedures), style (of management), skills (corporate strengths), staff (people), and shared values (culture). On the basis of this framework, Peters and Waterman developed a set of eight attributes that characterize all excellent innovative U.S. companies.

1. A Bias for Action

Even though these companies may be analytical in their approach to decision making, they are not paralyzed by the analysis. They have a "can do" and "let's try" approach that favors experimentation. Managers do not rely on the formal information and control systems. They get out of their offices and keep in touch informally: "MBWA—management by wandering around," it is called at Hewlett-Packard. An open-door policy at all levels is typical, as is the organizational fluidity that allows the setting up of small task forces (mainly of volunteers) with short deadlines who are expected to come up with an answer to a problem *and then implement their proposals.*

2. Close to the Customer

These companies offer good products because they do not regard the customer as a damn nuisance, best ignored. They regularly listen to their customers, from whom they get some of their best product ideas. They have what amounts to an obsession about customer service. IBM, for example, trains its salespeople not to be salespeople but "customer problem solvers." Its claim, to give the best customer service of any company in the world, is backed up by a fleet of special assistants (including some of the best salespeople), who are on 3-year assignments doing only one thing—dealing with every customer complaint within 24 hours.

3. Autonomy and Entrepreneurship

The innovative companies foster many leaders and many innovators throughout the organization. 3M, for example, is a hive of "product champions" who have been allowed to be creative and who are feverishly trying to make their ideas successful. Top management does not try to control so tightly that everyone feels stifled. They support practical risk taking, and they encourage internal competition. They have many innovations on the go, and they can tolerate it when inevitably many fail; that is how they ensure that *some* succeed. The comparison with Burns's organic system of management (see p. 46) is very clear.

4. Productivity Through People

The excellent companies treat the ordinary members of the organization as the basic source of quality and productivity gains. They do not regard capital investment and labor substitution as the fundamental source of efficiency improvement. They strongly oppose an "us-them" attitude in industrial relations, and they treat workers as people. They are not soft; the people orientation has a tough side. They are very performance conscious, but the personal achievements stem from mutually high expectations and peer review, rather than from exhortation and complicated control systems.

McDonald's, for example, compares a well-run restaurant to a winning baseball team and always refers to workers as "crew members." It believes that senior managers should be out in the field, paying attention to employees, to training, and to the standard of service offered. It works hard to restrain and cut the corporate management, believing that the less there is, the better. Its commitment to productivity through people is illustrated by "McDonald's Hamburger University," out of which many crew members graduate, and the annual competition for the best "All-American Hamburger Maker."

5. Hands-On, Value Driven

The basic philosophy of the excellent firms, the shared values of all the participants, may sound very "soft" and abstract, but it has far more to do with their achievements than economic resources, technological developments, organizational structure, or control systems. All these factors have to change over the years, but the philosophy must be established and maintained from top to bottom of the firm. Those at the top work hard to maintain the values in a very public, hands-on way. Their chief executives are famed throughout the company for getting involved in the actual processes (e.g., design, selling), thus publicly demonstrating their commitment to high standards.

This explicit understanding of and commitment to a system of values is probably the single most important key to excellence. Less successful firms either do not know what their values are or have a set of objectives but seem only to get fired up about quantitative ones (e.g., earnings per share, growth measures). These can motivate the top 10, 50, even the top 100 managers, but larger firms need to propagate clear values throughout the whole organization. The content of the dominant beliefs is narrow in scope but is exhibited by all the firms. It includes a belief in being the best producer (whether the product is an aircraft, a hamburger, or an advertising campaign) and in giving superior quality and service. The importance of the nuts and bolts of doing the job well, of informal methods of improving communication to achieve goals, and of economic growth and profits is also featured strongly.

6. Stick to the Knitting

Excellent companies do not wish to become conglomerates. "Never acquire a business you don't know how to run" was how a retiring chairman of Johnson & Johnson put it to his successor. They have seen the way in which corporations such as ITT have suffered through trying to spread into new business sectors by large acquisitions. Excellent companies move out mainly through internally generated diversification, one manageable step at a time.

7. Simple Form, Lean Staff

As big as these companies are, the underlying structural forms and systems are elegantly simple. Top-level staffs are lean: corporate staffs of fewer than 100 people running multibillion-dollar enterprises. Complicated structures that blur the lines of authority, such as matrix organization, are eschewed. The straightforward divisional form, with the product divisions having all the functions of a business, is used. The hiving off of successful new products into separate divisions is encouraged and rewarded at surprisingly small volumes (e.g., at about $20 million turnover at 3M).

8. Simultaneous Loose-Tight Properties

The excellent companies are both centralized and decentralized. On the one hand, for the most part, they have pushed autonomy downward, to the division, to the product development team, to the shop floor. On the other hand, they are fanatical centralists around the few core values they see as key to the enterprise: quality, reliability, action, regular informal communication, and quick feedback. These are ways of exerting extremely tight control and of ensuring that nothing gets very far out of line. The attention to the customer is one of the tightest properties of all—not through massive forms and large numbers of control variables, but through self- and peer discipline, making this the focus of activity. Thus, the "soft" concept of a philosophical value is, in fact, harder in its impact than setting target ratios in a control system. As one chief executive said, "It's easy to fool the boss, but you can't fool your peers."

These findings, Peters and Waterman underline, show that the excellent companies are, above all, "brilliant on the basics." They do not let techniques substitute for thinking, nor analysis impede action. They work hard to keep things simple in a complex world. They tolerate some chaos in return for quick action and regular innovation. They prize their values as their most essential asset.

One conclusion that Peters and Waterman came to, rather reluctantly, was that associated with almost every excellent company was a strong leader who was instrumental in forming the culture of excellence in the early stages of the firm's development. Even so, they strongly believed that firms can change toward excellence. Yet Peters starts a later book, *Thriving on Chaos,* with the statement, "There are no excellent companies"! This is because the business world is changing so fast that no company is safe, not even those earlier designated as excellent, many of which have been in difficulties. All firms must continue to face up to the need for a revolution in organizations by emphasizing a new set of basic aims. These are (a) enhanced responsiveness through greatly increased flexibility and (b) continuous short-cycle innovation aimed at creating new markets for both new and mature products of world-class quality and service.

To help in achieving the necessary changes, Peters proposes 45 specific prescriptions across five major business areas (customer responsiveness, fast-paced innovation, flexibility by empowering people, loving change, building new systems). For example, one of the 10 prescriptions for "creating total customer responsiveness" is "be an internationalist." Even small firms must, early on, look for business opportunities abroad: selling, designing, and manufacturing. A prescription under "learning to love change" is "create a sense of urgency," and one for "building new systems for a world turned upside down" is "revamp the chief control tools."

These aims may sound like a tall order, but firms have no choice but to change and innovate in order to survive. If managers doubt this, they should look at what their fastest growing competitors are doing and see the writing on the wall.

Bibliography

Peters, T. J., *Thriving on Chaos: A Handbook for Management Revolution,* Macmillan, 1988.

Peters, T. J., *The Pursuit of WOW,* Macmillan, 1994.

Peters, T. J., *The Tom Peters Seminar,* Vintage Books, 1994.

Peters, T. J., and Waterman, R. H., *In Search of Excellence: Lessons From America's Best Run Companies,* Harper & Row, 1982.

Rosabeth Moss Kanter

Rosabeth Moss Kanter is a Professor of Business Administration at the Harvard Business School and a consultant to many organizations. A sociologist working in the tradition of Max Weber (see p. 3), she has carried out a historical study of U.S. work communes. Her detailed study of the human aspects of the functioning of a major present-day U.S. manufacturing company, *Men and Women of the Corporation,* was the 1977 winner of the C. Wright Mills Award for the best book on social issues.

The study focused on three key roles in the company (code-named the Industrial Supply Corporation—"Indsco"): those of managers, secretaries, and wives. The *managers,* with a small minority of exceptions, were men; the *secretaries* and the *wives* were women, and Kanter's work analyzes their relationships. On the one hand, it might seem strange to consider wives as part of the corporation, but in fact (though not in theory) this is how they were defined and treated. On the other hand, the husbands of the relatively rare female managers were not put in this position; they were considered to be independent of Indsco.

Managers, particularly as they rise to the top, are required to cope with increasing uncertainty. Greater routinization applies primarily to the lower levels; managers have to be allowed to exercise discretion. They are, therefore, the recipients of the owners' and main board's trust. At Indsco, the top managers inevitably chose people like themselves in whom to put this trust. The managers spent a lot of time interacting with each other—between one third and one half of their time actually in meetings. Interacting with people like oneself is always easier, and there was a decided wish to avoid those with whom communication was felt to be uncomfortable. Deviants and nonconformists were suspect; those who dressed differently raised questions because of the messages they might be conveying. Predictability had the highest value. It was acceptable to be somewhat controversial as long as the manager was consistent and fitted in with the basic values of hard work (staying late at the office if necessary, or taking work home) and loyalty (being committed to a long-term career with the company).

The response to the uncertainties of performance and the need for easy communication are great pressures for management to become a closed circle. Homogeneity is the prime criterion for selection, and social conformity a standard for conduct. Women were clearly put in the category of the incomprehensible and unpredictable and, with rare exceptions, were excluded. Many managers reported that they felt uncomfortable dealing with them. "It took more time," "They changed their minds all the time," and "I'm always making assumptions that turn out to be wrong" were typical comments. Some managers were prepared to admit that this was really saying something about themselves, but this then became another example of their preference for dealing with their own kind.

The secretary had a very distinctive role in the corporation. She has been defined as the "office wife." This is a revealing analogy because the term *wife* denotes a traditional, not a bureaucratic, relationship (using Weber's terms; see p. 4). The secretarial promotion ladder (a bureaucratic component of the role) was very short; most women got there before the age of 30 and were then stuck. The only way forward was a promotion in the status of her boss. This status determined both the formal rank and the actual power of the secretary; the tasks remained more or less the same at all levels.

The secretary, therefore, had to live her organizational life through her boss. In Weber's terms, this is the patrimonial traditional pattern even though it is embedded in a formal bureaucratic system. Very untypically in a bureaucracy where people normally work with those just above and just below themselves in status and salary, the boss-secretary relationship allows two people working closely together to have very wide discrepancies in remuneration. The relationship encourages considerable dependency, and secretaries are expected to show loyalty and devotion to their bosses. They are expected to value such nonmaterial rewards as prestige, personal feelings of being wanted and "loved," and having a salary rather than wages (even though that salary may be less than many wages).

Although the corporate wife had no official employment relationship with Indsco, she still had a clear career progression. There were three phases, each with its own problems. The first was the *technical phase,* corresponding to the husband's specialist or early managerial job. At that stage, he is engaged in a job, extremely demanding of time and energy, in which she can play no part. Conversely, he is underinvolved at home, and she tends to leave him out of the activities there. This mutual exclusion is the major strain and resentment.

The second was the *managerial phase* of the wife's career, which came when the husband entered middle and upper management and she was expected to perform social and hostess duties. At this stage, her behavior, her social adequacy, has a considerable bearing on the progress of her husband's career. Friendships are no longer just a personal matter, but have business implications—as, for example, when an old friendship between two of the managers and their wives had to be dropped because one manager now far outranked the other. Gossip is important, and every wife is faced with the problem of how far she is going to let her true feelings determine her social life and how far to let her relationships be determined by company "political" considerations.

The third phase was the *institutional phase,* with the husband at the top of the organization or in a position where he must represent it to the outside. Here, the issue for both husband and wife is the public nature of almost all their activities. What for others would be defined as pleasure (playing golf, attending a symphony concert, giving a party) are part of the business and indeed are allowable for tax deduction as a business expense. Charitable and community service activities, wherein the wife's role is especially prominent, may generate useful business. The corporation and its needs and relationships pervade the couple's whole life. Yet, because so much of the top manager's work is concerned with evaluating and being evaluated on personal grounds of trust and integrity, the wife is faced with the task of carrying out these activities as though they were highly personal, not ritualistic and contrived. Her job is to contribute to the image of her husband as a whole, real man. Top wives have also to suppress their private beliefs, and one wife, for example, told how proud she was that she never at any time during her husband's career unburdened herself of her private views to anyone.

From her study of Indsco, Kanter sees three important general needs for change in the modern industrial corporation: (a) improving the quality of working life (to stem the steady decrease in the number of those who say their jobs are satisfying), (b) creating equal employment opportunities for women and minorities, and (c) opening opportunities and releasing aspirations for employees to make better use of their talents in contributing to the corporation. To achieve these objectives, changes in organizational structures are needed.

One way to enhance opportunities would be to open the circle of management to promotion from a wider range of personnel—for example, women and clerical workers. This should be based on their appraised competence to do such jobs and ignore the segregated and restricted career paths that trap them in lower level jobs. Changes would be required in the appraisal, promotion, and career systems and in the design of jobs. Ways need to be found to create intermediate jobs that would act as career bridges into management.

Then, empowering strategies concerned with flattening the hierarchy, decentralization, and creating autonomous work groups are necessary. Number-balancing strategies would aim to raise the proportion of women and other minorities in higher jobs. It is important to combat tokenism by ensuring that several such group members, not just a single representative, are hired and later promoted at the same time. All these strategies for change are required if "affirmative action" policies are to be effective.

But Kanter is well aware of the difficulties in getting change in large corporations, and this awareness led her on to a study of "change masters"—corporate entrepreneurs capable of anticipating the need for and of leading productive change. She carried out an in-depth study of 10 major companies, each with a well-known reputation for progressive human resources policies. The companies included General Electric, General Motors, Honeywell, Polaroid, and Wang Laboratories.

By examining in detail 115 innovations and the factors that encouraged them, Kanter found a crucial distinction between organizations that can and do innovate and those whose style of thought is against change and prevents innovation. Innovative firms have an "integrative" approach to problems. They have a willingness to see problems as wholes and in their solutions to move beyond received wisdom, to challenge established practices. Entrepreneurial organizations are willing to operate at the edges of their competence, dealing with what they do not yet know (e.g., new investments, new markets, new products). They do not measure themselves by the standards of the past, but by their visions of the future.

They contrast very strongly with firms with a "segmentalist" approach. These see problems as narrowly as possible, independently of their context. Companies like this are likely to have segmented structures: many compartments strongly walled off from one another—production department from marketing department, corporate managers from divisional managers, management from labor, and men from women. As soon as a problem is identified, it is broken up and the parts dealt with by the appropriate departments. Little or no effort is given to the problem as an integrated whole. As a segmentalist manager, you are not going to start dealing with others' aspects of the problem, and you would regard it as a personal failure if they were to start worrying about yours. So, entrepreneurial spirit is stifled and the solution is unlikely to be innovative. It will follow the solid structure laid down. (This analysis is comparable to the organic vs. mechanistic distinction of Burns; see p. 46.)

In describing cases of integrative organizations in which innovations thrive, Kanter suggests a number of important elements necessary to reduce the segmentalism apparent in so many noninnovative, older, troubled firms. The aim is to reawaken the spirit of enterprise and to arouse the potential entrepreneurs that exist in all organizations. The methods include encouragement of a culture and of pride in the firm's own achievements, reduction of layers in the hierarchy, improvement of *lateral* communication, and giving of increased information about company plans. Decentralization is very important, as is the empowerment of entrepreneurial people lower down the organization to have the authority and the resources to exploit their ideas—even if this means cutting across established segments and boundaries.

In later books, Kanter elaborates the need for organizations to change in order to be successful. They have to employ the four F's: being focused, fast, friendly, and flexible. The *focused* aspect means developing internal synergies in leaner, more integrated organizations. This involves encouraging cooperative efforts in a less diversified business that can apply one unit's competence to another's problems. They are also *fast* in actively promoting "newstreams"—that is, creating official channels to speed the flow of new business possibilities within the firm. Thus, the opportunities for innovation extend well beyond the R&D department, and many more people at more levels are given the chance to lead new projects, thus encouraging "interpreneurship." *Friendly* companies find it easier to establish working alliances with other organizations. This allows them to extend their range without increasing in size. It gives them information access, windows on technology, speed of action, and mutual accommodation to innovation. *Flexible* organizations have given up bureaucracy, have reduced hierarchy, and work flexibly with a smaller fixed core of employees and a larger number of partnership ties.

This all adds up to a new approach of postentrepreneurial management based on three principles:

1. Minimize obligations and maximize options. Keep fixed costs low and use variable means to achieve goals.

2. Derive power through influence and alliances, rather than through full control or total ownership.

3. Keep things moving by encouraging continuous regrouping of people, functions, and products to produce innovative combinations.

Only in this way will corporations learn to thrive in the global economy.

Bibliography

Kanter, R. M., *Men and Women of the Corporation,* Basic Books, 1977.

Kanter, R. M., "Power Failure in Management Circuits," *Harvard Business Review,* (July-August 1979), 65-75; reprinted in D. S. Pugh (ed.), *Organization Theory,* Penguin Books, 1997.

Kanter, R. M., *The Change Masters: Corporate Entrepreneurs at Work,* Touchstone Books, 1985.

Kanter, R. M., *When Giants Learn to Dance,* Simon & Schuster, 1989.

Kanter, R. M., *World Class,* Simon & Schuster, 1995.

Karl E. Weick

Karl Weick's lively view of *managing* and of *organizing,* active words
he prefers to the more static words *management* and *organization,*
matches the liveliness of his personal interests, which he says range
from jazz big bands to "railroading." In its essentials, his is the view of
an American psychologist who has used his discipline imaginatively to
deepen the understanding of this field of endeavor. Weick is Rensis
Likert Collegiate Professor of Organizational Behavior and Psychology
at the University of Michigan.

As he sees organizations, they are "sensemaking systems," which inces-
santly create and re-create conceptions of themselves and of all around
them that seem sensible and stable enough to be manageable. Their members continually reaffirm to one another the truths of this reality as they see
it and the correctness of what should be done about it. Sensemaking is more
than interpretation; it includes generating what is interpreted. People build
up a view of themselves and what is going on and at the same time interpret
what was their own view in the first place. As Weick frequently puts it,
"People know what they think when they see what they say."

So, sensemaking is rolling hindsight. It is a continual weaving of
sense from beliefs, from implicit assumptions, from tales from the past,
from unspoken premises for decision and action, and from ideas about
what will happen as a result of what can be done. Once put into words,
it is constrained and framed by those same words because they are only
approximately what they refer to. Often, words have multiple meanings,
so all the time people are working with puns. Further, words are inclined
to convey discrete categories: They are not equal to depicting the
unbroken complex flow of life in organizations.

The sense that is made is shaped also by selective perception—that
is, by noticing some things and not others. Commitments that have been
made, then, have to be justified retrospectively. There is a constant
process of putting together reasoned arguments and arguing about them,
most obviously in meetings that have a value as sensemaking occasions.
The sense that is made, though, has its limits. People with time to spend
on a problem make sense of it in a way most understandable to themselves, so others become less able to follow what is afoot. Showing up

at meetings therefore produces a situation that is manageable only by those who have been showing up.

The whole sensemaking process gives ostensible orderliness to what is going on and has gone on. The development of a "generic sensemaking," within which although individuals differ yet they sufficiently concur, maintains a sense of organization.

Organizational sensemaking has at least seven distinguishing characteristics. It is:

1. *Grounded in identity construction* because sensemakers perpetually redefine their notion of themselves.

2. *Retrospective,* a never-ending reconstruction of experience. We are in the position of explorers who never know what they are exploring until it has been explored.

3. *Enactive of sensible environments* because people make sense of their worlds. By so doing, they create, or enact, a part of the very environment they face. They implant their own reality. So, an organization imposes the environment that imposes on it, and the bigger it becomes the more it runs into what it has itself enacted. A manufacturer that defines itself as the monopoly supplier of a product will, by that enactment, hamper itself from perceiving that innovative substitutes are a threat to its market. Most firms in the Swiss traditional watch industry, for example, just did not enact their environment to include cheap digital watches, and so suffered.

4. *Social* because it occurs with and in relation to other people inside and outside the organization.

5. *Ongoing* because it never stops and therefore never starts. Sensemaking is always in process.

6. *Focused on and by extracted cues*—that is, growing from familiar points of reference. Controlling these cues is a source of power because controlling what others respond to frames the view they will take and what they will do.

7. *Driven by plausibility rather than accuracy* because "the sensible need not be sensable." People go along with what to them is plausible and credible even if it cannot be checked. It might also have some accuracy, but because an equivocal and changing world has always moved on before a precise account of it can be formulated, absolute accuracy is impossible. Hence, accuracy takes second place to acceptability, to a version good enough to guide action for the time being.

Excellent illustrations of the impact of the enacted nature of organizational sensemaking are given by an examination of crisis situations. These are so complex that the enactments of the individuals involved will inevitably be partial, and their interactions may well exacerbate the crisis. Weick uses the example of the industrial disaster at the Union Carbide plant in Bhophal, India, to show how the preconceptions of everybody involved, from senior managers to operators, determined which action was taken. Their enacted views of their situation led to disaster. He wryly quotes the operating manual. After telling operators to dump the gas into a spare tank if a leak cannot be stopped, this manual states: "There may be other situations not covered above. The situation will determine the appropriate action." In fact, it was the other way around: The actions of the managers and operators determined the disaster situation. For example, after earlier safety violations had been corrected, top management regarded the plant as "safe." This preconception allowed them to undertake methods of reducing the operating costs of "a safe plant" in ways which, in the event, contributed to the disaster. Again, the operators had long dismissed an operating gauge as dysfunctional, having had trouble with it. They therefore neglected its correct reading in the disaster situation—a blind spot which had an important bearing on their attempts to make sense of what was happening. This is not to blame them; we often cannot know what "the appropriate action" should be until we are involved in doing something, seeing what happens and making sense of it.

Weick also makes use of a published study in the knitwear industry in Scotland to illustrate the seven characteristics of sensemaking given above. A number of small manufacturers in and around one town make cashmere sweaters. The managers of each see their own firm as having a distinct *identity,* signified by color and design of product, within an industry having a collective high-quality identity that distinguishes it from other makers of sweaters. The industry claims to have a business strategy centered on a specific high-income market, a strategy that has developed *retrospectively* from experience of sales, rather than has been planned with foresight. The sales agents whom the firms employ sell classically designed clothes and therefore feed back information from that particular market that confirms the prior beliefs the makers hold about it. Thus, the latter constantly *reenact* their environment, affirming this by *social* (including sociable) contacts in and between firms, the whole a continual *ongoing* process during which *cues* from designers, trade shows, and shops, as well as from the agents, reinforce the particular way in which the situation is perceived and so sustain its *plausibility.*

This is a long-established industry where sensemaking is molded by handicraft traditions. In younger organizations with professionally qualified employees, sensemaking has freer range, especially when innovative, nonroutine decisions are to be made. Here, the enactment of environments and the self-fulfilling prophecies that result should be most conspicuous. If, however, these newer organizations follow the current fashion and set up self-managed teams, their sensemaking will become less generic and more fragmented. Each team will make sense of things in its own way.

Paradoxically, if sensemaking constructs relatively stable interpretations, then this would render a flexible organic form of organization (see Burns, p. 46) steadily less so, and steadily less effective if it continued to be in an unstable environment. This might account for the tendency of organic organizations to drift toward the mechanistic form.

Whatever the form of organization, some of its elements will be tightly coupled together, whereas the coupling of others will be comparatively loose. Weick derives the concept of *loose coupling* from work by March (see p. 125) and others. It means that if some parts or activities in an organization change, the effect of this on other parts or activities will be limited, or be slow to show, or both. The mutual influence of loosely coupled systems is low.

Loose coupling facilitates adaptation. In a loosely coupled organization, there can be differential change, some aspects changing faster or more than others, so that, overall, there is a flexible response by the organization. Because bonds *within* loosely coupled subassemblies are stronger than those *between* them (e.g., within work groups or departments, as against between work groups or departments), there is both stability and flexibility.

Whatever the form of organization, it will have to work with ambiguous, uncertain, equivocal, and changing information. Despite their facade of numbers and objectivity and accountability, organizations and those who manage them wade among guesswork, subjectivity, and arbitrariness. Weick believes that language could better reflect this constant ambiguous flux by making more use of verbs and less of nouns. Indeed, he urges people to "stamp out nouns": to think of managing rather than management, of organizing rather than organization, as noted earlier.

He offers managers and others in organizations 10 further "pieces of advice":

1. *Don't panic in the face of disorder.* Some degree of disorder is necessary so that disorderly, ambiguous information can be taken in and coped with, rather than tidily screened out.

2. *You never do one thing all at once.* Whatever you do has many ramifications, not just the one you have in mind. And whereas some consequences happen right away, others show up indirectly and much later.

3. *Chaotic action is preferable to orderly inaction.* When someone says, "What shall I do?" and is told, "I don't know, just do something," that is

probably good advice. Because sense is made of events retrospectively, an action, any action, provides something to make sense of. Inaction is more senseless.

4. *The most important decisions are often the least apparent.* Decisions about what is to be retained in files, in databases, in memories indeed, provide the basis for future action. Such decisions may not be conspicuous, yet they sustain the past from which the future is begun.

5. *There is no solution.* Because there are no simple answers and because rarely is anything right or wrong, learn to live with improvisation and just a tolerable level of reasonableness.

6. *Stamp out utility.* Good adaptation now rules out some options for the future. Concentrating overmuch on utility now can rule out sources of future utility. Resources and choices are used up. Better to retain some noise and variability in the system, even at a cost to present efficiency, so that fresh future repertoires of action may be opened up.

7. *The map is the territory.* When the manager's map of what causes what, drawn from past experience, is superimposed on the future, it becomes for the user the territory that it maps. Simplification though it is, such a map has been worked over more than any other product has, and is as good a guide as can be had.

8. *Rechart the organizational chart.* Do not be boxed in by its conventional form. See things as they work out and people as they are to you. See the chart in the way it functions. For example, in the box on the chart for chairperson, write "hesitancy"; in the box for general manager, write "assertiveness"; and so on as people come over to you.

9. *Visualize organizations as evolutionary systems.* See what is evolving and what you can and should change. Likewise, recognize what is not and what you cannot.

10. *Complicate yourself!* Consider different causes, other solutions, new situations, and more complex alternatives and take pleasure in the process of doing so.

Weick does his best to follow his own 10th piece of advice and to move on always toward other ways of looking at organizing and organizers.

Bibliography

Weick, K. E., *The Social Psychology of Organizing,* Addison-Wesley, 1969; 2nd ed., 1979.

Weick, K. E., "Enacted Sensemaking in Crisis Situations," *Journal of Management Studies, 25,* (1988), 305-317; reprinted in D. S. Pugh (ed.), *Organization Theory,* Penguin Books, 1997.

Weick, K. E., *Sensemaking in Organizations,* Sage, 1995.

4 *Decision Making in Organizations*

The task of administration is so to design this environment that the individual will approach as close as practicable to rationality (judged in terms of the organization's goals) in his decisions.

Herbert A. Simon

An organization is a collection of choices looking for problems, issues and feelings looking for decision situations in which they might be aired, solutions looking for issues to which they might be the answers, and decision-makers looking for work.

James G. March

It makes more sense to talk about participative and autocratic situations than it does to talk about participative and autocratic managers.

Victor H. Vroom

An organization can be considered as a set of games between groups of partners who have to play with each other.

Michel Crozier

Although writers have considered a range of aspects of organizational functioning, a continuing school of thought maintains that the analysis of decision making is the key to understanding organizational management processes.

This approach was inaugurated by Herbert Simon and his colleagues at Carnegie-Mellon University. For Simon, management is decision making. His colleague, James March, develops this approach to consider the nonrationality of decision processes.

Victor Vroom proposes a theory of appropriate decision-making styles, and Michel Crozier examines the nature of the power that is at the basis of the decision-making "game."

Herbert A. Simon

Herbert Simon is a distinguished American political and social scientist whose perceptive contributions have influenced thinking and practice in many fields. He began his career in public administration and operations research, but as he took appointments in successive universities, his interests encompassed all aspects of administration. He is Professor of Computer Science and Psychology at Carnegie-Mellon University, Pittsburgh, where he and his colleagues have been engaged in fundamental research into the processes of decision making, using computers to simulate human thinking. Simon's outstanding intellectual contribution was publicly recognized when, in 1978, he was awarded the Nobel Prize in economics.

For Simon, "management" is equivalent to "decision making," and his major interest has been an analysis of how decisions are made and of how they might be made more effectively.

He describes three stages in the overall process of making a decision:

1. Finding occasions calling for a decision—the *intelligence* activity (using the word in the military sense)
2. Inventing, developing, and analyzing possible courses of action—the *design* activity
3. Selecting a particular course of action from those available—the *choice* activity

Generally speaking, intelligence activity precedes design, and design activity precedes choice; but the sequence of stages can be much more complex than this. Each stage in itself can be a complex decision-making process. The design stage can call for new intelligence activities. Problems at any stage can generate a series of subproblems, which in turn have their intelligence, design, and choice stages. Nevertheless, in the process of organizational decision making, these three general stages can be discerned.

Carrying out the decisions is also regarded as a decision-making process. Thus, after a policy decision has been taken, the executive having to carry it out is faced with a wholly new set of problems involving decision making. Executing policy amounts to making more detailed policy. Essentially, for Simon, all managerial action is decision making.

On what basis do administrators make decisions? The traditional theory of economists assumed complete rationality. Their model was of "economic man" (which, of course, embraced woman), who deals with the real world in all its complexity. He selects the rationally determined best course of action from among all those available to him in order to maximize his returns. But, clearly, this model is divorced from reality. We know that people's thinking and behavior have a large nonrational element. The need for an administrative theory is precisely because human rationality has practical limits. These limits to rationality are not static, but depend on the organizational environment in which the individual's decision takes place. It then becomes the task of administration to design this environment so that the individual will approach as closely as practicable to rationality in decisions as judged in terms of the organization's goals.

In place of "economic man," Simon proposes a model of "administrative man." Whereas economic man maximizes (selects the best course from those available), administrative man "satisfices" (looks for a course of action that is satisfactory or "good enough"). In this process, decision makers are content with gross simplifications, taking into account only those comparatively few relevant factors their minds can manage to encompass. "Most human decision-making, whether individual or organizational, is concerned with the discovery and selection of satisfactory alternatives; only in exceptional cases is it concerned with the discovery and selection of optimal alternatives." Most decisions are concerned, not with searching for the sharpest needle in the haystack, but with searching for a needle sharp enough to sew with. Thus, administrators who "satisfice" can make decisions without searching for all the possible alternatives and can use relatively simple rules of thumb. In business terms, they do not look for "maximum profit" but "adequate profit"; not "optimum price" but "fair price." This makes their world much simpler.

What techniques of decision making are then available? In discussing this problem, Simon makes a distinction between two polar types of decisions: *programmed* and *nonprogrammed* decisions. These are not mutually exclusive, but rather make up a continuum stretching from highly programmed decisions at one end to highly unprogrammed decisions at the other. Decisions are programmed to the extent that they are repetitive and routine or a definite procedure has been worked out to deal with them. They thus do not have to be considered afresh each time they occur. Examples are the decisions involved in processing a customer's order, determining an employee's sickness benefit, or carrying out any routine job.

Decisions are unprogrammed to the extent that they are new and unstructured or where there is no cut-and-dried method for handling the problem. This may be either because the decision has not occurred before or because it is particularly difficult or important. Examples are decisions to introduce a new product, to make substantial staff redundancies, or to move to a new location. All these decisions would be nonprogrammed (though entailing many programmed subdecisions) because the organization would have no detailed strategy to govern its responses to these situations, and it would have to fall back on whatever general capacity it had for intelligent problem solving.

Human beings are capable of acting intelligently in many new or difficult situations, but they are likely to be less efficient. The cost to the organization of relying on nonprogrammed decisions in areas where special-purpose procedures and programs can be developed is likely to be high, and an organization should try to program as many of its decisions as possible. The traditional techniques of programmed decision making are habit, including knowledge and skills, clerical routines, and standard operating procedures, and the organization's structure and culture—that is, for example, its system of common expectations, well-defined information channels, and established subgoals. The traditional techniques for dealing with nonprogrammed decisions rely on the selection and training of executives who possess judgment, intuition, and creativity. These categories of techniques have been developed over thousands of years (the building of the pyramids must have involved the use of many of them). But since World War II, Simon argues, a complete revolution in techniques of decision making has got under way, comparable to the invention of powered machinery in manufacturing.

The revolution has been a result of the application of such techniques as mathematical analysis, operational research, electronic data processing, information technology, and computer simulation. These were used first for completely programmed operations (e.g., mathematical calculations, accounting procedures) formerly regarded as the province of clerks. But more and more elements of judgment (previously unprogrammed and the province of middle management) can now be incorporated into programmed procedures. Decisions on stock control and production control have been in the forefront of this development. With advances in computer technology, more and more complex decisions will become programmed. Even a completely unprogrammed decision, made once and for all, can be reached via computer techniques by building a model of the decision situation. Various courses of action can then be simulated and their effects assessed. "The automated factory of the future," Simon maintains, "will operate on the basis of programmed decisions produced in the automated office beside it."

Bibliography

March, J. G., and Simon, H. A., *Organizations,* John Wiley, 1958.

Simon, H. A., *Administrative Behavior,* 2nd ed., Macmillan, 1960; 3rd ed., Free Press, 1976.

Simon, H. A., *The New Science of Management Decision,* Harper & Row, 1960; Prentice Hall, 1977.

Simon, H. A., *The Shape of Automation,* Harper & Row, 1965.

James G. March

James March is Professor of Management at Stanford University, California. His breadth of mind is indicated by his being linked also with the Political Science and Sociology Departments. His interests have long focused on decision making in organizations, ever since his early work at Carnegie-Mellon University. Its renowned contributors to the understanding of decision making include also Herbert A. Simon (p. 117) and Richard Cyert, both colleagues of March's and both still at Carnegie-Mellon, Cyert for many years as its president.

March himself brings to his lively analyses of decision making a unique blend of the logical and the poetical. His work is logical in argument, poetical in imagery and expression. He believes that decision making can be understood in much the same nonrational way as a painting by Picasso or a poem by T. S. Eliot. It is far from a rationally controlled process moving steadily to a culminating choice. The confusion and complexity surrounding decision making is underestimated. Many things are happening at once. Views and aims are changing, and so are alliances among those concerned. What has to be done is not clear, nor is how to do it. In this topsy-turvy world, in which people do not comprehend what is going on, decisions may have little to do with the processes that supposedly make them, and organizations "do not know what they are doing."

It is a world in which rationality has cognitive, political, and organizational limits. Cognitively, attention is the key scarce resource. Individuals cannot attend to everything at once, nor can they be everywhere at once. So, they attend to some parts of some decision making, not to all of them. What they attend to depends on the alternative claims on them because giving attention to one decision means overlooking others. As March puts it, "Every entrance is an exit somewhere else." Therefore, timing is crucial—timing when to join in and which matters to raise.

March shares with his former colleague Simon the conception of *bounded* rationality. Not only is attention scarce, but mental capacity is also limited. The mind of the decision maker can only encompass so much. It can only cope with a limited amount of information and with a limited number of alternatives. That being so, even if decision making is intended to be rational, its rationality has severe bounds. Decisions will be taken knowing much less than in principle could be known.

Along with scarce attention and bounded rationality come erratic preferences. People change their minds about what they want. Even if they know what they want, they may ignore their own preferences and follow other advice or other traditions. They may state their preferences in an ambiguous way. Their preferences may conflict with the preferences of others.

Here, the cognitive limits to rationality connect with the political limits. March and his other former colleague Cyert recognize that a firm, and indeed any other kind of organization, is a shifting, multiple-goal political coalition. "The composition of the firm is not given; it is negotiated. The goals of the firm are not given; they are bargained." The coalition, to use their word, includes managers, workers, stockholders, suppliers, customers, lawyers, tax collectors, and other agents of the state, as well as all the subunits or departments into which an organization is divided. Each group has its own preference about what the firm should be like and what its goals should be. Hence, negotiation and bargaining, rather than detached rationality, are endemic.

This is where the political limits to rationality connect with the organizational limits. These are the limits set by *organized anarchies*. Although all organizations do not have the properties of organized anarchy all of the time, they do for part of the time, and especially if they are publicly owned or are educational, such as universities, colleges, and schools. Organized anarchies have "three general properties." First, because preferences are unclear, the organization discovers its goals from what it is doing, rather than by defining them clearly in advance. Second, because it has "unclear technology," "its own processes are not understood by its members," and it works by trial and error more than by knowing what it is doing. Third, because of "fluid participation," who is involved in what is constantly changing. Take a college, for instance. Pronouncements on strategy are more reviews of what courses are already taught than they are statements of future goals; new teaching techniques, such as video games, are tried without knowing whether they will work and without their being understood by authorizing committees; and what such committees understand and approve depends on who turns up at meetings.

Given these cognitive, political, and organizational characteristics, decision-making processes are bound to be affected. Not only in those organizations prone to organized anarchy, but even in business firms, such decision processes have four peculiarities: (a) quasi resolution of conflict, (b) uncertainty avoidance, (c) problemistic search, and (d) organizational learning.

Quasi resolution of conflict is the state of affairs most of the time. The conflicts inherent in the political nature of organizations and therefore in the making of decisions are not resolved. Rather, devices for their quasi resolution enable them to be lived with. One such device is "local rationality." Because each subunit or department deals only with a narrow range of problems—the sales department with how to sell, and the personnel department with how to recruit, and so on—each can at least purport to be rational in dealing with its "local" concerns. Of course, these local rationalities can be mutually inconsistent, as when accounting's insistence on remaining within budget destroys marketing's advertising campaign. Thus, they may not add up to overall rationality for the organization as a whole.

A second such device can ease this difficulty. It is "acceptable-level decision rules." The acceptable level of consistency between one decision and another is low enough for the divergences to be tolerable. What is needed is an outcome acceptable to the different interests, rather than one that is optimal overall.

A third such device, "sequential attention to goals," also helps. As the conflicts between goals are not resolved, attention is given first to one goal and then to another, in sequence. For example, smooth production is first emphasized, and then later on the priority switches to satisfying customers by design variations that disrupt production.

Uncertainty avoidance, too, pervades decision making. All organizations must live with uncertainty. Customer orders are uncertain, so are currency fluctuations, so is future taxation, and so on. Therefore, decision making responds to information here and now and avoids the uncertainties of longer term forecasting. Pressing problems are dealt with, and planning for the longer run is avoided. Market uncertainties are avoided by exclusive contracts with customers and by conforming with everyone else to recognized pricing and negotiating practices. For the same reason, *search is problemistic* and shortsighted. The occurrence of a problem spurs a search for ways to deal with it, and once a way is found, then search stops. Farsighted regular search, such as the steady accumulation of market information, is relatively unimportant. Such information is likely to be ignored in the urgency of any particular sales crisis. Moreover, search is "simple-minded." When a problem arises, search for a solution is concentrated near the old solution. Radical proposals are brushed aside, and a safer answer is found, not much different from what there was before. When a U.S. university sought a new dean to head a major faculty, prominent outsiders were passed over and an established insider chosen because of fears that outsiders might make too many changes. Business organizations, too, regularly choose both managers and workers to fit in with the least amount of change.

Finally, decision-making processes are learning processes. In them, *organizational learning* takes place. Decision makers do not begin by knowing all they need to know. They learn as they go. They learn what is thought practicable and what is not, what is permissible and what is not. By trial and error, they find out what can be done and adapt their goals to it.

Perhaps it should not be surprising that all this leads March, together with Cohen and Olsen, to propose a *garbage can model of organizational choice,* famed for its name as well as for what it postulates. For when people fight for the right to participate in decision making and then do not exercise it, when they request information and then do not use it, when they struggle over a decision and then take little interest in whether it is ever carried out, something curious must be going on.

So, the opportunity or need to arrive at a decision, to make a choice, can be seen as "a garbage can into which various kinds of problems and solutions are dumped by participants, as they are generated." There may be several garbage cans around with different labels on them.

In the model so vividly depicted, a decision is an outcome of the interplay between *problems, solutions, participants,* and *choices,* all of which arrive relatively independently of one another. Problems can arise inside or outside the organization. Solutions exist on their own, irrespective of problems (people's preferences wait for their moment to come; the computer waits for the question it can answer). Participants move in and out. Opportunities for choices occur any time an organization is expected to produce a decision—for example, when contracts must be signed or money must be spent.

The decisions come about by *resolution,* by *oversight,* or by *flight.* If by resolution, then the choice resolves the problem, although this is likely to take time. If by oversight, the choice is made quickly, incidentally to other choices being made. If by flight, the original problem has gone (flown) away, leaving a choice that can now be readily made but that solves nothing. Probably, most decisions are made by oversight or flight, not by resolution.

Whether or not a decision happens is because of the "temporal proximity" of what streams into the garbage can; that is, a decision happens when a suitable collection of problems, solutions, participants, and choices coincides. When it does, solutions are attached to problems and problems to choices by participants who happen to have the time and energy to do it. So, the decision that is made may be more or less "uncoupled" from the apparent process of making it, being a result of other coincidental reasons.

Seen like this, "an organization is a collection of choices looking for problems, issues and feelings looking for decision situations in which they might be aired, solutions looking for issues to which they might be the answer, and decision-makers looking for work." Although this may be so anywhere, nowhere is it more so than in an organized anarchy, such as a university.

March admits that the picture may be overdrawn, but he contends it is real enough to mean that the rational "technology of reason" should be supplemented with a "technology of foolishness." Sometimes, people *should* act *before* they think, so that they may discover new goals in the course of that action. They *should* make decisions with consequences for the future in the knowledge that they do not know what will be wanted in the future. In terms of ostensible rationality, this is foolish. But decision making needs scope for foolishness. Playfulness allows this. Playfulness is a deliberate (but temporary) suspension of the normal rational rules so that we can experiment. We need to play with foolish alternatives and *in*consistent possibilities. We need to treat goals as hypotheses to be changed, intuitions as real, hypocrisy as a transitional inconsistency, memory as an enemy of novelty, and experience not as fixed history but as a theory of what happened, which we can change if that helps us learn. From time to time, we should be foolishly playful inside our garbage cans.

Bibliography

Cohen, M. D., March, J. G., and Olsen, J. P., "A Garbage Can Model of Organizational Choice," *Administrative Science Quarterly, 17,* (1972), 1-25.

Cyert, R. M., and March, J. G., *A Behavioral Theory of the Firm,* Prentice Hall, 1963.

March, J. G., *Decisions and Organizations,* Blackwell, 1988.

March, J. G., *A Primer on Decision Making,* Free Press, 1994.

March, J. G., and Olsen, J. P., *Ambiguity and Choice in Organizations,* 2nd ed., Oxford University Press, 1980.

Victor H. Vroom

Victor Vroom has been involved for many years in research, teaching, and consulting on the psychological analysis of behavior in organizations. A Canadian by birth, he has been at McGill University, a number of U.S. universities, and is currently Searle Professor of Organization and Management and Professor of Psychology at Yale University. His interests in the effects of personality on participation in decision making began early, and his doctoral dissertation on this topic won him the Ford Foundation Doctoral Dissertation Competition in 1959. He has also won the McKinsey Foundation Research Design Competition and the J. M. Cattell Award of the American Psychological Association.

Vroom's dissertation corroborated previous findings that participation in decision making has positive effects on attitudes and motivation, but in addition it showed that the size of these effects was a function of certain personality characteristics of the participants. Authoritarians and people with weak independence needs are unaffected by the opportunity to participate, whereas equalitarians and those with strong independence needs develop more positive attitudes and greater motivation for effective performance through participation. The study did point out, though, that a number of different processes related to participation might be affected differently.

Much more recently, Vroom (in collaboration with P. W. Yetton and A. G. Jago) has explored in much greater depth the processes of management decision making and the variations in subordinate participation that can come about. Possible decision processes that a manager might use in dealing with an issue affecting a group of subordinates are as follows (although there are some variations if the issue concerns one subordinate only):

AI   You solve the problem or make the decision yourself, using information available to you at that time.

AII   You obtain the necessary information from your subordinate(s) and then decide on the solution to the problem yourself. You may or may not tell your subordinates what the problem is when getting the information from them. The role played by your subordinates in making the decision is clearly one of providing necessary information to you, rather than of generating or evaluating alternative solutions.

CI   You share the problem with relevant subordinates individually, getting their ideas and suggestions without bringing them together as a group. Then, *you* make the decisions that may or may not reflect your subordinates' influence.

CII You share the problem with your subordinates as a group, collectively obtaining their ideas and suggestions. Then, *you* make the decision that may or may not reflect your subordinates' influence.

GII You share a problem with your subordinates as a group. Together, you generate and evaluate alternatives and attempt to reach agreement (consensus) on a solution. Your role is much like that of chairperson. You do not try to influence the group to adopt "your" solution, and you are willing to accept and implement any solution that has the support of the entire group.

Processes AI and AII are designated autocratic processes, CI and CII consultative processes, and GII a group process. (GI applies to single subordinate issues.) Having identified these processes, Vroom and Yetton's research program then proceeded to answer two basic questions:

1. What decision-making processes *should* managers use to deal effectively with the problems they encounter in their jobs? This is a normative or prescriptive question. To answer it would require setting up a logical "model" with a series of steps or procedures by which a manager could rationally determine which was the most effective process to inaugurate.

2. What decision-making processes *do* managers use in dealing with their problems, and what factors affect their choice of processes and degree of subordinate participation? This is a descriptive question, and the answer is important in delineating how far away from a rational approach managers are in their decision making. We could then ask what activities of training or development could lead managers to a more effective decision-making style.

In their answer to the first question, Vroom and his collaborators have made a most distinctive contribution. They have developed a detailed normative model of decision-making processes that is based on rational principles consistent with existing evidence on the consequences of participation for organizational effectiveness. They begin by distinguishing three classes of consequences that influence decision effectiveness:

1. *The quality or rationality of the decision.* Clearly, a process that jeopardized this would be ineffective.

2. *The acceptance or commitment on the part of the subordinates to execute the decision effectively.* If this commitment is necessary, then processes that do not generate it even though they give a high-quality decision would be ineffective.

3. *The amount of time required to make the decision.* A decision process that took less time, if it were equally effective, would normally be preferable to one that took longer.

These consequences generate a set of rules for the model that may then be applied to the characteristics of a manager's problem under consideration. The model will then indicate which decision process is appropriate to the particular case. The model can be expressed in the form of a decision tree, as shown on Figure 4.1. In the decision model, the problem characteristics are presented as questions. The manager starts at the left-hand side and moves to the right along the path determined by the answer to the question above each box. At the final point of the line, the model shows which of the decision processes should be used to reach, in the least time, a quality decision that will be found acceptable.

As will be seen from the decision model, all decision processes (autocratic, consultative, group) are applicable in some circumstances, and how often each should be used will depend on the types of decisions the manager has to make. The normative model requires that all managers, if they are to be rational and effective, have to be able to operate across the whole range. In later work, Vroom and Jago have elaborated the model to give greater discrimination among options and thus allow more detailed and more effective targeting of the decision process to the manager's problem. They have also made the more elaborate model available for use via a computer program.

The research undertaken by Vroom and his collaborators to answer their second question—How do managers actually behave?—is based on two methods. In the first method, many managers were asked to recall decision problems and how they tackled them in terms of the questions of the decision model. The second method involved many managers assessing a set of standardized problem descriptions and giving their preferred solutions.

The most striking finding of these descriptive studies was that, although there were certainly average differences between managers in

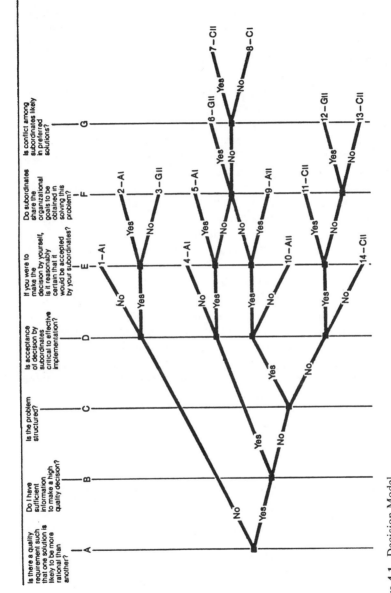

Figure 4.1. Decision Model
SOURCE: Vroom and Yetton (1973).

129

their use of various decision processes, these were small in comparison with the *range* of processes used by any individual manager. No managers indicated they would use the same process on all decisions, and most used all five of the decision processes above under some circumstances. "It makes more sense to talk about participative and autocratic situations than it does to talk about participative and autocratic managers."

The descriptive research also enabled a comparison of what managers do (or say they would do) and what the model would designate as rational behavior. On average, a "typical" manager was found to use the same decision process as that required by the decision model in 40% of the situations. In a further 25% of the situations, they used a process called "feasible" in that it satisfied the constraints of the model on protecting decision quality and acceptability but would not be the least time-consuming. Only in about 33% of the situations did the typical manager initiate a process that will risk quality or acceptability. In addition, it was found that the constraints necessary to achieve acceptability were much more frequently ignored than those necessary to achieve quality.

Vroom has designed a leadership development program, based on his normative model, that will enable managers to analyze their own decision processes against that of the model and to see where they depart from the rational constraints for effective decision making. The model proposes far greater variation for each problem situation than the typical manager exhibits. Using the model as a basis for making decisions would require such a manager to become both more autocratic and more participative, according to the problem.

Bibliography

Vroom, V. H., "A New Look at Managerial Decision-Making," *Organizational Dynamics,* 5 (1974), 66–80; reprinted in D. S. Pugh (ed.), *Organization Theory,* Penguin Books, 1997.

Vroom, V. H., *Some Personality Determinants of the Effects of Participation,* Garland, 1987.

Vroom, V. H., and Jago, A. G., *The New Leadership: Managing Participation in Organizations,* Prentice Hall, 1988.

Vroom, V. H., and Yetton, P. W., *Leadership and Decision-Making,* University of Pittsburgh Press, 1976.

Michel Crozier

The distinctively French view of organizations contributed by Michel Crozier arises both from his French birth and experience and from the many periods he has spent in the United States. These periods away from France give him a perspective on his own society. He is Director of the Center for the Sociology of Organizations in Paris, under the auspices of the Centre National de la Recherche Scientifique (CNRS), and has a long record of research in France. This research has covered a wide range of organizations and administrative and social problems, but with an emphasis on studies of public administration and state-owned industries. His early training in sociology was in the United States, however, and he has spent many subsequent periods at Stanford and Harvard.

Although Crozier's view has its origins in research in France, it penetrates bureaucracies everywhere. He does not see them as monolithic rational structures, but rather as systems in which, despite all efforts at control, individuals and groups of individuals have room for maneuver. Interaction between the system and the actors in the system is constant.

This view is distinctively founded on the concept of the power *game*. An organization is seen as a series of enmeshed power games, an "ensemble" of games. This idea is no mere colorful image. Games are very real to those in organizations. Indeed, an organization is not so much the direct creation of deliberate design as the result of the ensemble of games. The game channels power relationships and enables cooperation, reconciling the freedom of those in the organization with the constraints it places on them.

Games are played between groups of partners of many kinds—for example, between superiors and subordinates such as managers and workers, or between departments and sections. The players evolve different strategies that govern what they do. Superiors may follow a strategy of "divide and rule"; subordinates may follow a defensive strategy to protect whatever scope they may have to do things in their own way, free of interference from bosses or new regulations; occupational groups such as maintenance engineers may follow conservative (or aggressive) strategies toward technical modernization, and so on. Crozier calls this a *strategic model* of organization.

Players go so far, but not too far, in pursuing their strategies. Although all are free to gain whatever advantage can be got from a strategy rationally designed to serve their interests, the continuance of the organization is necessary for them to be able to play at all. These are not life-and-death struggles, but games for position within a system; therefore, limits are accepted. These are the rules of the game, which players in each game must respect if it is to continue. They are not formally set-down rules, but principles that can be discovered by analyzing the players' recurrent behavior, in the same way as their strategies can be seen in what they do. There may not be complete consensus on the rules, and some players may be endeavoring to change them, but they are sufficiently acknowledged and persistent for newcomers to learn them and to absorb the associated norms and values that define acceptable and unacceptable strategies.

The players in a game are far from equal—some are more powerful than others—and their roles differ further between games, so players who are powerful in one game may be weak in another. Their strategies, however, share a common fundamental objective: to gain whatever advantage is possible, within the constraining rules of the game, by restricting the choices of alternatives open to others while preserving or enhancing their own choices. The aim is to maneuver others into positions where their actions can be determined while retaining one's own freedom of action. All attempt to defend and extend their own discretion and to limit their dependence while placing others in the reverse position.

The most revealing case among those described by Crozier is that of the maintenance workers in what he terms the "industrial monopoly," the French nationalized tobacco industry. At the time of Crozier's research (at the end of the 1950s and beginning of the 1960s), this monopoly was dispersed throughout the country in many small and very similar factories. Each employed 350 to 400 people, of which perhaps one third were direct production workers. These workers were women, and their job was to operate the semiautomatic machines turning out cigarettes and so on.

The organization was very stable, and each small factory worked in a controlled environment. Finance, raw material procurement, distribution, and sales were all centrally controlled from Paris, so each local plant could get on with its task of production, unimpeded by problems. Except one: machine stoppages.

These stoppages occurred because of breakdowns and because of tobacco leaf variations that required constant adjustment of machines. The stoppages were the only major happenings that could not be dealt with by impersonal bureaucratic rules or bureaucratic action from Paris. Yet if machines stopped, work stopped, and the factory stopped making what it was there for. Who could do something about it? Only the dozen or so male maintenance workers under the factory's technical engineer, who alone knew how to set and repair the machines. No bureaucrat in Paris, no local factory director, not even the production workers on the machines knew what the maintenance workers knew. They acquired the tricks of their trade from one another and kept them to themselves. They did not explain to anyone else what they did. In their eyes, it was an unforgivable sin for a production worker herself to "fool around" with her machine, which she should not touch beyond operating it in the normal way. Thus, the maintenance workers succeeded in making the production workers directly, and everyone else indirectly, dependent on them. All the others were constrained by the maintenance workers, being the only ones able to deal with stoppages, while the maintenance workers themselves preserved their freedom of choice over what to do.

They could do so because they were powerful; and they were powerful because of their "control over the last source of uncertainty remaining in a completely routinized organizational system." Machine stoppages occurred unpredictably, and theirs was the choice of what to do. This choice gave them power because those who face and cope with uncertainties have power over others who are dependent on the choices. In the long run, power is closely related to those uncertainties on which the life of an organization depends, and the strategies of the groups in the power games are aimed at controlling the "ultimate strategic sources of uncertainties." *Uncertainty explains power.*

The maintenance workers, therefore, had power because whereas everything else was under bureaucratic control, the uncertain machine stoppages were not. These had to be dealt with on the spot as they happened. They presented the maintenance workers with an opportunity that was conspicuous because it was the sole uncertainty in each factory. In other organizations, the sources of uncertainty may not be so conspicuous, but in all organizations they come and go and, as they do so, the power of those who confront them waxes and wanes. Maintenance workers are only one example; the same applies to the rise and fall of financial experts, of production control specialists, and so on.

Why is it, then, that powerful experts are not able to cling to power indefinitely? If the uncertainty continues, and with it their know-how, they could indeed keep their grip on power, but this is unlikely because their success is self-defeating. The rationalization inherent in organizations breeds constant attempts to bring areas of uncertainty within the range of formal controls, and experts are themselves agents of the rationalization that diminishes their own power. The more they succeed in recording their own know-how in bureaucratic procedures and regulations, the more their own power to deal with the uncertainties themselves is curtailed. Their choices become restricted. Therefore, the maintenance workers in the tobacco factories strove to keep their rules of thumb to themselves and to prevent their becoming bureaucratized. Even though officially laid down instructions for the setting and maintenance of machines were kept at the head office in Paris, these were completely disregarded by the maintenance workers, and there were no copies in the factories themselves—for *the routinization of uncertainty removes power.*

This aphorism shapes strategies up and down hierarchies, as well as between occupational groupings. The battle between superiors and subordinates involves a basic strategy by which subordinates resist rules that encroach on their discretion while pressing for rules that will limit the discretion of their superiors over them.

It is possible for opposed strategies to interlock in a series of bureaucratic vicious circles that block change. Administrators try to extend bureaucratic regulation; those subjected to it resist. The directors of the tobacco factories typically pressed for the modernization of procedures, whereas the technical engineers resisted anything that might alter the position of their maintenance workers. Crozier sees French society as a whole as an example of this, for its tendencies to bureaucratic centralization and impersonality provoke strategies by those affected, and these strategies, in turn, provoke greater bureaucratization. In every branch of administration, each level of hierarchy becomes a layer protected from those above and beneath. Those beneath restrict communication to those above and stall any threatening changes, whereas those above make ill-informed decisions that are not carried out as intended, but from the consequences of which they are shielded.

These workings give rise to a peculiar rhythm of change in bureaucratic organizations, certainly in France and perhaps elsewhere too. It is an alternation of long periods of stability with very short periods of crisis and change. Conflicts are stifled until they explode. Explosive crises are therefore endemic to such bureaucracies, and necessary to them as a means for change. At such times in French bureaucracies, personal authority supersedes the rules, as someone, such as General de Gaulle, is able to force some change out of the crisis. *Authoritarian reformer figures* wait amid the bureaucratic routine for that moment of crisis when the system will need them.

Yet, Crozier is optimistic. He hopes that if reforms were made in training and recruitment for French public administration and in its caste system, the elites could be opened up. He argues that the large organizations of the modern world are not necessarily inimical to change because change has never been faster, and it is fastest in those societies with the largest organizations. But there is always a risk that bureaucratic structures lead to forms of power games that block the changes that are needed.

Bibliography

Crozier, M., *The Bureaucratic Phenomenon,* University of Chicago Press, 1967.

Crozier, M., "Comparing Structures and Comparing Games" in G. Hofstede and S. Kassim (eds.), *European Contributions to Organization Theory,* Van Gorcum, 1976; reprinted in D. S. Pugh (ed.), *Organization Theory,* Penguin Books, 1997.

Crozier, M., and Friedberg, E., *Actors and Systems,* University of Chicago Press, 1980.

5 *People in Organizations*

Management succeeds or fails in proportion as it is accepted without reservation by the group as authority and leader.

Elton Mayo

The entire organization must consist of a multiple overlapping group structure with *every* work group using group decision-making processes skillfully.

Rensis Likert

The average human being learns, under proper conditions, not only to accept but to seek responsibility.

Douglas McGregor

The successful manager must be a good diagnostician and must value a spirit of enquiry.

Edgar H. Schein

The primary functions of any organization, whether religious, political, or industrial, should be to implement the needs of man to enjoy a meaningful existence.

Frederick Herzberg

Only organizations based on the redundancy of functions (as opposed to the redundancy of parts) have the flexibility and innovative potential to give the possibility of adaptation to a rapid change rate, increasing complexity and environmental uncertainty.

Eric Trist

Organizations are systems of interdependent *human beings*. Although this has been recognized implicitly by the writers of the previous sections, and explicitly by some, their main concern has been with the "formal system"—its aims, the principles on which it should be constituted to achieve them, and the methods by which it should function.

136

People have then been considered as one of the essential resources required to achieve the aims. But people are a rather special sort of resource. They not only work for the organization—they *are* the organization.

The behavior of the members of an organization clearly affects both its structure and its functioning, as well as the principles on which it can be managed. Most important, human beings affect the aims of organizations in which they participate—not merely the methods used to accomplish them. The writers in this section are social scientists specifically concerned with analyzing the behavior of people and its effects on all aspects of the organization. They have studied human attitudes, expectations, value systems, tensions and conflicts, and the effects these have on productivity, adaptability, cohesion, and morale. They have regarded the organization as a "natural system"—an organism whose processes have to be studied in their own right—rather than as a "formal system"—a mechanism designed to achieve particular ends.

Elton Mayo is the founding father of the "human relations movement," which brought into prominence the view that workers and managers must first be understood as human beings. Rensis Likert and Douglas McGregor reject the underlying assumptions about human behavior on which formal organizations have been built and propose new management methods based on a more adequate understanding of human motivation.

Edgar Schein's concern has been to understand and manage the relationship between the individual's career and the organization's culture, whereas Frederick Herzberg determines how people's characteristically human needs for growth and development may be satisfied in work.

Eric Trist and his colleagues at the Tavistock Institute demonstrate the utility of designing groups within organizations, which, while taking account of technical concerns, can also make provision for social and psychological aspects of human behavior.

Elton Mayo and the Hawthorne Investigations

Elton Mayo (1880–1949) was an Australian who spent most of his working life at Harvard University, eventually becoming Professor of Industrial Research in the Graduate School of Business Administration. In this post, he was responsible for the initiation and direction of many research projects, the most famous being the 5-year investigations of the Hawthorne works of the Western Electric Company in Chicago. Immediately prior to his death, Mayo was consultant on industrial problems to the British government.

Elton Mayo has often been called the founder of both the human relations movement and of industrial sociology. The research that he directed showed the importance of groups in affecting the behavior of individuals at work and enabled him to make certain deductions about what managers ought to do. `

Like most of his contemporaries, Mayo's initial interests were in fatigue, accidents, and labor turnover and the effect on these of rest pauses and physical conditions of work. One of his first investigations was of a spinning mill in Philadelphia, where labor turnover in one department was 250%, compared with an average of 6% for all the other departments. Mayo introduced rest pauses, and production and morale improved. When the operatives took part in fixing the frequency and duration of the pauses, a further improvement was registered and morale in the whole factory also improved. At the end of the first year, turnover in the department concerned was down to the average for the rest of the mill. The initial explanation was that the rest pauses, in breaking up the monotony of the job, improved the mental and physical condition of the men. After subsequent investigations, however, Mayo modified his explanation.

The major investigation that led to this modification and that laid the basis for a great many subsequent studies was the Hawthorne Experiment, carried out between 1927 and 1932. Prior to the entry of Mayo's team, an inquiry had been made by a number of engineers into the effect of illumination on workers and their work. Two groups of workers had been isolated, and the lighting conditions for one had been varied and for the other held constant. No significant differences in output were found between the two; indeed, whatever was done with the lighting, production rose in *both* groups.

At this point, the industrial research team directed by Mayo took over. The first stage of their inquiry is known as the Relay Assembly Test Room. Six female operatives engaged in assembling telephone relays were segregated to observe the effect on output and morale of various changes in the conditions of work. During the 5 years of experiment, various changes were introduced and a continuous record of output was kept. At first, a special group payment scheme was introduced; previously, the women had been grouped with 100 other operatives for incentive payment purposes. Other changes introduced at various times were rest pauses in several different forms (varying in length and spacing), shorter hours, and refreshments, in all more than 10 changes. Before putting the changes into effect, the investigators spent much time discussing them with the women. Communication between the workers and the research team was very full and open throughout the experimental period. Almost without exception, output increased with each change made.

The next stage in the experiment was to return to the original conditions. The operatives reverted to a 48-hour 6-day week, no incentives, no rest pauses, and no refreshment. Output went up to the highest yet recorded. By this time, it had become clear, to quote Mayo, "that the itemized changes experimentally imposed . . . could not be used to explain the major change—the continually increasing production." The explanation eventually given was that the women experienced a tremendous increase in work satisfaction because they had greater freedom in their working environment and control over their own pace-setting. The six operatives had become a social group with their own standards and expectations. By removing the women from the normal setting of work and by intensifying their interaction and cooperation, informal practices, values, norms, and social relationships had been built up, giving the group high cohesion. Also, the communication system between the researchers and the workers was extremely effective; this meant that the norms of output were those that the women thought the researchers desired. The supervisors took a personal interest in each worker and showed pride in the record of the group. The result was that the workers and the supervisors developed a sense of participation and, as a result, established a completely new working pattern. Mayo's generalization was that work satisfaction depends to a large extent on the informal social pattern of the work group. Where norms of cooperativeness and high output are established because of a feeling of importance, physical conditions have little impact.

This, however, is the explanation arrived at in later years. At the time of the actual experiment, the continually increasing output was regarded as something of a mystery, so an inquiry was instituted into conditions in the factory at large. This inquiry took the form of an interview program. It was quickly realized that such a program told the researchers little about the actual conditions in the factory but a great deal about the attitudes of various employees. The major finding of this stage of the inquiry was that many problems of worker-management cooperation were the results of the emotionally based attitudes of the workers, rather than of objective difficulties in the situation. Workers, thought Mayo, were activated by a "logic of sentiment," whereas management was concerned with the "logic of cost and efficiency." Conflict is inevitable unless this difference is understood and provided for.

The third stage of the investigation was to observe a group performing a task in a natural setting—that is, a non-experimental situation. A number of male employees in what became known as the Bank Wiring Observation Room were put under constant observation and their output recorded. It was found that they restricted their output; the group had a standard for output, and this was not exceeded by any individual worker. The attitude of the members of the group toward the company's financial incentive scheme was one of indifference. The group was highly integrated with its own social structure and code of behavior, which clashed with the code of management. Essentially, this code was composed of solidarity on the part of the group against management. On the one hand, not too much work should be done because that would be rate busting; on the other hand, not too little work should be done because that would be chiseling. There was little recognition of the organization's formal allocation of roles. This was confirmation of the importance of informal social groupings in determining levels of output.

Taken as a whole, the significance of the Hawthorne investigations was in "discovering" the informal organization that, it is now realized, exists in all organizations. The investigations demonstrated the importance to individuals of stable social relationships in the work situation. They confirmed Mayo in his wider thinking that what he calls the "rabble hypothesis" about human behavior (that each individual pursues only a narrow, rational self-interest) was completely false. They confirmed his view that the breakdown of traditional values in society could be countered by creating a situation in industry conducive to spontaneous cooperation.

For Mayo, one major task of management is to organize spontaneous cooperation, thereby preventing the further breakdown of society. As traditional attachments to community and family disappear and as the workplace increases in importance, the support given by traditional institutions must now be given by the organization. Conflict, competition, and disagreement between individuals are to be avoided by management's understanding its role as providing the basis for group affiliation. From the end of the Hawthorne project to his death, Mayo was interested in discovering how spontaneous cooperation could be achieved. This has been the basis of the human relations movement—the use of the insights of the social sciences to secure the commitment of individuals to the ends and activities of the organization.

The impact of Hawthorne and Mayo on both management and academics has been tremendous. It led to a fuller realization and understanding of the "human factor" in work situations. Central to this was the "discovery" of the informal group as an outlet for the aspirations of the worker. His work also led to an emphasis on the importance of an adequate communication system, particularly upward from workers to management. The investigations showed, to quote Mayo, that "management succeeds or fails in proportion as it is accepted without reservation by the group as authority and leader."

Bibliography

Mayo, E., *The Human Problems of an Industrial Civilization,* Macmillan, 1933; reprinted by Ayer, 1977.

Mayo, E., *The Social Problems of an Industrial Civilization,* Routledge & Kegan Paul, 1945; reprinted by Ayer, 1977.

Roethlisberger, F. J., and Dickson, W. J., *Management and the Worker,* Harvard University Press, 1949.

Rensis Likert and Douglas McGregor

Rensis Likert (1903–1981) was an American social psychologist who, in 1949, established the Institute of Social Research at the University of Michigan. Until his retirement in 1969, he was thus at the head of one of the major institutions conducting research into human behavior in organizations. On his retirement, he formed Rensis Likert Associates, a consulting firm, to put his ideas about the management of organizations into wider practice. His books are based on the numerous research studies that he and his colleagues have conducted. His last book was jointly written with his research collaborator and wife, Jane Gibson Likert.

Douglas McGregor (1906–1964) was a social psychologist who published a number of research papers in this field. For some years, he was President (Chief Executive) of Antioch College, and he has described how this period as a top administrator affected his views on organizational functioning. From 1954 until his death, he was Professor of Management at the Massachusetts Institute of Technology.

"Managers with the best records of performance in American business and government are in the process of pointing the way to an appreciably more effective system of management than now exists," proclaimed Likert. Research studies have shown that departments low in efficiency tend to be in the charge of supervisors who are "job centered"; that is, they "tend to concentrate on keeping their subordinates busily engaged in going through a specified work cycle in a prescribed way and at a satisfactory rate as determined by time standards." This attitude is clearly derived from that of Taylor (see p. 91), with its emphasis on breaking down the job into component parts, selecting and training people to do them, and exerting constant pressure to achieve output. Supervisors see themselves as getting the job done with the resources (which include the people) at their disposal.

Supervisors with the best record of performance are found to focus their attention on the human aspects of their subordinates' problems and on building effective work groups that set high achievement goals. These supervisors are "employee centered." They regard their jobs as dealing with human beings, rather than with the work; they attempt to know them as individuals. They see their function as helping employees do the job efficiently. They exercise general rather than detailed supervision and are more concerned with targets than methods. They allow maximum participation in decision making. If high performance is to be obtained, a supervisor not only must be employee centered but also must have high performance goals and be capable of exercising the decision-making processes to achieve them.

In summarizing these findings, Likert distinguished four systems of management. System 1 is the exploitive authoritative type, in which, for example, management uses fear and threats, communication is downward, superiors and subordinates are psychologically far apart, and the bulk of decisions is taken at the top of the organization.

System 2 is the benevolent authoritative type, in which, for example, management uses rewards, subordinates' attitudes are subservient to superiors, information flowing upward is restricted to what the boss wants to hear, and policy decisions are taken at the top but decisions within a prescribed framework may be delegated to lower levels.

System 3 is the consultative type, in which management uses rewards and occasional punishments, and some involvement is sought; communication is both down and up, but upward communication other than that which the boss wants to hear is given in limited amounts and only cautiously. In this system, subordinates can have a moderate amount of influence on the activities of their departments as broad policy decisions are taken at the top and more specific decisions at lower levels.

System 4 is characterized by participative group management. Management gives economic rewards and makes full use of group participation and involvement in setting high performance goals and improving work methods; communication flows downward, upward, and with peers and is accurate; and subordinates and superiors are very close psychologically. Decision making is widely done throughout the organization through group processes and is integrated into the formal structure by regarding the organization chart as a series of overlapping groups, with each group linked to the rest of the organization by means of persons (called "linking pins") who are members of more than one group. System 4 management produces high productivity, greater involvement of individuals, and better labor-management relations.

In general, high-producing managers are those who have built the personnel in their units into effective groups, whose members have cooperative attitudes and a high level of job satisfaction through System 4 management. But there are exceptions. Technically competent, job-centered, tough management can achieve high productivity (particularly if backed up by tight systems of control techniques). But the members of units whose supervisors use these high-pressure methods are likely to have unfavorable attitudes toward their work and the management and to have excessively high levels of waste and scrap. They also show higher labor turnover and greater labor-management conflict, as measured by work stoppages, official grievances, and the like.

Management, according to Likert, is always a relative process. To be effective and to communicate, leaders must always adapt their behavior to take account of the *persons* they lead. No specific rules will work well in all situations; only general principles must be interpreted to take account of the expectations, values, and skills of those with whom the manager interacts. Sensitivity to these values and expectations is a crucial leadership skill, and organizations must create the atmosphere and conditions that encourage all managers to deal with the people they encounter in a manner befitting their values and their expectations.

To assist in this task, management now has available a number of measures of relevant factors that have been developed by social scientists. Methods are available to obtain objective measurements of such variables as (a) the amount of member loyalty to an organization; (b) the extent to which the goals of groups and individuals facilitate the achievement of the organization's goals; (c) the level of motivation among members; (d) the degree of confidence and trust between different hierarchical levels and between different subunits; (e) the efficiency and adequacy of the communication process; and (f) the extent to which superiors are correctly informed of the expectations, reactions, obstacles, problems, and failures of subordinates—together with the assistance they find useful and the assurance they wish they could get.

These measures and others enable an organization to know at any time the state of the system of functioning human beings that underpins it (called the "interaction-influence system"), whether it is improving or deteriorating and why, and what to do to bring about desired improvements. This objective information about the interaction-influence system enables problems of leadership and management to be depersonalized and the "authority of facts" to come to the fore. A much wider range of human behavior can now be measured and made objective, whereas previously impressions and judgments had to suffice.

Douglas McGregor examines the assumptions about human behavior that underlie managerial action. The traditional conception of administration (as exemplified by the writings of Fayol; see p. 87) is based on the direction and control by management of the enterprise and its individual members. It implies certain basic assumptions about human motivation, which McGregor characterizes as "Theory X." These basic assumptions are:

1. The average human being has an inherent dislike of work and will avoid it if possible. Thus, management needs to stress productivity, incentive schemes, and "a fair day's work" and to denounce "restriction of output."

2. Because of this human characteristic of dislike of work, most people must be coerced, controlled, directed, and threatened with punishment to get them to put forth adequate effort toward the achievement of organizational objectives.

3. The average human being prefers to be directed, wishes to avoid responsibility, has relatively little ambition, and wants security above all.

Theory X has persisted for a long time (although it is not usually stated as baldly as this). It has done so because it has undoubtedly provided an explanation for *some* human behavior in organizations. However, many readily observable facts and a growing body of research findings (e.g., those described by Likert) cannot be explained on these assumptions. McGregor proposes an alternative "Theory Y," with the underlying principle of "integration" to replace direction and control. The assumptions about human motivation of Theory Y are:

1. The expenditure of physical and mental effort in work is as natural as play or rest. The ordinary person does not inherently dislike work; according to the conditions, it may be a source of satisfaction or punishment.

2. External control is not the only means for obtaining effort. "People will exercise self-direction and self-control in the service of objectives to which they are committed."

3. The most significant reward that can be offered to obtain commitment is the satisfaction of the individual's "self-actualizing needs" (see Schein, p. 148). This can be a direct product of effort directed toward organizational objectives.

4. The average human being learns, under proper conditions, not only to accept but also to seek responsibility.

5. Many more people are able to contribute creatively to the solution of organizational problems than do so.

6. At present, the potentialities of the average person are not being fully used.

McGregor develops an analysis of how the acceptance of Theory Y as the basis for running organizations would work out. He is particularly concerned with effects on performance appraisals, salaries and promotions, participation, and staff-line relationships. On this last topic, he makes the important point that there will be tension and conflict between staff and line as long as the staff departments are used as a service to top management to *control* the line (which is required by Theory X). With Theory Y, the role of the staff is regarded as that of providing professional help to *all levels* of management.

The essential concept, which both Likert and McGregor are propounding, is that modern organizations, to be effective, must regard themselves as interacting groups of people with "supportive relationships" to each other. In the ideal, all members will believe that the organization's objectives are of personal significance to them. They will regard their jobs, which contribute to the objectives, as meaningful, indispensable, and difficult. Therefore, to do their jobs effectively, they need and obtain the support of their superiors. Superiors, in turn, regard their prime function as the giving of this support to make their subordinates effective.

In later work, Likert and Likert extend the System 1 to 4 classification by identifying the "System 4 Total Model Organization" (System 4T). This designation refers to organizations that have a number of characteristics in addition to those of System 4. These include (a) high levels of performance goals held by the leader and transmitted to subordinates; (b) high levels of knowledge and skill of the leader with regard to technical issues, administration, and problem solving; and (c) the capacity of the leader to provide planning, resources, equipment, training, and help to subordinates. System 4T is also characterized by an optimum structure in terms of differentiation and linkages, and stable group working relationships.

System 4T is currently the best method for dealing with conflict because of its approach to getting appropriate data related to *group* needs (thus removing person-to-person conflict) and engaging in group decision making to resolve the differences in the best interests of the entire organization. If members of one or both of the two groups show an inability to use group decision-making techniques sufficiently well, then higher levels must provide further training in group processes. The interaction-influence system will develop a capacity for self-correction because superiors recognize those groups that are not performing their linking-pin and problem-solving functions effectively and can arrange for coaching and training. Correction is possible because the failures are picked up, not by after-the-fact data (e.g., falling production, rising costs, lower earnings), but through the interaction-influence system, in the early stages before poor performance and conflict arise.

Likert's argument is that the nearer to System 4T the organization approaches, the more productivity and profits will improve, and conflict will be reduced. Likert also suggests a System 5 organization of the future, in which the authority of hierarchy will completely disappear. The authority of individuals will derive only from their linking-pin roles and from the influence exerted by the overlapping groups of which they are members.

Bibliography

Likert, R., *The Human Organization: Its Management and Value,* McGraw-Hill, 1967.

Likert, R., *New Patterns of Management,* Garland, 1987.

Likert, R., and Likert, J. G., *New Ways of Managing Conflict,* McGraw-Hill, 1976.

McGregor, D., *The Human Side of Enterprise,* McGraw-Hill, 1960.

McGregor, D., *Leadership and Motivation,* MIT Press, 1966.

McGregor, D., *The Professional Manager,* McGraw-Hill, 1967.

Edgar H. Schein

Edgar H. Schein has for many years been Professor of Management at the Sloan School of Management of the Massachusetts Institute of Technology. A social psychologist by training, in his early years at MIT he was a junior colleague of Douglas McGregor's (see p. 142), whose personality and work had much influence on him. Working in that tradition, Schein has been an influential researcher, consultant, and writer on issues concerned with organizational behavior, particularly individual motivation, career dynamics, and organizational culture.

Schein's analysis of motivation begins, like McGregor's, with an examination of the underlying assumptions that managers make about the people they manage. He suggests three sets of assumptions, roughly in order of their historical appearance, and adds a fourth that he considers more appropriate.

1. The *rational-economic model* is the mental picture held by managers who consider workers to be primarily motivated by economic incentives as manipulated by the organization. The worker is essentially passive, lazy, and unwilling to take responsibility and must therefore be controlled by the manager. This is the basis of Taylor's approach to management (see p. 91), which is expounded by McGregor (see p. 145) as Theory X. This approach led to the possibility of mass-production industry but broke down when unions became powerful and jobs became more complex, requiring more of an employee than being just a "pair of hands."

2. The *social model* developed from awareness of the worker's needs for identity through relationships with others, particularly the working group. The group's norms and pressures have much more power over production than do formal incentive systems and management controls. The work of Mayo and the Hawthorne investigations (see p. 138) had an important impact in changing managerial ideas, as did Trist and his colleagues' study of mining (see p. 158). The implications for managers are spelled out in Likert's work on the need for "employee-centered" leadership and participative group management (see Likert and McGregor, p. 142).

3. The *self-actualizing model* is a further development that underlines the fact that, typically, organizations remove the meaning of any work that employees do. The inherent need of workers to exercise their under-

standing, capacities, and skills in an adult way is thus frustrated, and alienation and dissatisfaction ensue. The analysis of the clinical psychologist Abraham Maslow has been very influential here. He maintained that "self-actualization" (the realization of one's distinctive psychological potential) is the highest form of human need, going beyond economic and social fulfillment. The implications of this approach are developed for managers in McGregor's Theory Y (see p. 145), Argyris's Model II (see p. 178), and Herzberg's job enrichment (see p. 154).

4. The *complex model,* developed by Schein, maintains that earlier theories are based on conceptions that are too simplified and generalized. Human needs fall into many categories and vary according to a person's state of personal development and life situation. So, motives will vary from one person to another, one situation to another, and one time to another. Incentives can also vary in their impact; money, for example, usually satisfying basic economic needs, can also serve to satisfy self-actualization needs for some. What motivates millionaires to go on to make their second or fifth million? Employees are also capable of learning new motives through organizational experiences and can respond to different kinds of managerial strategies.

The most important implications for managers is that they need to be good diagnosticians. They should be flexible enough to vary their own behavior in relation to the need to treat in an appropriate way particular subordinates in particular situations. They may require to use any of the economic, social, or self-actualizing models. They may use "scientific management" in the design of some jobs but allow complete group autonomy for the workers to organize themselves in others. They would thus use a "contingency approach," as exemplified by Lawrence and Lorsch (see p. 53) and Vroom (see p. 126), among others.

According to Schein, the key factor that determines the motivation of individuals in organizations is the *psychological contract.* This is the unwritten set of expectations operating at all times between every member of an organization and those who represent the organization itself to that member. It includes economic components (e.g., pay, working hours, job security), but it will also include more implicit concerns, such as being treated with dignity, obtaining some degree of work autonomy, and having opportunities to learn and develop. Some of the strongest feelings leading to strikes and to employee turnover have to do with violations of these implicit components even though the public negotiations are about pay and conditions of work.

The organization, too, has implicit expectations—for example, that employees will be loyal, will keep trade secrets, and will do their best on behalf of the organization. Whether individuals will work with commitment and enthusiasm is the result of a matching between the two components. On the one side is their own expectations of what the organization will provide to them and what they should provide in return; on the other side is the organization's expectations of what it will give and get. The degree to which these correspond will determine the individual's motivation. The degree of matching is liable to change, and the psychological contract is therefore continually being renegotiated, particularly during the progress of a person's career.

The "career development perspective" taken by Schein sees the continual matching process between the individual and the organization as the key to understanding both human resource planning for the organization and career planning for the individual. This matching is particularly important at certain key transitions in a career, such as initial entry into the organization, moving from technical to managerial work, and changing from being "on the way up" to "leveling off."

A crucial element in the matching is the nature of the *career anchor* the individual holds. This is the self-perceived set of talents, motives, and attitudes, based on actual experiences, that each individual develops, particularly in the early years of an organizational career. It provides a growing area of stability within the individual's attitudes that anchors the interpretation of career and life options. Typical career anchors found by Schein in a detailed longitudinal study of MIT management graduates include those of technical competence, managerial competence, security, and autonomy. Career anchors affect considerably the way in which individuals see themselves, their jobs, and their organizations. For example, one graduate using a technical competence anchor was still, in mid-career, only concerned with technical tasks. He refused to become involved in aspects of sales or general management even though he was now a director and part owner of the firm in which he worked. Another graduate, using managerial competence as an anchor, left one firm although his bosses were quite pleased with his performance. But he considered that he only actually worked 2 hours a day, and he was not satisfied with that.

The understanding of the dynamics of career development is important in enabling Human Resource Planning and Development to improve the matching processes between individual and organizational needs so that early-, mid-, and late-career crises can be dealt with more effectively.

A distinctive aspect of the way in which an organization functions, which shapes its overall performance as well as the feelings that individuals have about it, is its *culture*. This is the pattern of basic assumptions developed by an organization as it learns to cope with problems of external adaptation and internal integration. These assumptions are taught to new members as the correct way to perceive, think, and feel in order to be successful. They cover a wide range of issues—for example, how to dress, how much to argue, how far to defer to the boss's authority, and what to reward and what to punish. Organizations develop very wide differences on these topics.

Leaders play a key role in maintaining and transmitting the culture. They do this by a number of powerful mechanisms. What they pay attention to, measure, and control; how they react to a range of crises; whom they recruit, promote, and excommunicate; all these send important messages about the kind of organization they are running. The key to leadership is managing cultural change.

The considerable difficulties that almost inevitably beset the establishment of an effective organization after a merger of two companies underline the need to understand the nature of cultural differences and how cultural change can be consciously managed. The big danger is that the acquiring company will impose not only its own structures and procedures but also its own philosophy, value systems, and managerial style on a situation for which it has no intuitive "feel." Thus, a large packaged foods manufacturer purchased a chain of successful fast-food restaurants. It imposed many of its manufacturing control procedures on the new subsidiary, which drove costs up and restaurant managers out. These were replaced by parent-company managers who did not really understand the technology and hence were unable to make effective use of the marketing techniques. Despite 10 years of effort, they could not run it profitably, and it had to be sold at a considerable loss.

Similar problems occur when organizations diversify into new product lines, new areas, or new markets. Afterward, managers frequently say that cultural incompatibilities were at the root of the troubles, but somehow these factors rarely get taken into account at the time. One reason is that the culture of an organization is so pervasive that it is very difficult for members to identify its components in their own situation. They only recognize their own characteristics when they run up against problems because of differences in others. Schein presents a series of diagnostic procedures that would enable managers (usually with the help of an outside consultant) to uncover the cultural assumptions of their own organization and thus to gain insight into its compatibility with others.

Bibliography

Schein, E. H., *Career Dynamics: Matching Individual and Organizational Needs,* Addison-Wesley, 1978.

Schein, E. H., *Organizational Psychology,* 3rd ed., Prentice Hall, 1980.

Schein, E. H., *Organizational Culture and Leadership,* Jossey-Bass, 1985.

Frederick Herzberg

Frederick Herzberg is Distinguished Professor of Management at the University of Utah. After training as a psychologist, he studied industrial mental health. For many years, he has, with colleagues and students, been conducting a program of research and application on human motivation in the work situation and its effects on the individual's job satisfaction and mental health. He questions whether current methods of organizing work in business and industry are appropriate for people's total needs and happiness.

Herzberg and his colleagues conducted a survey of 200 engineers and accountants representing a cross section of Pittsburgh industry. They were asked to remember times when they felt exceptionally good about their jobs. The investigators probed for the reasons why the respondents felt as they did and asked for a description of the sequence of events that gave that feeling. The questions were then repeated for sequences of events that made them feel exceptionally bad about their jobs. The responses were then classified by topic to determine what types of events led to job satisfaction and to job dissatisfaction.

The major finding of the study was that the events that led to satisfaction were of quite a different kind from those that led to dissatisfaction. Five factors stood out as strong determinants of job satisfaction: achievement, recognition, the attraction of the work itself, responsibility, and advancement. Lack of these five factors, though, was mentioned very infrequently in regard to job *dis*satisfaction. When the reasons for the dissatisfaction were analyzed, they were found to be concerned with different factors: company policy and administration, supervision, salary, interpersonal relations, and working conditions. Because such distinctly separate factors were found to be associated with job satisfaction and job dissatisfaction, Herzberg concludes that these two feelings are not the opposites of one another; rather, they are concerned with two different ranges of human needs.

The set of factors associated with job dissatisfaction are those stemming from the individual's overriding need to avoid physical and social deprivation. Using a biblical analogy, Herzberg relates these to the

"Adam" conception of the nature of humanity. When Adam was expelled from the Garden of Eden, he was immediately faced with the task of satisfying the needs that stemmed from his animal nature: the needs for food, warmth, avoidance of pain, safety, security, belongingness, and so on. Ever since then, people have had to concern themselves with the satisfaction of these needs, together with those that, as a result of social conditioning, have been added to them. Thus, for example, we have learned that, in certain economies, the satisfaction of these needs makes it necessary to earn money, which has, therefore, become a specific motivating drive.

In contrast, the factors associated with job satisfaction are those stemming from people's need to realize their human potential for perfection. In biblical terms, this is the "Abraham" conception of human nature. Abraham was created in the image of God. He was capable of great accomplishments, of development, of growth, of transcending his environmental limitations, and of self-realization. People have these aspects to their natures too; they are, indeed, the characteristically human ones. They have needs to understand, to achieve, and through achievement to experience psychological growth, and these needs are very powerful motivating drives.

Both the Adam and the Abraham natures look for satisfaction in work, but they do so in different ranges of factors. The Adam nature seeks the avoidance of dissatisfaction and is basically concerned with the job environment. It requires effective company policies, working conditions, security, pay, and so on and is affected by inadequacies in these. Because they are extrinsic to the job itself, Herzberg refers to them as "job hygiene" or "maintenance" factors. Just as lack of hygiene will cause disease but the presence of hygienic conditions will not, of itself, produce health, so lack of adequate "job hygiene" will cause dissatisfaction but its presence will not, of itself, cause satisfaction. Satisfaction in work is provided through the Abraham nature, which is concerned with the job content of the work itself, with achievement, recognition, responsibility, advancement, and so on. These are the "motivator" or growth factors, and their presence will cause satisfaction. Their absence will not cause dissatisfaction (if the job hygiene factors are adequate) but will lead to an absence of positive satisfactions. It is thus basic to Herzberg's approach that job satisfaction and job dissatisfaction are not opposites because they are concerned with different factors in work serving different aspects of human nature. The opposite of job satisfaction, therefore, is not job dissatisfaction but simply no job satisfaction. The opposite of job dissatisfaction, similarly, is lack of job dissatisfaction.

The finding of the original study—that the factors associated with job satisfaction were basically different in kind from those associated with job dissatisfaction—has been repeated in several subsequent studies. Collating the information based on 12 different investigations, involving more than 1,600 employees in a variety of jobs in business and other organizations and in a number of countries, Herzberg presents results to show that the overwhelming majority of the factors contributing to job satisfaction (81%) were the motivators concerned with growth and development. A large majority of the factors contributing to job dissatisfaction (69%) involved hygiene or environmental maintenance.

How, then, may this "motivation-hygiene" approach be used to increase the motivation and job satisfaction of employees? First, it is clear that this cannot be done through the job hygiene factors. Certainly, these can and should be improved because they will reduce job dissatisfaction, but adequate company policies, working conditions, pay, and supervision are increasingly thought of as a right to be expected, not as an incentive to greater achievement and satisfaction. For this, the rewarding nature of the work itself, recognition, responsibility, and opportunities for achievement and advancement are necessary. Herzberg recognizes that these phrases may be used nowadays in relation to jobs, but they are often used in a superficial way or as inspirational talk without much effective action. He therefore advocates an industrial engineering approach based on the design of jobs but from the opposite point of view from that of Taylor (see p. 91). Instead of rationalizing and simplifying the work to increase efficiency, the motivation-hygiene theory suggests that jobs be enriched to include the motivating factors to bring about an effective use of people and to increase job satisfaction.

The principles of *job enrichment* require that the job be developed to include new aspects that provide the opportunity for the employee's psychological growth. It is important that the new aspects are capable of allowing this. Merely to add one undemanding job to another (as is often the case with job enlargement) or to switch from one undemanding job to another (as in job rotation) is not adequate. These examples are merely horizontal job loading. In contrast, job enrichment calls for vertical job loading, in which opportunities for achievement, responsibility, recognition, growth, and learning are designed into the job. The approach would be to look for ways of removing some controls while retaining or increasing individuals' accountability for their own work;

giving a person a complete natural unit of work; granting additional authority to an employee in the job; increasing job freedom; making reports directly available to the worker personally rather than to the supervisor; and introducing new and more difficult tasks not previously undertaken.

A number of experiments have been reported by Herzberg and his colleagues in which these changes have been introduced with considerable effect. For example, in a study of the job of "stockholder correspondent" of a large corporation, the following suggestions were considered but rejected as involving merely horizontal job loading: (a) firm, fixed quotas could be set for letters to be answered each day, (b) the employees could type the letters themselves as well as compose them, (c) all difficult inquiries could be channeled to a few workers so that the rest could achieve high rates of output, and (d) the workers could be rotated through units handling different inquiries and then sent back to their own units. Instead, changes leading to the enrichment of jobs were introduced, such as the following: (a) correspondents were made directly responsible for the quality and accuracy of letters, which were sent out directly over their names (previously a verifier had checked all letters, and the supervisor had rechecked and signed them and was responsible for their quality and accuracy); (b) subject matter experts were appointed within each unit for other members to consult (previously, the supervisor had dealt with all difficult and specialized questions); and (c) verification of experienced workers' letters was dropped from 100% to 10%, and correspondents were encouraged to answer letters in a more personalized way instead of relying on standard forms. In these ways, the jobs were enriched, with resulting increases in both performance and job satisfaction.

In other studies, laboratory technicians ("experimental officers") were encouraged to write personal project reports, in addition to those of the supervising scientists, and were authorized to requisition materials and equipment directly; sales representatives were made wholly responsible for determining the calling frequencies on their customers and were given a discretionary range of about 10% on the prices of most products; and factory supervisors were authorized to modify schedules, to hire labor against agreed manning targets, to appoint their deputies, and so on. In each case, the results in both performance and satisfaction were considerable.

The more subordinates' jobs become enriched, the more superfluous does "on the job" supervision in the old sense become. But this does not downgrade the supervisors' jobs; in the companies studied, they found themselves free to develop more important aspects of their jobs with a greater managerial component than they had had time to before. It soon becomes clear that supervising people who have authority of their own is a more demanding, rewarding, and enjoyable task than checking on every move of circumscribed automatons. For management, the challenge is task organization to call out the motivators, and task support to provide adequate hygiene through company policy, technical supervision, working conditions, and so on, thus satisfying both the Adam and the Abraham natures of humanity in work.

Bibliography

Herzberg, F., *Work and the Nature of Man,* World, 1966.

Herzberg, F., "One More Time: How Do You Motivate Employees?" *Harvard Business Review, 46,* (1968), 53–62.

Herzberg, F., *Managerial Choice: To Be Efficient and To Be Human,* Olympus, 1982.

Herzberg, F., Mausner, B., and Snyderman, B., *The Motivation to Work,* John Wiley, 1959.

Paul, W. J., Jr., Robertson, K. B., and Herzberg, F., "Job Enrichment Pays Off," *Harvard Business Review, 47,* (1969), 61–78.

Eric Trist and the Work of the Tavistock Institute

Eric Trist (1909–1993) was a social psychologist who, for more than 20 years, was the senior member of the Tavistock Institute of Human Relations, London, a leading center for the application of social science to social and industrial problems. He subsequently was a Professor at the University of Pennsylvania and at York University, Ontario. At the Tavistock, he conducted, with a number of colleagues (including F. E. Emery, A. K. Rice, and E. J. Miller), a program of combined research and consultancy investigations into group and organizational functioning. This combination of research and consultancy is referred to as "action research." The work of Trist and his colleagues uses a systems approach to understanding organizational behavior.

In collaboration with K. W. Bamforth (an ex-miner), Trist studied the effects of mechanization in British coal mining. With the advent of coal cutters and mechanical conveyors, the degree of technical complexity of coal getting was raised to a higher level. Mechanization made possible the working of a single long face in place of a series of short faces, but this technological change had a number of social and psychological consequences for the work organization and the worker's place in it, to which little thought was given before the change was introduced. The pattern of organization in shortwall working was based on a small artisan group of a skilled man and his mate, assisted by one or more laborers. The basic pattern around which the work relationships in the longwall method were organized is the coal-face group of 40 to 50 men, their shot-firer, and "deputies" (supervisors). Thus, the basic unit in mining took on the characteristics in size and structure of a small factory department and, in doing so, disrupted the traditional high degree of job autonomy and close work relationships with a number of deleterious effects.

The mass production character of the longwall method necessitates a large-scale mobile layout advancing along the seam, basic task specialization according to shift, and very specific job roles with different methods of payment within each shift. In these circumstances, there are considerable problems of maintaining effective communications and good working relations between 40 men spatially spread over 200 yards in a tunnel and temporally spread over 24 hours in three successive shifts. From the production engineering point of view, it is possible to write an equation that 200 tons equals 40 men over 200 yards over 24 hours, but the psychological and social problems raised are of a new order when the work organization transcends the limits of the traditional, small face-to-face group undertaking the complete task itself. The social integration of the previous small groups having been disrupted by the new technology, and little attempt being made to achieve any new integration, many symptoms of social stress occur. Informal cliques, which develop to help each other out, can only occur over small parts of the face, inevitably leaving some isolated; individuals react defensively, using petty deceptions with regard to timekeeping and reporting of work; they compete for allocation to the best workplaces; mutual scapegoating occurs across shifts, each blaming the other for inadequacies (because, in the new system, with its decreased autonomy, no one individual can normally be pinpointed with the blame, scapegoating of the absent shift becomes self-perpetuating and resolves nothing). Absenteeism becomes a way for the miner to compensate himself for the difficulties of the job.

This study of the effects of technological change led Trist to develop the concept of the working group as being neither a technical system nor a social system, but as an interdependent sociotechnical system. The technological demands place limits on the type of work organization possible, but the work organization has social and psychological properties of its own that are independent of the technology. From this point of view, it makes as little sense to regard social relationships as being determined by the technology as it does to regard the way in which a job is performed as being determined by the social-psychological characteristics of the workers. The *social* and *technical* requirements are mutually interactive, and they must also have *economic* validity. The attainment of optimum conditions for any one of these three aspects does not necessarily result in optimum conditions for the system as a whole because interference will occur if the others are inadequate. The aim should be joint optimization.

In further studies of mining, Trist found that it was possible, within the same technological and economic constraints, to operate different systems of work organization with different social and psychological effects, thus underlining the considerable degree of organizational choice available to management to enable them to take account of the social and psychological aspects. A form of operation known as the "composite longwall method" was developed that enabled mining to benefit from the new technology while at the same time allowed some characteristics of the shortwall method to be continued. In the composite system, groups of men are responsible for the whole task, allocate themselves to shifts and to jobs within the shift, and are paid on a group bonus. Thus, the problems of overspecialized work roles, segregation of tasks across shifts with consequent scapegoating, and lack of group cohesion were overcome. For example, it became common for a subgroup that had finished its scheduled work for a shift before time to carry on with the next activity in the sequence to help those men on the subsequent shift who were members of their group. The composite longwall method was quite comparable in technological terms with the conventional longwall method, but it led to greater productivity, lower cost, considerably less absenteeism and accidents, and greater work satisfaction because it was a sociotechnical system that was better geared to the workers' social and psychological needs for job autonomy and close working relationships.

This sociotechnical system approach was also applied to supervisory roles by Rice in studies of an Indian textile firm. He found that it was not enough to allocate to the supervisor a list of responsibilities (see Fayol, p. 86) and perhaps to insist on a particular style of handling workers (see Likert and McGregor, p. 142). The supervisor's problems arise from a need to control and coordinate a system of worker-task relationships, and in particular to manage the "boundary conditions"— that is, those activities of this system that relate it to the larger system of which it is a part. To do this effectively, it is necessary to have an easily identifiable arrangement of tasks so that it is possible to maximize the autonomous responsibility of the group itself for its own internal control, thus freeing the supervisor for the key task of boundary management.

In an automatic weaving shed, for example, in which the occupational roles had remained unchanged since hand weaving, the activities of the shed were broken down into component tasks, with the number of workers required determined by work studies of the separate tasks. Those in different occupational tasks worked on different numbers of looms; weavers operated 24 or 32, battery fillers charged the batteries of 48, smash hands served 75, jobbers 112, the bobbin carrier 224, and so on. This apportionment resulted in the shift manager's having to interact on the job regularly with all the remaining 28 workers on the shift, jobbers having to interact with 14, smash hands with 9, a weaver with 7, and so on, all on the basis of individual interactions aggregated together only at the level of the whole shift, with no stable internal group structure. Rice carried through a reorganization to create four groups of six workers, each with a group leader, and each with an identifiable group task and a new set of interdependent work roles to carry it out. The boundaries of these groups were more easily delineated, and thus the work leader's task in their management was facilitated. As a result, there was a considerable and sustained improvement in efficiency and a decrease in damage.

These studies and others of the Tavistock Institute have led Emery and Trist to conceptualize the enterprise as an "open socio-technical system"—"open" because it is a system concerned with obtaining inputs from its environment and exporting outputs to its environment, as well as operating the conversion process in between. They regard the organization, not in terms of a closed physical system that can obtain a stable resolution of forces in static equilibrium, but in the light of the biological concept of an open system (due to von Bertalanffy) in which the equilibrium obtained by the organism or the organization is essentially dynamic, having a continual interchange across the boundaries with its environment. Indeed, they would regard the primary task of the management of the enterprise as a whole as that of relating the total system to its environment through the regulation of the boundary interchanges, rather than that of internal regulation. A management that takes its environment as given and concentrates on organizing internally in the most efficient way is pursuing a dangerous course. This does not mean that top management should not be involved in internal problems, but that such involvement must be oriented to the environmental opportunities and demands.

The problem is that environments are changing at an increasing rate and toward increasing complexity. Environmental factors over which the organization has no control, or even knowledge, may interact to cause significant changes. Emery and Trist have classified environments according to their degree of complexity from that of a placid, randomized environment (corresponding to the economist's perfect competition) to that of a "turbulent field" in which significant variances arise not only from competitive organizations involved but also from the field (e.g., market) itself.

They present a case history of an organization that failed to appreciate that its environment was changing from a relatively placid to a relatively turbulent one. This company in the British food canning industry had, for a long period, held 65% of the market for its main product—a canned vegetable. On this basis, the company invested in a new automatic factory and, in doing so, incorporated an inbuilt rigidity—the necessity for long runs. But even while the factory was being built, several changes in the environment were taking place over which the organization had no control. The development of frozen foods, and the increasing affluence that enabled more people to afford them, presented consumers with an alternative. Greater direct competition came from the existence of surplus crops, which U.S. frozen food manufacturers sold off very cheaply because of their inappropriateness for freezing, their use by a number of small British *fruit* canning firms with surplus capacity because of the seasonal nature of imported fruit, and the development of supermarkets and chain stores with a wish to sell more goods under their house names. As the small canners provided an extremely inexpensive article (having no marketing costs and a less expensive raw material), they were able within 3 years to capture over 50% of a shrinking market through supermarkets' own label channels. This is a clear example of the way in which environmental factors interact directly to produce a considerable turbulence in the field of the organization's operations, which, in the case of the vegetable canning factory, required a large redefinition of the firm's purpose, market, and product mix before a new dynamic equilibrium was obtained.

Emery and Trist maintain that enterprises like the food cannery are designing their organizational structures to be appropriate to simpler environments, rather than the complex turbulent ones they are actually facing. A new *design principle* is now required. Organizations by their very nature require what is known in systems theory and information theory as "redundancy." By this is meant duplication, replaceability, and interchangeability, and these resources are needed to reduce error in the face of variability and change. The traditional technocratic bureaucracy is based on *redundancy of parts*. The parts are broken down so that the ultimate elements are as simple as possible; thus, an unskilled worker in a narrow job who is inexpensive to replace and who takes little time to train would be regarded as an ideal job design. But this approach also requires reliable control systems—often cumbersome and costly.

An alternative design, based on the *redundancy of functions,* is appropriate to turbulent environments. In this approach, individuals and

Table 5.1 Features of Old and New Approaches

Old Approach	New Approach
The technological imperative	Joint optimization
People as extensions of machines	People as complementary to machines
People as expendable spare parts	People as a resource to be developed
Maximum task breakdown, simple narrow skills	Optimum task grouping, multiple broad skills
External controls (supervisors, specialist staffs, procedures)	Internal controls (self-regulating subsystems)
Tall organization chart, autocratic style	Flat organization chart, participative style
Competition, gamesmanship	Collaboration, collegiality
Organization's purposes only	Members' and society's purposes also
Alienation	Commitment
Low risk-taking	Innovation

SOURCE: Trist (1981).

units have wide repertoires of activities to cope with change, and they are self-regulating. For the individual, they create roles rather than mere jobs; for the organization, they bring into being a *variety-increasing* system, rather than the traditional control by variety reduction. For this approach to be achieved, there has to be continuing development of appropriate new values concerned with improving the *quality of working life* by keeping the technological determinants of worker behavior to a minimum to satisfy social and psychological needs by the involvement of all involved. Autonomous working groups, collaboration rather than competition (between organizations, as well as within them), and reduction of hierarchical emphasis are some of the requirements for operating effectively in modern turbulence. Table 5.1 sets out the key features of the old and new approaches.

The sociotechnical systems approach to jointly achieving effective functioning in a turbulent environment and to increasing the quality of working life has also been undertaken at a wider "macro-social" level. For example, working with the Norwegian social psychologists E. Thorsrud and P. G. Herbst, the Tavistock group has studied the Norwegian shipping industry.

Many technological designs are available for sophisticated bulk carriers. The one chosen was the one that best met the social and psychological needs of the small shipboard community that had to live together in isolated conditions 24 hours a day for considerable periods while efficiently achieving the work tasks. A common mess and a recreation room were established, deck and engine-room crews were integrated, and status differences between officers and men were reduced and even eliminated through the development of open career lines and the establishment of "all officer" ships. Also, training for future jobs onshore could begin at sea.

Without these improvements in the quality of working life, not enough Norwegians would have gone to sea to sustain the Norwegian Merchant Marine, which is critical for Norway's economy. Poorly educated and transient foreign crews could not cope with technically sophisticated ships, and alcoholism was dangerously high. These issues could not have been effectively tackled by any one single company; all firms in the industry, several seafaring unions, and a number of maritime regulatory organizations all had to be involved to sustain the macrosocial system development that was required.

The work of Trist and the Tavistock group has been most consistent in applying systems thinking over a large range of sites: the primary work system, the whole organization system, and the macrosocial domain. In doing so, they have illuminated the dynamic nature of organizations and their functioning, the crucial importance of boundary management, and the need for a new approach to organizational design that can accommodate environmental change.

Bibliography

Emery, F. E., and Thorsrud, E., *Democracy at Work,* Martinus Nijhoff (Leiden), 1976.

Emery, F. E., and Trist, E. L., "Socio-Technical Systems," in C. W. Churchman and M. Verhulst (eds.), *Management Science, Models, and Techniques,* Vol. 2, Pergamon, 1946; reprinted in F. E. Emery (ed.), *Systems Thinking,* Penguin Books, 1969.

Emery, F. E., and Trist, E. L., "The Causal Texture of Organizational Environments," *Human Relations, 18,* (1965), 21–32; reprinted in F. E. Emery (ed.), *Systems Thinking,* Penguin Books, 1969.

Herbst, P. G., *Alternatives to Hierarchies,* Martinus Nijhoff (Leiden), 1976.

Rice, A. K., *Productivity and Social Organization,* Garland, 1987.

Trist, E. L., "The Socio-Technical Perspective," in A. van de Ven and W. F. Joyce (eds.), *Perspectives on Organization Design and Behavior,* Wiley-Interscience, 1981.

Trist, E. L., and Bamforth, K. W., "Some Social and Psychological Consequences of the Longwall Method of Coal Getting," *Human Relations, 4,* (1951), 3–38; reprinted in D. S. Pugh (ed.), *Organization Theory,* Penguin Books, 1997.

Trist, E. L. et al., *Organizational Choice,* Garland, 1987.

6 *Organizational Change and Learning*

We contend, bureaucratization and other forms of organizational change occur as a result of processes which make organizations more similar without necessarily making them more efficient.

Paul J. Dimaggio and Walter W. Powell

The real problem of strategic change is ultimately one of managerial process and action; of signalling new areas for concern and anchoring those signals in issues for attention and decision, of mobilizing energy and enthusiasm in an additive fashion to ensure that new problem areas found and defined eventually gain sufficient legitimacy and power to result in contextually appropriate action.

Andrew Pettigrew

Organizational defensive routines are anti-learning and over-protective.

Chris Argyris

Today's problems come from yesterday's "solutions."

Peter Senge

Imaginization—an invitation to develop new ways of thinking about organization and management—an invitation to re-image ourselves and what we do.

Gareth Morgan

Organizations do change, whether for better or worse, and writers on organizations have examined the ways in which change comes about. Some have concentrated on the factors in the organization's context and environment that appear to both impel particular changes to occur and set constraints for them. Others have underlined that appropriate change that assists the organization to become more effective only comes about through considerable effort on the part of the organization's managers. They have to understand the need for change and be consciously working

165

to achieve it. In addition, modern organizations are in situations that require continuous development. Not only do they need to change, but they also have to acquire a capacity for learning.

Paul DiMaggio and Walter Powell argue that organizations change to be more like each other because the pressures from the state, from other institutions, from professional standards, and so on require managers to conform to accepted practice. In contrast, Andrew Pettigrew underlines the particular complexity of the interacting factors of context, content, and process with which managers have to grapple to execute an effective strategic change.

Chris Argyris points to the power of "defensive routines," the psychological blocks to considering change, which limit an organization's ability to draw on the full potential of its members. He suggests ways in which they might be overcome to produce an organization more open to change and able to participate in new learning.

Peter Senge is concerned with establishing the characteristics of a "learning organization," one that through a systems approach is able to learn continuously.

Gareth Morgan maintains that understanding an organization is greatly helped by applying a range of different images to it. This "imaginization" is the key to being better able to conceive of possible changes.

Paul J. DiMaggio and
Walter W. Powell

Paul J. Dimaggio and Walter W. Powell are American professors of sociology based at Yale and Arizona State universities, respectively. They are leading exponents of the particular approach to the study and understanding of organizations known as "institutional theory."

Institutional theory begins from Weber's views on the functioning of bureaucracy (see p. 5). Weber argues that the "rational-legal" bureaucratic type of organizational structure has become dominant in modern society because it is the most efficient form. It is based on rationally calculating how to organize to achieve desired ends. It has a hierarchy of authority, experts who have specific areas of responsibility, and a system of rules, which together control the organization's activities. It uses the files of the "bureau" to record the past behavior of the organization and to capture the professionally determined best available knowledge relevant to its goals. It can therefore carry out its activities unambiguously, predictably, continuously, and speedily. Because it is efficient, bureaucracy is used by governments needing both to control their staff and citizenry and to give equal protection under the law. It is also used by capitalist business firms that are in competition and therefore need to operate efficiently.

Writers in the first section of this book, such as Chandler (see p. 18), Mintzberg (see p. 27), and others, seek to describe and explain different types of organizational structures. But DiMaggio and Powell point out that bureaucracy has spread continuously during the 20th century, becoming the usual organizational form. They therefore ask, not why do organizational structures differ, but why there is such a startling degree of homogeneity in organizational forms and practices. Organizations of the same type in any organizational field (e.g., business firms in the same industry, governmental departments, hospitals) may have displayed considerable diversity in approach when they were first set up. But once a field becomes established, there is an inexorable push toward bureaucratic homogeneity.

But, unlike Weber, DiMaggio and Powell question whether this convergence is a result of the efficiency of the bureaucratic form that leads all to strive toward it. Rather, they maintain that the convergence is a result of institutional pressures from the environment on managers in an organizational field to become more similar to one another, *whether this leads to greater efficiency or not.* This emergence of a common structure and approach among organizations in the same field is referred to as *institutional isomorphism.* This is the constraining process that forces one unit in a population to come to resemble those other units that face the same set of environmental conditions. It is important because among the major factors that organizations must respond to are other organizations in their environments. Through these organizations, managers get their ideas about how to run organizations and obtain legitimacy for the actions they take. Legitimate actions are those that conform to the common view; they do not have to be effective.

Institutional isomorphism produces conformity through three mechanisms: *coercive* isomorphism (which stems from political influence), *mimetic* isomorphism (which results from responses to uncertainty), and *normative* isomorphism (which results from the professionalization of managers and specialists). Each of these mechanisms describes a process by which ideas from institutions in the organization's environment become legitimated and adopted.

Coercive isomorphism results from pressures, both formal and informal, from other important organizations in the environment. These pressures are of various sorts. They may have the force of law, as for example, pollution control regulations and antidiscrimination legislation. They may come from external institutions, as when governmental support agencies require certain accounting procedures to be in place before giving support to charities, or when important customers require particular delivery systems from their suppliers. The pressure may come from internal authority, as for example, in the case of common control information required by the head office of a corporation from all its subsidiaries. The pressures may be persuasive, but still very real, as when standards for school curricula or new products are publicly recommended.

One result of coercive pressures may be that the conformity obtained is only superficial. Indeed, in some cases there may be a general collusion that something is being done rather than actual change taking place. For example, health and safety regulations may ensure that all organizations appoint a specialist officer but may otherwise allow the issue to be relatively neglected throughout a whole sector. Even so these institutional pressures act coercively to produce a convergence in structures and procedures.

Mimetic isomorphism is based on imitation. All organizations face uncertainty, having to deal with problems with ambiguous causes and unclear solutions. This leads to what March (see p. 123) has identified as *problemistic search*—a short-term, shortsighted, simpleminded activity to find ways of dealing with a particularly urgent problem. A common result of such searches is to copy what others in a similar situation are reported as doing successfully because this gives legitimation. For example, following their application in a firm generally regarded as successful, new management practices as propagated by consultants may then be regarded as legitimate and be taken up by many organizations.

So, techniques such as job enrichment or zero-based budgeting, and new philosophies such as "excellence" or human resource management, quickly spread. A dramatic example of such imitation is the way in which the concept of quality circles was neglected by U.S. managements until it proved popular and effective in Japan, when it was then rapidly legitimated and embraced by Western firms. Such imitation may lead to a quick, viable solution with less expense. But it is often undertaken when no such benefit is obvious because being the same as the rest reduces management's feelings of uncertainty and can produce benefits in terms of image. As an example, Powell studied a public television station that, on a consultant's recommendation, switched from a functional structure to a divisional one (see Chandler, p. 18). Station executives were skeptical of any efficiency gains: Some services had to be duplicated across divisions, for example. But they adopted the change because they wanted to give the image that the station was becoming more "business minded." Again, all these pressures to imitate foster an organizational conformity.

Normative isomorphism results primarily from the continuing professionalization of the organization's managers and specialists. They wish to demonstrate that they are fully professional and up-to-the-minute in regard to good standards, whether in information technology, accounting requirements, or marketing techniques. Having had a common training, professionals are, in many ways, much closer to their professional counterparts in other organizations than they are to their managerial colleagues in their own. They therefore propagate common norms of legitimate practice that push all organizations to converge.

An important way in which normative isomorphism is encouraged is through the selection of the top personnel of organizations. A filtering often takes place. This might come about through the practice of recruiting high fliers from a narrow range of training institutions—for example, Ivy League business schools in the United States and *grandes écoles* in France. Another filter comes from promoting to top positions only from a narrow range of specialisms (e.g., financial, legal). Professional careers may themselves be controlled at entry level and at key progression points. All these filters create a pool of individuals in senior jobs with very similar backgrounds, training, and experience.

These similarities have been shown among superintendents in a U.S. public school system and among the board members of the *Fortune* top 500 companies. Some entrants to senior jobs are different, having managed to avoid the filters (e.g., black senior officials, female board members, Jewish naval officers). These are likely to be subjected to considerable persuasive pressures to gain legitimacy by acting in exactly the same way as the others. As before, the results are that the norms practiced lead to organizational isomorphism.

These pressures for institutional isomorphism are so considerable, maintain DiMaggio and Powell, that the processes can be expected to continue even in the absence of evidence that the changes increase organizational effectiveness. Indeed, if organizations do become more effective, the reason is often that they are rewarded for their similarity to other organizations in their field. This can make it easier for them to transact business with other organizations, to attract professional staff, and to be acknowledged as legitimate and respectable—this last being very important to public agencies in attracting financial support. But none of these factors ensures that they are actually more efficient than deviant organizations.

Bibliography

DiMaggio, P. J., and Powell, W. W. "The Iron Cage Revisited: Institutional Isomorphism and Collective Rationality in Organizational Fields," *American Sociological Review, 48,* (1983), 147-160; reprinted in W. W. Powell and P. J. DiMaggio (eds.), *The New Institutionalism in Organizational Analysis,* University of Chicago Press, 1991; reprinted in D. S. Pugh (ed.), *Organization Theory,* Penguin Books, 1997.

Powell, W. W., and DiMaggio, P. J., (eds.), *The New Institutionalism in Organizational Analysis,* University of Chicago Press, 1991.

Andrew Pettigrew

Andrew Pettigrew is Distinguished Professor of Organizational Behavior at the University of Warwick Business School, England, where he founded the Center for Corporate Strategy and Change and was for many years its Director. The center has been a leader in strategic change research in Britain. In its work on understanding the processes of change, it takes a historical approach grounded in a detailed study of the context of an organization in its industrial environment.

Pettigrew maintains that strategic change is a complex, situation-dependent, continuous process. As Figure 6.1 shows, it has to be understood in terms of three essential dimensions: (a) context (both internal and external), (b) content (e.g., objectives, assumptions), and (c) process (e.g., implementation patterns). Because management decision making is a political process, change is inevitably suffused with organizational politics. In major decisions, who is powerful among the decision group will determine the outcomes.

The bases of power in organizations may vary. *The Politics of Organizational Decision Making* is a detailed study of how one decision came to be made: the acquisition of a new computer system by a British chain store. In this decision, the technical manager was very powerful. One important source of his power was his ability to understand and control the information on options that went to the board. This is an example of a common power base: the emergence of a strong specialization in a then new technology, which reduces the power of the nonspecialists. But other bases of power are also available, and what they are have to be examined in each case by studying the management processes in the context in which they take place. No easy generalizations can be made in relating these to the outcome decisions (see Hickson, p. 13).

This focus on the processes of strategic change was continued by Pettigrew in detailed studies of change in a number of divisions of ICI, the British industrial conglomerate. Change may be viewed as a sequence of four stages, each with its own problems:

1. *Developing concern.* This involves problem sensing leading to legitimating the notion of change and getting it on the corporate agenda. It is a

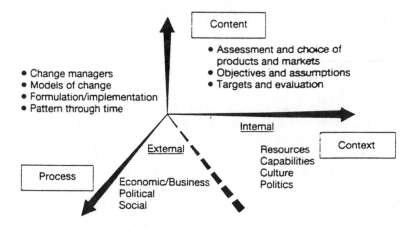

Figure 6.1. Dimensions for Understanding Strategic Change
SOURCE: Pettigrew and Whipp (1991).

time-consuming and politically sensitive process and one in which the top management plays a critical role. One contribution that leaders of ICI such as Lord Beeching and Sir John Harvey-Jones made was to continually flag up key problems facing ICI that required it to change.

2. *Acknowledging and understanding the problems.* The building of a climate of opinion necessary for change was shown to be a long process requiring many iterations and encountering blocks and unpredictable areas of movement along the way. Major change always affects power structures, career paths, and reward systems and is therefore unlikely to be straightforward in its application. In two ICI divisions, management training and development were used to equip the managers with the capacity to carry through the operational changes.

3. *Planning and acting.* It is very important in this stage to have established a desired future state of the organization around which planning can take place and commitment can be generated. In one division of ICI, this involved giving out clear, simple messages within a broad philosophy of downsizing and reorganization for profitability and maintaining them without dilution.

3. *Stabilizing change.* In this stage, management needs to ensure that the rewards, information flows, and pattern of power and authority support the new position. Because changes are often initiated by key figures, a danger is that they last only as long as these individuals remain in post. A key task is thus to ensure continuity by the development and appointment of appropriate successors.

Pettigrew also examined the contribution of the various organizational development (OD) groups that were operating in the different divisions of ICI. Their success and continued existence varied considerably between the divisions. One chastening lesson is not to expect too much from such OD specialists. As one supportive senior manager put it, "Using OD is in the first case an act of faith."

In a further study with his colleague Richard Whipp, now of Cardiff Business School, five key problems of managing strategic change were identified. Each of these is complex in itself and, in addition, has to be related to the other four: (a) assessing the environment, (b) leading change, (c) linking strategic and operational change, (d) treating human resources as assets and as liabilities, and (e) developing a coherent approach.

These five problem areas are examined in detailed studies of firms attempting to manage strategic change in the British vehicle, book publishing, merchant banking, and assurance industries. Among the firms studied were Jaguar, Peugeot Talbot, Longman's, Kleinwort Benson, Hill Samuel, and the Prudential. Each area has many factors and mechanisms to be examined, and these are different for each industry and for each firm.

When tackling the first problem, *assessing the environment,* it is not enough for companies to regard this as a technical exercise that can be left to appropriate specialists. Understanding the environment must be regarded as a multifunctional activity in which all top managements participate as a continuous learning process. This is because, for key firms in an industry, there is a large subjective element in which their understanding, and therefore their company's activities, actually determine what the environment will become (see Weick, p. 11). Thus, the understanding of Longman's staff as to the nature of their environment led to actions on their part that altered the shape of the book trade and that helped redefine the nature of that market.

Again, the 1970s change in the way in which the Prudential Assurance Company viewed the basis for competitive behavior in the assurance industry—away from actuarial risk toward product diversification—enabled it to redefine itself as the "Prudential Corporation." It was thus better placed to move forward to the structural changes necessary to operate in the changing market.

The second problem, that of *leading change,* is also complex and situation specific, best done in a series of incremental steps in which many managers are involved. It requires building a climate accepting of change within the firm, and in addition building the capability to mount the changes. This is quite the opposite from the "heroic leader" notion of leading change which is inappropriate. Thus, the regeneration of the car company Peugeot Talbot required the establishment of new, open working relationships among senior management; a reworking of the relations with the parent company; a rebuilding of the confidence of the staff, shell shocked after earlier major contractions; and the progressive elaboration of a new model program through improved communications and structures. Such a change from survival to regeneration could not be accomplished by one person or through a single program. It involved the emergence, over a period of years, of new leaders both at the top and at lower levels within the company.

The third key problem then becomes the *linking of strategic and operational change.* This is difficult because the implementation of strategic intentions over time inevitably transforms them, and what is done during implementation may overwhelm the original strategy. Indeed, often what are considered to be strategies are merely the *post hoc* labeling of what was done. "That worked, so it was our strategy to do it." Great attention is required to ensure that operational aspects do not undermine the general strategy. Actionable targets must become the responsibility of change managers operating at many levels. They have to be supported by rethought communication mechanisms and new reward systems. A major problem is that both strategic and operational change processes have to happen over the same time span and inevitably become "political" as they press for change and meet opposition.

The problem is highlighted in the contrast between the two merchant banks studied. In the 1970s, Kleinwort Benson had begun to sense trends in their environment, to identify the need for strategic development, and to foster a strategic change commitment among senior staff. In the 1980s, these capacities allowed the firm to adopt a broad strategic position (the expansion of international banking) and to work to drive the implications of that strategy throughout the organization. It was able to learn from failures (e.g., the slowness of internal deliberations, which led to the failure to purchase a Far Eastern stockbroker) to make compensating changes linked to the strategy. By the time of the deregulation of the British stock market in the 1980s, it was able to take relatively swift action—for example, in the acquisition of specialist firms in new activities such as "interest rate swaps" and "Eurobonds."

Hill Samuel, however, did not construct a fresh corporate strategy in the 1970s. What strategy there was emerged from the amalgam of the operational activities that were continually growing and diversifying. It did not, therefore, develop a capacity to formulate and implement strategy. So, in the early 1980s, the linking of strategic and operational change was immensely difficult. The gap between the new ideas and the organization's capacity for change was very wide, and the new chief executive had to build up linkages personally. Over a period, he had some success, but the strategic and operational linkages were still comparatively immature. Thus, the senior management never resolved differences over location, and when the board offered to sell the company to a Swiss bank, the CE resigned. Although that deal fell through, the firm was then purchased by the TSB, a British bank.

It is vital to regard *human resources as both assets and liabilities*—the fourth problem—and to take appropriate action. The organization's members must provide the knowledge base for learning, but it is also necessary to undertake "unlearning" when the established conceptions and skills are no longer appropriate. Shedding outmoded techniques and attitudes is not easy. Jaguar, for example, had to launch a major program of human resource management (HRM) in the 1980s when it undertook the challenge to become a profitable, high-quality car manufacturer. It had to move away from the traditional British motor industry's conflict-focused industrial relations view of personnel management. The new HRM approach involved recruiting staff, training staff, and developing commitment of all to the firm's mission. This was done through the use of new specialisms, such as manpower and salary planning, and internal communications services. Schemes for profit sharing, employee share-holding, and open learning to develop new skills were established. These added up to a very demanding set of changes that needed considerable resources.

The fifth problem is that of *coherence*—the ability to hold the organization together while simultaneously reshaping it. Four elements of strategic thinking are required:

1. *Consistency* in ensuring that the attempts to tackle existing problems do not contain internal contradictions. For example, earlier in Peugeot Talbot's existence, its then owners, Chrysler UK, tried to make it into a high-volume car producer although it had not mastered the special production techniques required.
2. *Consonance* that the strategy should be well adapted to the environment. It should not become the victim of the organization's entrenched partial view of its competitive position, as was the case with Hill Samuel.

3. *Competitive advantage* that the strategy aimed for should give comparative advantage in the market. For example, Longman's growth strategy included the market-led decision to add the fields of professional and business publishing to its established strengths in educational publishing.
4. *Feasibility* of the strategy in the resources needed. This was a problem that Jaguar, for example, had to beware of in its rush for change and growth.

The underlying conclusion of these studies is the recognition of the interconnectedness of all the factors involved. It is not possible to provide a general checklist of do's and don'ts in managing strategic change. Only a full understanding of the situation in each case can identify the course of the changes.

Bibliography

Pettigrew, A., *The Politics of Organizational Decision Making,* Tavistock, 1973.
Pettigrew, A., *The Awakening Giant: Continuity and Change in ICI,* Blackwell, 1985.
Pettigrew, A., and Whipp, R., *Managing Change for Competitive Success,* Blackwell, 1991.

Chris Argyris

Chris Argyris is a psychologist who, for many years, has been James Bryant Conant Professor of Education and Organizational Behavior at Harvard University, where he is now Professor Emeritus. He began his career at Yale University, and his important contributions to the field have been recognized with the establishment at that university of a chair named in his honor: the Chris Argyris Chair in the Social Psychology of Organizations.

Argyris has consistently studied how the personal development of individuals is affected by the kind of situation in which they work. Each person has a potential that, if fully realized, would bring benefits not only to the individual but also to the working group and employing organization. Unfortunately, businesses and other organizations are usually run in such a way that such benefits are prevented from appearing. This is because the typical approach of the managements of organizations and their lack of interpersonal competence prevent people from becoming mature in outlook. Employees too often remain shortsighted in their actions on the job, shirking responsibility and being uninterested in opportunities. They develop "defensive routines" that protect their current ways of working and that inhibit them from considering any changes—even changes that would improve their present position.

In such organizations, individuals cannot progress from infantile behaviors. In their limited routine tasks, they look forward to the end of the day's work but are unable to foresee the success or failure of the whole enterprise over a period of years. To their superiors, their infuriating inability to see beyond the end of their noses and their own relatively trivial work difficulties is inexplicable. They have come to accept a passive and dependent position, without initiative.

Faced with this lack of response, even among lower managers or specialists, executives are liable to become yet more autocratic and directive. Their existing strong "pyramidal values" are reinforced. The increased use of management controls deprives employees of any opportunity of participating in the important decisions that affect their working life; this deprivation leads to feelings of psychological failure. It is not they themselves but control systems (e.g., work study, cost accounting) that define, inspect, and evaluate the quality and quantity of their performance. And as subordinates tell less and less about what is happening, as everyone pays more attention to keeping up appearances ready for the next business process reengineering investigation or tense budget allocation committee meeting, defensive routines come to be the norm.

These are some of the problems that human beings have in relating to organizational life. Together with Donald A. Schon, Argyris has also examined some of the built-in contradictions that arise from the functioning of the organization itself, which has the paradoxical requirement of both wanting to maintain stability and also to be dynamic or changing. Thus, typically, organization members may be told: Take initiatives *but* do not violate rules; think beyond the present *but* be rewarded and penalized on present performance only; think of the organization as a whole *but* do not cross into others' areas of responsibility; cooperate with others *but* compete with others when required.

The main problem is not that these contradictions exist, but that, in the usual poor state of managerial interpersonal competence, they cannot be raised and discussed as issues. Although many managers may *talk* about the openness of communication and the participative approach of their organizations (what is called their "espoused" theory), what they actually do may be very different. Very strong defensive routines are built into management's thinking, ensuring resistance to the openness that leads to interpersonal change.

Argyris and Schon have demonstrated that the basis of many managers' actions (called their "theory-in-use") can be subsumed under four rules of behavior, referred to as Model I: (a) Design goals unilaterally and try to achieve them; (b) maximize winning and minimize losing by controlling the task with as little dependence on others as possible; (c) minimize generating or expressing negative feelings in public, keep your own thoughts and feelings a mystery; and (d) be rational and "objective" and suppress the voicing of feelings by others, thus protecting yourself and them from facing important issues that often have an emotional content to them.

Managers who operate on Model I have a very unilateral view of their world in which they are striving to have complete control. Their aim is to defend themselves and to impose on others. They thus generate mistrust and rigidity and are therefore confirmed in their Model I view that open discussion of issues is best avoided. The only learning that occurs is learning how to conform (called "single-loop" learning), and the process becomes "self-sealing."

Argyris and Schon propose a Model II theory-in-use that does allow organizational learning. The norms here are to (a) take action on valid information and be open about obtaining it, (b) take action after free and informed choice with all who are competent and relevant taking part, and (c) generate internal commitment to the choice with monitoring of implementation and preparedness to change. Managers who operate in a Model II world are not defensive and thus can participate in double-loop learning. They look for contributions from others who are competent; they are able to confront their own basic assumptions and take part in testing them in public, which allows their changing.

The issue then becomes: If managers operating in a Model I mode are by definition unaware of this fact because they are using defensive routines to resist change, how may they be helped to develop effective learning in Model II? Argyris proposes a training program to bring out into the open these contradictions in situations in which managers' feelings of vulnerability are reduced. Managers are helped by interpersonal consultants to confront the large gap that usually exists between what is said and done in a decision-making group and what is actually thought by the members. They can then analyze the defensive routines that they habitually use to stop openness and innovation and can practice taking a Model II approach in their work.

Using this approach, Argyris conducted a case study lasting more than 5 years, as described in his book *Knowledge for Action.* It was both a consulting and a research program—a combination known as "action research." He worked with the owner-directors of a management consulting firm to develop their Model II skills. He shows that his seminars helped them overcome their defensive routines on many occasions (not all). Inevitably, some managers became more competent at Model II behavior than others. Often, in change programs, it is found that top managers put the need for change high in their espoused theory but their theory-in-use stays the same. Unusually, in this case the senior managers made the most progress. They are at the forefront of making the firm better capable of organizational learning.

Bibliography

Argyris, C., *Organization and Innovation,* Irwin, 1965.

Argyris, C., *Strategy, Change, and Defensive Routines,* Ballinger, 1985.

Argyris, C., *Personality and Organization,* Garland, 1987.

Argyris, C., *Knowledge for Action: A Guide to Overcoming Barriers to Change,* Jossey-Bass, 1993.

Argyris, C., and Schon, D., *Organizational Learning: A Theory of Action Perspective,* Addison-Wesley, 1978.

Peter Senge

Peter Senge, a systems theorist, is Director of the Systems Thinking and Organizational Learning Program of the Sloan School of Management at the Massachusetts Institute of Technology. He argues that, in the present-day complex world, organizations must be able to learn how to cope with continuous change in order to be successful: They have to become *learning organizations*. His concern is to describe the art and practice of such a learning organization.

It is not easy for organizations to learn because they are afflicted with learning disabilities, such as the following:

- *The excessive commitment of individuals to their own positions.* This limited view leads to people focusing only on their own role and taking little responsibility for the results produced when all the positions interact.

- *The allocation of blame externally,* away from the immediate group: The enemy is out there. It may be other departments (marketing and manufacturing mutually blaming each other) or governmental regulations or unfair competition from another country. But blaming external factors hampers learning and is almost always not the complete story.

- *The illusion of taking charge.* Being "proactive" rather "reactive" is attractive to managers but could simply mean fighting the enemy out there in the same way but more aggressively. Without analysis reflecting on the internal changes necessary, it may simply be disguised reactiveness.

- *A focus on immediate events as explanations.* This precludes seeing the longer term patterns of change that lie behind the events and attempting to understand the causes of those larger patterns.

- *Unawareness of slow, gradual processes that present greater threats than immediate events.* It is said that a frog placed in boiling water will immediately jump out, but if placed in warm water that is gradually heated to boiling will stay and boil because its sensing apparatus is geared to sudden changes, not to gradual ones. Senge argues that something of the same sort happened to the U.S. auto industry from the mid-1960s to the mid-1980s in regard to Japanese and German competition. Over the 20 years, this foreign competition rose from near zero to a 38% share of the market before U.S. manufacturers took them seriously.

- *The delusion that learning comes only from experience.* People do learn from experience, but in a complex system they can no longer directly experience the consequences of many of their important decisions. Decisions on investment in R&D or on strategic positioning may have large ramifications over a decade or more. It is not therefore possible to learn only on the basis of trial and error.
- *The myth of the top management being agreed and united.* This myth leads to suppression of disagreements and encourages watered-down compromises to maintain the appearance of a cohesive team. If disagreement does come to the surface, it is expressed in polarized terms, with those involved finding fault and blaming each other. Thus, as Argyris (p. 179) shows, real double-loop learning does not take place.

To combat these considerable disabilities, Senge proposes five disciplines that organizations need to practice to become learning organizations.

The first discipline concerns *personal mastery.* Individuals need to exercise the highest levels of mastery, not over other people, but over themselves. They need to have a good understanding of themselves and what they wish to achieve. This personal learning is the basis for organizational learning because no organization's capacity for learning can be greater than that of its members. But few organizations encourage such self-discipline, with the result that organizations contain vast untapped resources of energy and learning potential.

The second discipline necessitates the continual challenge and review of the deeply entrenched tacit *mental models* that members of the organization bring to all its activities. Stereotypes of customer behavior, accepted recipes for product development, and the neglect of the possibilities of discontinuous change are examples of mental models that have to be continuously reviewed in an effort to make thinking more open to a wider range of new ideas. Directors at the Anglo-Dutch Shell Oil Company attribute their considerable success over the last two decades in the unpredictable world oil business to their ability to challenge the mental models of their managers.

The third discipline concerns the *building of a shared vision* for the organization and its members of the future that they wish to create. A shared vision has been the key to all successful organizations—the "value driven" nature of excellent organizations, as Peters and Waterman put it (p. 102). It has to be more than the usual artificial "vision statement"—a genuine vision of what they want to achieve that firms such as Ford, IBM, Polaroid, and Apple Computer have displayed.

The fourth discipline is a commitment to *team learning*—an open dialogue of cooperation in groups, rather than "turf battles." Only then can the intelligence of the team exceed that of its members, rather than reduce it drastically.

The discipline that unites the others and brings all together in an understandable pattern is that of *systems thinking.* This is the fifth discipline, which provides the title for Senge's book and is the foundation for organizational learning. It is necessary to think in a systems way, which is rather different from people's usual focus on immediate events.

Systems thinking has a number of laws. The first is: Today's problems come from yesterday's "solutions." Often, problems arise from "solutions" that merely shift the problem to another part of the system. A solution to the problem of high stock inventory that involved drastic reductions might result in salespeople spending large amounts of their time pacifying irate customers awaiting late deliveries. The impounding by the police of a large shipment of drugs may result in an increase of drug-related crime as the reduced availability forces the price up and thus increases the crime levels of addicts desperate to maintain their supply. So, other laws of the fifth discipline are, The harder you push, the harder the system pushes back; The easy way out usually leads back in; and, The cure can be worse than the disease.

A more sophisticated understanding of how complex systems work is required, and managers need training to encourage systems thinking. Another law of the fifth discipline is, Behavior grows better before it grows worse. Treating the symptoms may bring temporary relief, but at the cost of later larger problems. There is a fundamental mismatch between the behavior of complex systems and people's ways of thinking about them. This is because, for important issues, "cause and effect are not closely related in time and space." The result of a decision taken now may have its effects only after some time and in a different part of the organization anyway. Thus, the decision to cut the budget of the training department in a particular year may seem a sensible economy, but in the following year, the result might be a large decrease in the operational efficiency of a new computer billing system through inadequate preparation.

The basic contribution of the fifth discipline of systems thinking is the art of seeing the forest *and* the trees. Managers do not often take the time to step back from the trees to see the forest and, unfortunately, when they do step back, they just see lots of trees! Senge analyzes the sad story of the Peoples' Express Airlines, an innovative, low-cost, high-quality airline service in the Eastern United States, to illustrate the necessity for systems thinking. The airline was founded in 1980 and was immediately successful, growing in 5 years to become the fifth largest carrier in the United States. But in 1986, it was taken over by another airline, having made a loss of $133 million in the first 6 months of that year.

What went wrong? Many theories were proposed, including a too great "people orientation" by the management, lack of an adequate strategy in relation to takeovers, and an innovative seat reservation system introduced by other airlines that allowed price competition. But each of these theories is only partial. A proper analysis requires consideration of the interactions of five sets of factors (air fleet, human resources, competition, finance, and policy levers) and generates a list of more than 40 variables that must be considered in a systemwide way. A simulation was built at MIT that allows many of the variables to be changed to evaluate their impact on the system as a whole. Working with simulation suggests that what is required is an organization capable of self-analysis—for example, in understanding that one cannot innovate with dramatically new ideas in human resource policies *and* become a major player in the airline industry within a few years. A firm can grow too fast and so not be able to learn to understand and manage the turbulent changes involved, and thus to think and act systemically.

A key contribution to an organization's capacity to learn is thus the use of computer-based simulations, called "microworlds." These allow for "play" in developing a more complex systemic understanding of the organization's position and what the change possibilities are. This understanding leads to the realization of another of the laws of the fifth discipline: You can have your cake and eat it too—but not at once.

Bibliography

Senge, P. N., *The Fifth Discipline: The Art and Practice of the Learning Organization,* Century Business, 1992.

Senge, P. N., "Mental Models," *Planning Review, 20,* (1992), 4-10, 44; reprinted in D. S. Pugh (ed.), *Organization Theory,* Penguin Books, 1997.

Gareth Morgan

Born in Wales, Gareth Morgan lives and works in Canada. He is Distinguished Research Professor at York University, Toronto, having moved there from the University of Lancaster in England. He has written books and many articles analyzing organizations and management and has been a consultant and seminar leader to numerous organizations.

Everyone in an organization has in mind an implicit picture of that organization, a mental image of what it is like. Morgan contends not only that an organization is seen differently by different people but also that it can be seen in different ways by any one person. If multiple images of an organization are used, much greater understanding is gained because organizations are many things at once and so multiple images envisage more of what is going on. They can reveal new ways of managing and designing organizations that were not apparent before.

Morgan himself puts forward eight possible images of organizations: (a) as machines, (b) as living organisms, (c) as brains, (d) as cultures, (e) as political systems, (f) as psychic prisons, (g) as systems in flux and transformation, and (h) as instruments of domination. The name of each image is a metaphor likening an organization to something and, by doing so, opening up a fresh way of thinking about it.

If an organization is thought of as a *machine,* the emphasis is on the orderly arrangement of who does what and who has authority over whom. This is a mechanical kind of thinking concerned with clear hierarchy, authority and responsibility, discipline, stability, and equitable treatment of personnel. It is extolled by classic management theorists such as Fayol and Taylor (see p. 86 and p. 91) and analyzed by sociologists such as Weber and Burns (see p. 3 and p. 46). The strength of an organization seen and set up in this form is that it works well where a machine would work well—that is, where tasks are straightforward and repetitive, as in a fast-food hamburger chain or an accounts office. Its limitation is that it dehumanizes work.

If an organization is seen as a *living organism,* a biological metaphor, then there is less preoccupation with orderliness and more attention given to adaptiveness. Tasks and lines of authority can be changed to

184

continuously realign the organization responsively with its changing environment. This view is extolled by Peters and by Kanter (see p. 99 and p. 105). It is the organic type described by Burns (see p. 46) and one of those described by Mintzberg (see p. 29). Its strength is that it fosters an organization that is an open flexible system, giving full scope to human capacities, especially appropriate to competitive and turbulent conditions, as in the aerospace and microelectronics industries. Its limitations are that it can overlook its own built-in conflict potential and that, as "population ecologists" such as Hannan and Freeman (see p. 72) have argued, an organization is not infinitely adaptable but can become obsolete and "die."

An image of an organization as a *brain* does not mean that it has central planning teams or a research department. Rather, it presumes that intelligence is spread throughout the organization. In this, the brain is similar to a holograph in which any part can reproduce the whole and stand for it. So, in all its parts, the organization does not just learn, but can learn to learn better. There can be double-loop learning (Argyris, p. 179) that goes farther than single-loop learning (which only corrects errors) into another feedback loop that questions the operating norms, the ways of working, that lead to error in the first place. Such an organization would accept uncertainty and self-criticism and be able to see farther than the "bounded rationality" postulated by Simon and by March (see p. 118 and p. 121). Were an organization to have a rigid structure, these advantages, unfortunately, might not be realized. Such a structure would have opposing assumptions embedded in it. It would have specialist departments, each holding on to its own specialized information, each unable to learn from the others or to question its own ways of working.

Seeing an organization in terms of *cultures,* Morgan's fourth image, brings to attention not only its overall corporate culture but also the subcultures of its constituent sections and groups and the societal culture of which its own culture is a part. People who share a culture interpret situations and events in similar ways, sustaining their common outlook with evocative figures of speech, symbols, and ceremonies. As an obvious instance, even an unoccupied room symbolizes what is expected, having either ordered chairs and notepads or, alternatively, chairs arranged casually. This cultural view reveals the wide organizational life that is beyond the overtly rational and shows possibilities of change. Even the relationships of an organization with its environment can be reinterpreted, rethought, and thus changed, as when a railway switches from thinking about passengers or a hospital about patients and both begin to think about customers instead.

The fifth image recognizes an organization as a *political system.* An organization can be autocratic or democratic or anywhere in between. There are departmental interests, management interests, and the interests of those lower down, personal career interests, and many more. All interests have a potential for conflict and for wheeling and dealing. They exploit both the legitimate authority classified by Weber (p. 5) and the power drawn from controlling resources and know-how analyzed by Pfeffer and Salancik (p. 62) and Hickson (p. 13). The strength of this image is that it helps people to accept the reality of organizational politics and to ask whose interests are being served.

Organizations give purpose and structure to the lives of their members. Our roles become our realities, as Morgan puts it. There lies the danger, for individuals can believe that they are more in control than is really so. In this, they deceive themselves because they can be in a *psychic prison,* attributing to the organization an existence and power of its own and allowing their thinking to be confined by it. Their thinking may indeed be the result of forces in their unconscious as psychoanalysis has shown. The strength of this prison image is that it exposes to people how they can become trapped in this way in a certain psychic reality and suggests to them that it is possible to break out of it. Managers can see that their organization is of their own making and take a fresh look at what they are doing.

To see an organization as *a system in flux and transformation,* a seventh possible image, sees it as just like everything else in the universe. There are various conceptions of how change takes place. It can be seen as brought about through one-way cause and effect or—and this is better—by mutual causality in which "causes" loop back on themselves. Or by "autopoiesis," whereby the organization changes itself by changing its own environment. Or by dialectical change, whereby any phenomenon generates its opposite, as when the power of the employers led to the formation of trade unions. This image warns against an organization being seen as struggling against the environment; rather, it must survive in interdependence with others in that environment.

Finally, Morgan draws a picture of organizations as *instruments of domination.* He points out that the building of the Great Pyramid in Egypt was both a triumph of skill and effort and a sacrifice of the labor and lives of many to glorify a few. Organizations achieve much, but as they do so, they can cripple people by accidents, diseases, and stress. They can abruptly dispose of them after years of service, and pollute their habitat. The strength of this image is its recognition that domination of the many by the few is intrinsic to the very concept of hierarchy that exists in virtually every organization.

Morgan shows how the problems of a small firm in the public relations industry may be illuminated by using a range of metaphors. The firm was founded by two senior partners (holding 80% of the equity between them) and two junior partners. It was immediately successful, on the basis of the client-centered all-around competencies of the founders in giving a creative service. New staff, when recruited, were encouraged to develop their overall generalist skills, as well as their specializations. Although this process was time-consuming and expensive, it did give great flexibility to the firm and allowed greater work interest for the staff. Commitment was high, and all worked hard and for long hours. Its success allowed the firm to grow in a few years to 150 staff.

Major conflicts began when the senior partners, feeling that the demands of the organization were too great in view of their family commitments, suggested a change to a more formalized structure. Their proposals included job definitions, set procedures for the change of staff between projects, greater control over when staff were away from the office, and in general "more system." The junior partners objected that the firm was successful precisely because of the present "creative chaos" and that they saw no need for change. They offered to take more of the workload from the senior partners in exchange for more equity participation in the company. But the senior partners were not prepared to relinquish control in this way. In the event, despite the convention that the partners operated by consensus, the senior partners installed the changes. They appeared to be accepted, but within a year the junior partners had left to found their own agency in the original creative chaos style. The firm continued, but less successfully in that its work was now regarded by some clients as "sound but uninspiring."

Several of the metaphors may be used to help in making sense of these developments. The *machine* metaphor would point to the increasing bureaucratization and ask what the appropriate level of system should be, in view of the size and dependence of the firm. The living *organism* metaphor would focus on the potential incongruence of the organization in its environment and ask whether it has the degree of creative chaos to be successful in its market niche. The *brain* metaphor would note the loss of the holographic character of the enterprise and ask how far it is now constrained to single-loop learning. The *culture* metaphor would lead to asking how far the values of the original culture have changed and whether there are ways of re-creating some of those characteristics in the new situation.

Using the *political* system metaphor points to the considerable differences in power between the partners that allowed the senior partners to impose their own decision when real conflicts appeared. What are the limitations on the organization's processes when this degree of power can be exercised? The *psychic prison* metaphor focuses on the psychological factors that shape relationships, including the senior partners' (probably unconscious) need for dominance and the junior partners' (probably equally unconscious) need to resist.

An important benefit from using a range of metaphors is that they supply competing explanations. Proposals for change from one may be tested against another. For example, if the changes in the company were generated by the owners' unconscious need for control, then the underlying problems cannot be solved by addressing only the issues of corporate culture or learning capacity (see Argyris, p. 178).

Managers can apply these ideas, says Morgan, by *imaginization*. This is "an invitation to re-image ourselves and what we do." In a book with this title, Morgan illustrates what he means and how he uses images in his own work as a consultant "to create new momentum in stuck situations."

It is a book full of lively cartoons and images, from yogurt pots to lions. One of them "imaginizes" an organization as a spider plant—a plant that throws out long trailing stems, each with, on its end, a miniature of the original plant. Managers seeing their organization in this way come up with ideas they have not considered before. One would be that expansion can be by setting up offshoots, instead of by increasing the size of the central plant pot. But then, what financial support should these new subsidiaries receive? If the organization already has a dispersed form, this image might prompt one to ask, Is the central pot is doing enough? Or too much? Are some offshoots withering and becoming a drain on the center? And so on. Different images raise different questions and so expose problems or opportunities that might otherwise be overlooked.

Bibliography

Burrell, G., and Morgan, G., *Sociological Paradigms and Organizational Analysis,* Heinemann, 1979.

Morgan, G., *Images of Organization,* Sage, 1986.

Morgan, G., *Imaginization: The Art of Creative Management,* Sage, 1993.

Name Index

Allan, S. A., 50
Argyris, Chris, 165, 166, 177-179, 181,
    188
Athos, Anthony, 100

Bamforth, Ken W., 158
Bartlett, Christopher, 1, 2, 39-43
Bond, Michael, 79-81
Braverman, Harry, 84, 85, 95-98
Burns, Tom, 30, 34, 35, 44, 45, 46-49,
    73, 101, 109, 114, 184, 185

Carroll, Glen, 76
Chandler, Alfred D., 1, 2, 18, 26, 167,
    169
Child, John, 8, 12, 65
Cohen, M. D., 124
Crozier, Michel, 41, 60, 131-135
Cyert, Richard M., 121, 122

Daems, H., 22
Davis, S. M., 50
DiMaggio, Paul J., 165, 166, 167-170
Donaldson, Lex, 14
Durant, William, 21

Edwards, Richard, 97
Emery, Fred E., 161

Fayol, Henri, 10, 32, 55, 84, 85, 86-90,
    160, 184
Freeman, John, 44, 45, 72-76, 185

Ghoshal, Sumantra, 1, 2, 39-43

Handy, Charles, 1, 2, 34-38
Hannan, Michael T., 44, 45, 72-76, 185
Herbst, P. G., 163
Herzberg, Frederick, 96, 136, 137, 149,
    153-157
Hickson, David J., 8, 13-15, 41, 64, 171,
    186
Hinings, C. R. (Bob), 8, 64
Hofstede, Geert, 44, 45, 77-83

Jago, A. G., 126, 128

Kanter, Rosabeth Moss, 84, 85, 105-110,
    185
Kotter, J., 50

Lane, H., 50
Lawrence, Paul R., 44, 45, 50-55, 149
Likert, Jane Gibson, 142, 146
Likert, Rensis, 53, 96, 136, 137,
    142-145, 146-147, 160
Lorsch, Jay W., 44, 45, 50-55, 149

March, James G., 63, 73, 114, 121-125,
    169, 185
Marx, Karl, 95
Maslow, Abraham, 149
Mayo, Elton, 96, 136, 137, 138-141
McGregor, Douglas, 53, 96, 136, 137,
    142, 146-147, 148, 149, 160
McMillan, Charles, 8

Miles, Raymond E., 44, 45, 66-71
Mintzberg, Henry, 1, 2, 27-33, 167, 185
Morgan, Gareth, 165, 166, 184-188
Morse, J. J., 50

Olsen, J. P., 124

Pascale, Richard, 100
Payne, Roy, 8
Peters, Thomas J., 84, 85, 99-104, 181, 185
Pettigrew, Andrew, 165, 166, 171-176
Pfeffer, Jeffrey, 44, 45, 62-65, 186
Pheysey, Diana, 8
Powell, Walter W., 165, 166, 167-170
Pugh, Derek, 2, 8-16, 24, 64, 65

Rice, A. K., 160

Salaman, Graeme, 97
Salancik, Gerald R., 15, 44, 45, 62-65, 186
Schein, Edgar H., 136, 137, 148-152
Schon, Donald A., 178-179
Senge, Peter, 165, 166, 180-183

Simon, Herbert A., 117-120, 121, 185
Sloan, Alfred P., 21
Smith, Adam, 19
Snow, Charles C., 44, 45, 66-71
Stalker, G. M., 46
Storrs, Constance, 86

Taylor, Frederick W., 84, 85, 89, 91-94, 96, 142, 148, 155, 184
Thompson, James D., 32, 44, 45, 56-61, 66, 67, 73
Thorsrud, E., 163
Trist, Eric, 136, 137, 158

Vroom, Victor H., 126-130, 149

Waterman, Robert H., Jr., 84, 85, 99-104, 181
Weber, Max, 1, 2, 3-7, 10, 30, 34, 53, 81, 105, 106, 167, 184, 186
Weick, Karl E., 84, 85, 111-115, 173
Whipp, Richard, 172, 173
Williamson, Oliver E., 1, 2, 23-26

Yetton, P. W., 126

Subject Index

Acceptable-level decision rules, 123
Acquisitions, 102
Action, bias for, 100
Action research, 158
Activities, structuring of, 10-12
Adaptation:
  loose coupling and, 114
  types of strategies for, 66-70
Adaptive response, 22
Adhocracy, 29, 32
Administrative problem, 20, 66, 67, 68, 70
Affirmative action policies, 108
Age, of managers, 12
Analyzer adaptation strategy, 69-70
Anarchies, organized, 122-123
Anglo work culture, 81-82
Asian work culture, 81
Aston Group, 1, 2, 8-16, 24, 64, 65
Authoritarian decision making, 126
Authoritative management, 143
Authority, 78
  acceptance of, 141
  centralization of, 9, 10, 12
  concentration of, 10, 11, 12, 60
  defined, 3
  discontinuous changes in the nature
    of, 35-37
  functional, 89
  integration and, 53
  multi-unit business enterprise and, 19
  organization as living organism and,
    184-185
  organizations of future and, 147
  power-distance culture and, 82
  scientific management and, 93
  technical, 48
  transnational company, 41
  types of, 3-6

worker's, 156, 157
Autocratic management, 127, 130, 177
Automation, 97
Autonomy, 149
  innovative companies and, 101, 103
  struggle for, 62
  work groups and, 108, 163

Blame, allocation of, 180
Boundary conditions, managing, 160-161
Boundary spanning units, 57, 59
Bounded rationality, 121-125, 185
Brain, image of organization as, 185, 187
British Broadcasting Corporation, 49
Buffering, 57, 59, 67
Bureaucracies, 5-6, 34
  boss-secretary relationship and, 106
  crises and, 135
  full, 11, 60
  homogeneity pressures, 167-170
  organizational climate in, 12
  organization size and, 11
  personnel, 11
  power games and, 134
  redundancy and, 162
  spread of, 167-168
  system-actor interactions in, 131
  workflow, 11
Bureaucratic insularity, 25
Business enterprise, large-scale, 18-22

Capitalism, 6
  de-skilling of work and, 95-98
  formative years of modern, 18-20
Career(s), normative isomorphism and,
    170

Career anchor, 150
Career bridges, into management, 108
Career development, 150, 164
Career system, 48-49
Centralization, 9, 10, 12
    club culture and, 34
    decision making and, 34
    degree of, 89
    departmental structure and, 20
    entrepreneurial organization and, 30
    excellent companies and, 103
    global companies and, 40
    interdependence of activities and, 59
    machine organization and, 30
    strategic apex toward, 30, 33
    power games and, 134
    state central planning and, 14
    transnational company and, 41
Certainty, need for, 56
Change:
    uncontrolled, 73
    See also Organizational change
Change masters, 108
Charismatic authority, 3-4
Choice:
    decision making and, 117
    freedom of, in power games, 132,
        133-134
    garbage can model of, 124-125
    power games and, 132
    strategic, 13, 14
Club culture, 34
Coercive isomorphism, 168-169
Coherence, strategic change and, 175-176
Collectivist culture, 78
Command, unity of, 89
Command activities, 87-88
Committee system, 48
Communication, 27
    ease of, 105, 106
    informal, 100, 102
    innovative organization and, 32
    lateral, 89, 109
    management style and, 143
    mechanistic firm, 47, 48
    multi-unit business enterprise and, 19
    organic organization, 47
    prospector firms, 69

resistance to openness in, 178
    strategic change and, 174
    work group output and, 139
Communication costs, 25
Community influence, organization
    replacing, 141
Competition:
    environmental niche and, 74-76
    internal, 101
    slow, gradual processes and, 180
Competitive advantage, 176
Competitive principle, 54
Complex model, of motivation, 149
Computer technology, de-skilling work
    and, 97
Concentration of authority, 10, 11, 12
Configuration of rule structure, 9
Conflict:
    differentiation and, 51-52, 53
    integration and, 51-52, 53
    political organization and, 33
    power games and, 134-135
    quasi resolution of, 123
    removing person-to-person, 146
    transnational companies and, 43
    worker-management, 140
Confucian dynamism, 81
Constricted decision making process, 15
Consultative management, 127, 143
Consumers, shaping, 97
Contracting out work, 35, 36-37
Contractual fringe, 36-37
Control:
    bureaucratic organizations and, 5-6
    machine organization and, 30
    mechanistic organization and, 46
    of strategic contingencies, 15
    transnational companies and, 42
Control activities, 87-88
Control systems, 25
Cooperation:
    management style and, 144
    management-worker, 93-94
    power games and, 131
    spontaneous, 141
    team learning and, 182
    worker management, 140
    work group norms of, 139-140

Cooperative efforts, 109
Coordination, bureaucratic organizations
    and, 5-6
Coordination activities, 87, 88
Creative innovation, 22, 101
Creative problem solving, 146
Creative staff, 49
Crisis situations, organizational
    sensemaking and, 113
Cross-national firms, 39-43
Cues, sensemaking and, 112
Cultural maps, 79
Culture(s):
    of excellence, 104
    national, 77-83
    See also Organizational culture
Custom, authority fixed by, 4
Customers, responsiveness to, 100-101,
    103, 104
Customer demands, fluctuations in, 15

Decentralization, 19, 20, 21
    degree of, 89
    excellent companies, 103
    federal organization and, 37
    innovative organization and, 32
    integrative organizations and, 109
    interdependence of activities and, 59
    multinationals and, 40
    opportunities for women and
        minorities and, 108
    prospector firms, 69
    transnational company, 41
Decision(s):
    commitment to execute, 128
    consequences of, 181, 182
    effectiveness, 127-130
    flight, 124
    nonprogrammed, 118-120
    oversight, 124
    programmed , 118-120
    quality or rationality of, 128
    time required to make, 128
    resolution, 124
Decision makers, specialized, 24-25
Decision making, 88, 116
    administrative man and, 118

attention to, 121
bounded rationality and, 121-125
classes of, 28
concentrated authority and, 10, 11
constricted, 15
control of strategic contingencies and,
    14-15
erratic preferences and, 122
fluid, 15
formal system and, 48
group, 146-147
nonrational, 121
personality effects on, 126
political processes in, 171
power and, 131-134, 171
satisficing and, 118
sensemaking and, 113, 115
sporadic, 15
stages in, 117
strategic choice and, 65
strategies, 60-61
subordinate participation and,
    126-127, 130, 143
techniques, 118-120
Decision rules, acceptable-level, 123
Decision tree, 128
Defender adaptation strategy, 67-68
Defensive routines, 166, 177-179
Defensive strategy, 20
Demand:
    global, 39-43
    influencing, 63
    mass markets and, 18
    shaping, 97
Departments:
    buffering function, 57
    conflicts between, 51-52
    coordinating activities, 88
    interdependence and, 57
    power games and, 131
    quasi resolution of conflict and, 123
    rigid organizational structure and, 185
Dependence on other organizations, 11,
    14
Dependencies, balancing, 62-65
Depersonalization, bureaucratic
    organizations and, 5-6
Design activity, decision making and, 117

Design principal, 162-163
Development, job satisfaction and, 154, 155
Differentiation, external environment
    and, 50-55
Directive management, 177
Disbanding, rate of, 74, 75
Discipline, 89
Disseminator, manager as, 27-28
Disturbance handlers, manager as, 28
Diversification, 29, 31-32, 63, 103
Divisions, 26, 103
    self-sufficient, 31-32
Documentation, formalization of, 9, 10, 11
Domination, instruments of, 186-187
Double-loop learning, 179, 185

Economic incentives, 145, 148, 149
Economic man, 118
Effective bureaucracies, 12
Efficiency:
    bureaucratic organizations and, 5
    competition forcing, 54
    decision making and, 119
    excellent organizations and, 101
    global companies and, 40
    scientific management and, 91-94
    supervisory style and, 142-144
Employee(s):
    empowering, 108, 109
    expectations and, 149-150
    initiative of, 178
    opportunities for, 107-108
    potential of, 146, 154, 177
    See also Motivation; Workers
Employee-centered supervisors, 142-144
Engineering problem, 66, 67, 68, 69
Entrepreneur, manager as, 28
Entrepreneurial organizations, 29, 30,
    101, 103, 108, 109
Entrepreneurial problem, 66, 67, 68, 69
Environment(s):
    alignment with, 66-71
    assessing for strategic change, 173
    coarse-grained, 76
    complexity, 161
    ecological perspective, 72
    interdependence with, 62-65

negotiating, 63
niche in, 74-76
opportunities in, 161
pressures for organizational
    homogeneity and, 168
rationality in decision making and, 118
scanning, 65
sensemaking and, 112
turbulent, 162-163
    See also External environment
Environmental problems, solutions to,
    50-55
Equalitarian decision making, 126
Equity, 89
Executives:
    commitment to high standards, 102
    long-term planning and, 19
    motivation and opportunity for, 21
    succession, 64, 65
    wife role and, 107
    See also Top management
Existential culture, 35
Expectations:
    manager's sensitivity to, 144
    organizational culture and, 185
    psychological contract in motivation
        and, 149
Experimentation, 100
Expert(s):
    in bureaucracies, 6
    career structure and, 48
    power games and, 133-134
    rational-legal bureaucracies and, 167
Expertise, 20
    international companies and, 40
    professional organization and, 31
    specialized, 13
External constraints, adapting to or
    altering, 63
External environment:
    coercive isomorphism and, 168
    interdependence with, 62-65
    transactions with, 56-57
    turbulent, 162-163
    uncertainty and, 56-61

Family, organization replacing, 141

Federal organization, 37-38
Feminine culture, 78
Feudal organizational form, 4
Fixed costs, 109
Flexible labor force, 37
Flexible organizations, 109
Flexible systems, 185
Fluid decision making process, 15
Focused companies, 109
Forecasting, 87-88
Formalization:
    of documentation, 9, 10, 11
    organization size and, 14
Formal system, 48
Founding, rate of, 74-75
France:
    nationalized tobacco industry, 132-134
    work cultures in, 82
Friendly companies, 109
Full bureaucracies, 11, 60
Function, differentiation of, 50
Functional authority, 89
Functional management, 94

Games, power, 131-134
Garbage can model, of organizational
    choice, 124-125
Generalists, environmental niche
    conditions and, 76
Germanic work culture, 82
Global business environment, 39-43, 104
Goals, 48, 87, 88
    bureaucratic organizations and, 5
    conflicting, 122, 123
    employee commitment to, 145
    hierarchy and, 25
    negotiation of, 122
    organized anarchies and, 122
    performance, 143, 146
    sequential attention to, 123
    subordination of individual, 89
    task culture and, 35
    variable means to achieve, 109
Groups, 9
    autonomy of, 149
    decision making, 127, 146-147
    effects on individual behavior, 138-141

formality of interaction, 12
supportive relationships among, 146
See also Work groups
Growth, job satisfaction and, 154, 155

Hawthorne Experiment, 138-141
Hawthorne Investigations, 96, 138
Hawthorne Investigations, 96
Hereditary transmission of authority, 4-5
Hierarchies, 18, 52
    command structure, 89
    concentrated authority in, 10
    conducting transactions and, 24
    curbing opportunism in, 25
    disappearance of, 147
    domination and, 187
    efficiency of, 5
    flattening, 108, 109
    means of coordination and, 58
    mechanistic organization and, 46, 47
    rational-legal bureaucracies and, 167
    studying, 9-12
    unitary structure of, 25
Human behavior:
    assumptions about, 145-146, 148-149
    measuring, 144-145
    rabble hypothesis about, 140-141
Human needs, 153-154
Human potential, 146, 154, 177
Human relations approach, 96-97, 137,
    141
Human resources, strategic change and,
    175

Identity construction, 112, 113
Ideology, missionary organization and,
    30, 33
Imaginization, 166, 188
Imitation, in problem solving, 169
Individual(s):
    aims of, 35
    autonomy for, 12
    career anchors and, 150
    commitment to positions, 180
    defensive routines of, 177-179
    expectations of, 149-150

group's effects on behavior of,
     138-141
interdependence of, 136-137
knowing employees as, 143
motivations of, 145-146, 148-149
needs of, 153-154
psychic prison and, 186
self-actualization and, 145, 148-149
studying organizations and, 9
Individual characteristics, authority
     based in, 4
Individualist culture, 78, 82
Industrial engineering, 94, 155
Industrial Revolution, 31, 81
Informants, studying organizations using,
     9
Information:
   coordinating activities, 88
   impactedness of, 24, 26
   management style and, 143
   manager activities and, 27-28
   problemistic search and, 123
Information cost of transactions, 23-26
Initiative, 89
Innovation/innovative firms, 12, 29, 32
   analyzer firms and, 70
   attributes of excellent, 100-104
   continuous, 99
   continuous short-cycle, 104
   defensive routines and, 178, 179
   firm characteristics, 108, 109
   international operations and, 39
   mechanistic firm, 47
   prospectors and, 68
   speeding flow of, 109, 110
   systems thinking and, 183
   technological, 46
Institutional economics, 23-24
Institutional isomorphism, 168-170
Integrated network structure, 41
Integration, differentiated firm and, 51-52
Integrative organizations, 109
Intelligence, profitability based on, 36
Intelligence activity, decision making
     and, 117, 119
Intensive technology, 58
Interaction-influence system, 144-145,
     147

Interdependence:
   with environment, 62-65
   management-worker, 93
   types of, 57-58, 59
International companies, 40
   national work culture and, 82-83
Internationalist, 104
Interpersonal manager role, 27
Intraorganizational power, strategic
     contingencies theory of, 14-15

Japanese firms:
   just-in-time delivery systems, 36-37
   missionary approach, 33
Job-centered supervisors, 142, 144
Job design, 155
Job dissatisfaction, determinants of,
     153-155
Job enlargement, 155
Job enrichment, 149, 155-157
Job hygiene factors, 154-155
Job rotation, 155
Job satisfaction, 107, 139-140, 144,
     153-155

Labor, division of, 96
Labor force:
   flexible, 37
   management relations with, 143
Labor process, capitalist organization of,
     95-98
Large-scale business enterprise, 18-22
Leader/leadership, 27
   acceptance of, 141
   authority and, 3-4
   charismatic, 4-5
   knowledge levels, 146
   transmission of performance goals,
     146
   excellent companies, 101, 104
   innovative companies, 101, 103
   missionary organization and, 33
   organizational culture and, 151
   sensitivity and, 144
   succession and, 4-5
Leading change, 173-174

Learning:
  assessing environment and, 173
  decision-making processes and, 124
  double-loop, 179, 185
  international operations and, 39
  organizational change and, 178-179
  single-loop, 178, 185
  strategic change and, 175
  team, 182
  transfer of, 40
Learning organization, 124, 166,
    180-183, 185
Liaison manager role, 27
Line-and-staff structure, 21, 22
Living organism, organization as,
    184-185, 187
Local rationality, 123
Long-linked technology, 58
Long-term planning, 19
Loosely coupled systems, 114

Machine, image of organization as, 184,
    187
Machine organization, 29, 30-31
Machine power, profitability based on, 36
Maintenance factors, 154
Management, 19, 84-85
  activities of, 87-88
  as art, 28
  boundary, 160-161
  closed circle, 106
  contingency approach, 149
  differentiated firms, 51-53
  excellent companies, 99-104
  functional, 94
  imitation of techniques of, 169
  ineffective bureaucracies, 12
  of labor processes, 96
  matrix organizations, 54-55
  mechanistic firm, 47, 48
  national cultures and, 77-83
  organic, 101
  performance and, 142-144
  postentrepreneurial, 109-110
  principals of, 89-90, 92-94
  promotion to, 106, 107-108
  relative process of, 144

roles, 27-28
  scientific, 85, 91-94, 96-97, 149
  stability of tenure, 89
  strategic choices of, 13
  systems of, 143-144
  work-activity studies, 27
  work-related attitudes, 77-83
  See also Supervisors; Top management
Management by objectives, 81-82
Management by results, 38
Management by wandering around, 100
Management organizations, ideal types
    of, 46-47
Managers:
  age of, 12
  bureaucratic organizations and, 5-6
  company roles of, 105-106
  discretion of, 105
  high-producing, 142-144
  human behavior assumptions of,
    145-146, 148-149
  imaginization and, 188
  multi-unit firm, 18-21
  organizational change and, 177-178
  power and, 14-15, 131
  professionalization of, 5-6, 19, 168,
    169-170
  selecting and training, 88, 106
  succession and, 4-5, 172
Managing, 111
Market(s):
  choosing viable, 66, 67
  conducting transactions and, 24
  continuously changing, 46
  entrepreneurial organizations and, 108
  short-cycle innovation and, 104
  uncertainties in, 123
Market-matrix organization, 71
Marxism, 95, 97
Masculine culture, 78-79
Mass markets, 18, 19
Mass production, 96, 148
Material order, 89
Matrix organizations, 54-55
McKinsey 7-s framework, 100
Mechanistic organization, 34, 46, 47-49,
    109, 114
Mediating technology, 58

Mental models, challenging, 181
Mergers, 63, 151
M-form, 25-26
Middle line, 29, 31-32
Mimetic isomorphism, 168, 169
Minorities, employment opportunities
    for, 107-108
Missionary organizations, 30, 33
Monitor, manager as, 27
Monopoly capitalism, 97
Monopoly-like position, 15
Moral outlook, capitalism and, 6
Motivation:
    assumptions about, 145-146, 148-149
    job enrichment and, 155-157
    job satisfaction and, 153-155
    need satisfaction and, 153-154
    pay and, 89, 145, 148, 149, 154, 155
Multidimensional organization structure,
    42
Multidivisional structure, 25-26
Multinational companies, 39-40
Multi-unit firm, 18-22

National cultures, differences between,
    77-83
Negotiator, manager as, 28
Niche, resources of, 74-76
Nonbureaucracies, 11
Nonprogrammed decisions, 118-120
Norm(s):
    power games and, 132
    professionalization and, 169-170
    of rationality, 56, 59-60
    work group cohesion and, 139
Normative isomorphism, 168, 169-170

Objectives, 21
Ongoing process, sensemaking as, 112, 113
Open system, 56, 161
Operating core, 29, 31
Operational change, 174-175
Opportunism, 25
Organic culture, 35
Organic organization, 46-47, 109, 114,
    185

Organic system of management, 101
Organization(s):
    activity types, 86-87
    age of, 75-76
    alignment with environment, 66-71
    authority relations within, 3-6
    dependence on other, 11, 14
    effective, 50, 54, 63, 146
    as evolutionary systems, 115
    excellent, 99-104, 181
    institutional aspects, 9
    learning, 124, 166, 180-183, 185
    loosely coupled, 114
    mental image of, 184-188
    movement between, 65
    people in, 136-137
    population of, 72-76
    replacing family and community, 141
    shared vision and, 181
    societal transactions and, 23-26
    as sensemaking systems, 111-115
    strategic choice in, 13, 14
    strategic model of, 132
    studying, 8-12
    technical core of, 56-57
    types, 3, 29-30, 34
Organizational climate, 11-22
Organizational change, 165-166
    complexity of interacting factors in,
        171-176
    defensive routines and, 166, 177-179
    leading, 173-174
    learning organization and, 180-183
    linking strategic and operational,
        174-175
    pressures for bureaucratic
        homogeneity and, 167-170
    slow, gradual process of, 180
    strategic, 171-176
Organizational culture, 34
    integrative organizations and, 109
    mergers and, 151
    organizational change and, 185, 187
    transnational companies, 42
Organizational roles, changing nature of,
    38
Organizational size:
    disbanding and, 75

information cost of transactions and, 23
organizational structuring and, 11
specialization and, 13, 14
stability and, 63
Organizational structure, 1
   complex turbulent environments and, 162-163
   contingency approach, 53
   decision-making strategies and, 60
   differentiation and, 50-55
   environmental adaptation and, 66-71
   environmental interdependence and, 62
   excellent companies, 103
   global business environment and, 39-43
   homogeneity pressures, 167-168
   interdependence of activities and, 59
   Japanese companies, 14
   multidivisional, 25-26
   multi-unit firm, 18-22
   organization size and, 11
   rational-legal bureaucratic, 5-6, 167
   rigid, 185
   role of management in developing, 19
   segmented, 108-109
   societal change and, 72-73
   strategic choice in, 13, 14
   studying, 9
   transactions and, 24-26
   See also Centralization; Decentralization
Organization management, 84-85
Organizations and environment approach, 50-55
Organized anarchies, 122-123
Organizing, 87, 88, 100-104, 111
Output:
   group standards for, 140
   informal social groupings and, 140
   pressure to achieve, 142

Participative management, 127, 130, 143, 178
Paternalistic organizations, 14
Pathological systems, 47

Patrimonial organization, 4, 106
Pay:
   capitalist system and, 95
   motivation and, 89, 145, 148, 149, 154, 155
   performance-based, 92
   scientific management and, 91, 92
   secretaries and, 106
People:
   interdependence of, 136-137
   management orientation to, 101
   management style adapting to, 144
   organizational images and, 184
   See also Individual(s)
Perception, selective, 111
Performance, 99
   equalitarians and, 126
   excellent organizations and, 101
   goals for, 143, 146
   pay connected to, 92
   supervisory style and, 142-144
Performance assessment, 59-60, 88
Personal bureaucracies, 60
Personality:
   charismatic leaders and, 4
   decision making and, 126
Personal mastery, 181
Personnel bureaucracies, 11
Planning, 73
   activities of, 87-88
   capacity of leader to provide, 146
   long-term, 19
   strategic change and, 172
Plausibility, sensemaking and, 112, 113
Playfulness, decision making and, 125
Political action, 63
Political assessment, 60
Political organizations, 30, 33
Political processes:
   administrative succession and, 64, 65
   coalitions and, 122
   conflicts and, 123, 186
   decision making and, 171
   institutional isomorphism and, 168, 169
   power and, 48-49, 186, 188
   strategic change and, 174
Pooled interdependence, 57-58

Population ecology of organizations,
    72-76
Positive strategy, 20
Power:
    alliances and, 110
    decision making and, 171
    defined, 3
    influence and, 110
    mechanistic firm, 47, 48
    multiple sources of uncertainty and, 60
    organizational size and, 63
    organizational types and, 29-33
    political system and, 48-49, 186, 188
    secretary and, 106
    strategic contingencies theory of,
        14-15, 64-65
    transnational organizations and, 41-42
Power-distance dimension, 77-83, 82
Power game, 131
Prices, determining in transactions, 24
Problemistic search, 123-124, 169
Procedures, standardization of, 9, 10, 11
Product(s):
    diversification and, 20
    entrepreneurial organizations and, 108
    ideas from customers about, 101
Product divisions, 103
Production:
    capitalist organization of, 96
    de-skilling workforce and, 96-97
    Hawthorne Experiment and, 138-141
    high-volume, 18, 20
    stable, 15
Productivity:
    supervisory style and, 142-144
    through people, 101-102
Professional core, 36
Professional managers, 5-6, 19, 168,
    169-170
Professional organization, 29, 31
Professional skills, profitability based
    on, 36
Professional workers:
    existential culture and, 35
    institutional isomorphism and, 168,
        169-170
Profit(s), 91
    capitalism and, 95-96, 97

maximizing, 69
Profit centers, 26
Programmed decisions, 118-120
Project teams, 69
Prospector adaptation strategy, 68-69
Prosperity, maximizing, 91
Psychic prison, organization as, 186, 188
Psychological contract, motivation and,
    149-150
Psychological needs, of workers, 163
Punishment, 143, 145

Quality circles, 169
Quality of working life, 163-164
Quasi markets, 62
Quasi resolution of conflict, 123

Rabble hypothesis, 140-141
Rational-economic level, motivation and,
    148
Rationality:
    bounded, 121-125, 185
    in decision making, 128, 130
    limits to, 118, 121-125, 185
    norms of, 56, 59-60
Rational-legal organizations, 5-6, 167
Reactor strategies, 70
Reciprocal interdependence, 57-58
Recognition, 155
Redundancy of functions, 162-163
Redundancy of parts, 162
Remuneration, see Pay
Research-based organizations, 32
Resource(s):
    allocation of, 18, 20, 28, 35
    capacity of leader to provide, 146
    interacting for central control of,
        62-63
    niche, 74-76
    task culture and, 35
Resource dependence perspective, 62-65
Responsibility, 155
Responsiveness:
    enhanced, 104
    multinationals and, 40
Retrospective, sensemaking and, 112, 113

Rewards, 143, 155
Risk, 12
    assessment of, 61
    assuming, 101
    minimizing, 69
Role culture, 34-35
Role specialization of, 9, 10, 11, 13
Role structure, configuration of, 9

Scalar chain, 89
Scientific management, 85, 91-94, 96-97,
    149
Secretaries, company roles of, 105, 106
Segmented structures, 49, 50-55, 108-109
Self-actualization needs, 145, 148-149
Sensemaking systems, 111-115
Sequential attention, 63
Sequential interdependence, 57-58
Sex roles, national cultures and, 79
Shamrock organization, 36
Single-loop learning, 178, 185
Social contacts, 112, 113
Social effects, systems of work
    organization and, 159-160
Social group, workers as, 139-140
Social model, motivation and, 148
Social needs of workers, 163
Social order, 89
Social systems, organizational
    functioning and, 48
Society:
    breakdown of values in, 141
    discontinuous changes in, 35-37
    keeping up with change, 72-73
    as network of transactions, 23
Sociotechnical system, work group as,
    159-164
Specialist(s):
    conflicts and, 51-52
    environmental niche conditions and,
        76
    innovative organizations and, 32
    organic organizations and, 46-47
    professional organization and, 31
    professionalization of, 168, 169-170
Specialist departments, 185
Specialization, 24, 89

analyzer firms and, 70
    of functions and roles, 9, 10, 11, 13
    Japanese companies and, 14
    organizational size and, 13, 14
    scientific management and, 93, 94
    strategic choice in, 13, 14
    technological, 171
    transnational company and, 41
Spokesperson, manager as, 28
Sporadic decision making process, 15
Staff-line relationships, Theory Y and,
    146
Standard(s):
    excellent firms and, 102
    professionalization and, 169
Standardization, 58
    of norms, 33
    of procedures, 9, 10, 11
    of work, 30
Standard products, 40
Strategic apex, 29, 30
Strategic change, 171-176
Strategic choice, 13, 14, 65
Strategic contingencies theory of
    intraorganizational power, 14-15,
    64-65
Strategic issues, centralized structure
    and, 21
Strategic model of organization, 132
Strategic tasks, transnational
    organizations and, 41-43
Strategies:
    defensive, 20
    organizational structure and, 18-22
    organized anarchies and, 122
    positive, 20
    power games and, 131-134
    worldwide, 39-43
Strikes, 149
Structure, see Organizational structure
Structuring activities, 10-12
Subordinates, see Workers
Subsidiaries, 37-38
    decision making in, 10, 11
    international companies and, 40, 41
Subunit power, 65
Sunk costs, 25
Supervisors:

employee-centered, 142-144
enriched jobs and, 156-157
job-centered, 142, 144
managing worker-task relationships,
    160
Support staff, 32
System 4T, 146-147
System in flux and transformation,
    organization as, 186
Systems, open, flexible, 185
Systems thinking, 182-183

Task(s):
    command activities and, 88
    de-skilling, 96
    differentiation of, 50
    mechanistic organization and, 46, 47
    organic organization and, 46-47
    organization as living organism and,
        184-185
    routine, 177
    science of work and, 92, 94
    sequence of, 57
Task culture, 35
Task forces, 69
Team, self-managed, 114
Team learning, 182
Technical authority, 48
Technical core, 56-58, 59, 67, 69
Technological change, 18, 19, 22
Technologies:
    de-skilling work and, 97
    innovation and, 46
    investment in, 67
    specialization in, 171
    types of, 58
    work organization and, 159
Technostructure, 29
Tenure, stability of, 89
Theory X, 145, 146, 148
Theory Y, 145-146, 149
3M, 101, 103
Top management, 99
    excellent companies, 103
    myth of cohesiveness of, 181
    tasks of, 21
    wife role and, 107

See also Executives
Traditional organizations, 4-5
Training, 164
    capacity of leader to provide, 146
    in group processes, 147
Transactions:
    cost of, 23-26
    external environment, 56-57
    satisfying member needs through, 50-51
Transnational organization, 41-43
Turnover, 149

U-form, 25
Uncertainties:
    avoidance of, 78, 82, 123
    buffering against, 57, 59
    coping with, 14
    differentiation and, 51, 53, 54
    environmental, 54, 56-61
    higher management and, 105, 106
    institutional isomorphism and, 168,
        169
    learning organization and, 185
    managing, 25
    pathological systems and, 47
    power in control over, 133-134
    reutilization and, 134
    strategic contingencies and, 64-65
    uncontrolled change and, 73
Unions, 148
Unity of command, 55, 89
Unity of direction, 89

Values:
    breakdown of societal, 141
    excellent firms, 102
    managers fitting in with, 105
    manager's sensitivity to, 144
    power games and, 132
    quality of work life and, 163
    work group cohesion and, 139
Vertical information system, 67
Vertical integration, 20, 22, 25, 67
Vision:
    shared, 181
    transnational companies and, 43

White-collar jobs, de-skilling, 97
Wives, company roles of, 105, 106
Women:
  equal employment opportunities for, 107
  selection for management, 106
Work:
  changing nature of, 36
  design of, 155
  de-skilling of, 95-98
  division of, 89, 93
  human motivations and, 145-146, 148
  science of, 92, 93
Work activities, stable coordination of, 56
Workers:
  assumptions about motivations of,
    148-149
  constant pressure on, 142, 144
  cooperation with management, 140
  decision making participation and,
    126-127, 130
  effect of group on individual behavior
    of, 138-141
  emotionally-based attitudes of, 140

exploitation of, 95-96, 143
feelings about organization, 150-151
focusing on human aspects of, 142,
  143
opportunities for, 155, 164
potentialities of, 146, 154, 177
power games and, 131
scientific selection of, 92
training, 92-93
See also Motivation; Employee(s)
Worker-task relationships, 160
Workflow bureaucracies, 11, 15, 60
Work groups:
  cohesion and, 139
  effective, 143, 144
  as interdependent sociotechnical
    systems, 159-164
  output standards, 140
  stable, 146
  technological demands and, 159
Working class, control of, 96
Work life, quality of, 107, 163-164

About the Authors

Derek S. Pugh is Visiting Research Professor of International Management at the Open University, United Kingdom, having previously been at the Universities of Edinburgh and Aston, the London Business School, and Open University Business School. He has been a visiting professor at business schools in France, Germany, Israel, and Italy and is a Fellow of the British Psychological Society, the Royal Statistical Society, the Italian Academy of Business Administration, and the International Academy of Management. He has served as Chairman and Honorary Vice-President of the Association of Teachers of Management of the United Kingdom and as editor of the newsletter of the British Academy of Management.

Professor Pugh is currently General Editor of The History of Management Thought series (Dartmouth Publishing). He is joint author and editor of 12 books, including the first three volumes of the Aston research program. His latest books are *Great Writers on Organizations: The Omnibus Edition* (1993, Dartmouth Publishing, with David J. Hickson), *How to Get a Ph.D.* (2nd ed., 1994, Open University Press, with Estelle M. Phillips), *Management Worldwide* (1995, Penguin Books, with David J. Hickson), and *Anglo-German Business Collaboration: Pitfalls and Potentials* (1996, Macmillan, with Dagmar Ebster-Grosz). His edited volume *Organization Theory: Selected Readings* (4th ed., Penguin Books) appears in 1997.

David J. Hickson is Research Professor of International Management and Organization at Bradford Management Center, England. His principal research interests are how societal culture affects managerial decision making in different nations and what influences the success of major decisions. His previous research has included processes of managerial decision making, power in organizations, and bureaucratization. He was founding Editor-in-Chief of the international research journal *Organization Studies;* a founder of the European research association in his field, the European Group for Organizational Studies (EGOS);

and a founding member of the British Academy of Management. He has held appointments in university business schools and research institutes in Canada, the United States, and the Netherlands, has an Honorary Ph.D. from the University of Umeå in Sweden, and has lectured widely around the world. He has published numerous research journal papers and book chapters and is author or editor of eight books, most recently *Management in Western Europe* (1993, DeGruyter) and *Management Worldwide: The Impact of Societal Culture on Organizations Around the Globe* (1995, Penguin Books, with Derek S. Pugh). Prior to becoming an academic, David Hickson worked in financial administration and qualified professionally as a chartered secretary and in personnel management.